Teacher Beliefs and Classroom Performance: The Impact of Teacher Education

A Volume in
Advances in Teacher Education

Editors: James Raths and Amy C. McAninch

Teacher Beliefs and Classroom Performance: The Impact of Teacher Education

Edited by

James Raths

University of Delaware

Amy C. McAninch

Rockhurst University

INFORMATION AGE PUBLISHING

80 Mason Street • Greenwich, Connecticut 06830 • www.infoagepub.com

Library of Congress Cataloging-in-Publication Data

Teacher beliefs and classroom performance : the impact of teacher
education / eds., James Raths and Amy McAninch.
    p. cm. — (Advances in teacher education)
    ISBN 1-59311-068-5 (pbk.) — ISBN 1-59311-069-3 (hardcover)
  1. Teachers—United States—Attitudes. 2. Teachers—Training
of—United States. I. Raths, James. II. McAninch, Amy Raths. III.
Series.
    LB1775.2.T42 2003
    371.1'001'9—dc22

                                                    2003016126

Printed in the United States of America

CONTENTS

FOREWORD

This volume of *Advances in Teacher Education* is about beliefs held by teachers. Most of the authors who have contributed to this collection of essays assume that beliefs are propositions that are felt to be true by the person embracing them, but that do not rest on the kind of evidence that justifies the use of the term "knowledge." Teacher beliefs are an important topic for a number of reasons.

First, as a sage once remarked, "it is not what we don't know that hurts us so badly; it is what we think we know (beliefs) that is false that does so much damage." Kennedy (1997) has suggested that teacher candidates enter their professional studies thinking they know a great deal about teaching and that these entering beliefs act as filters in the learning process. As new ideas are introduced, students weigh them in terms of their current understandings. If the new ideas clash with their beliefs, the ideas are resisted or rejected. In teacher education, if a teacher candidate believes that knowledge can be transmitted from the mind of the teacher to the mind of students, in a manner of an injection, pedagogical practices based on constructivist theories are unlikely to be adopted. In much the same way, in-service teachers rapidly filter new ideas through a web of ideology and beliefs that Doyle and Ponder (1977-1978) call the "practicality ethic." New curricular interventions are quickly scrutinized for their perceived "practicality" and are discounted and rejected if teachers believe they are impractical. Thus, teacher learning is at times compromised by these beliefs.

The second reason for studying teacher beliefs has to do with the public school's special role as a venue for carrying out democratic social

Advances in Teacher Education, pages vii–xii
Copyright © 2003 by Information Age Publishing
All rights of reproduction in any form reserved.

reform and as a means of social mobility. In 1954, the U.S. Supreme Court found that "separate was inherently unequal" and decreed that de jure segregation was unconstitutional. Its order, modified by the phrase "with all deliberate speed," took years and many subsequent court battles to begin to put into place. No doubt many teachers rose to the occasion and fought vigorously to realize greater educational opportunity for African-American students; however, other teachers harboring racist beliefs bemoaned racial integration and lamented the impact of *Brown v. the Board of Education* in their classroom and schools (see, for example, Wells & Crain, 1998). In another similar landmark event, the Congress passed Title 9 of the Elementary and Secondary Education Act (1972), which provided rights for women (girls) in public schools. Teachers with sexist views were challenged to implement the new policies. Similarly, the civil rights of students has been advanced by the stream of legislation in special education mandating the mainstreaming of students that heretofore had been "warehoused" in segregated classrooms, far removed from non-labeled, age-graded peers. Teachers who have strong beliefs regarding the integration of children with disabilities into the mainstream may fail to meet the needs of their students and actually obstruct federal law.

What must be recognized in each of these cases is that the teaching force is drawn from the general population. There is no reason to believe that entrants into teaching would be any more egalitarian in their beliefs regarding race, class, gender, and disability than the citizens in the communities in which they teach, yet they are called on to implement these policies safeguarding the civil rights of students. There is a strong push on the part of many teacher educators to address these beliefs and others of equal importance to twenty-first century America in schools at all levels, but especially in teacher education.

Finally, the processes by which beliefs are impacted are not well understood. For all the studies of teacher beliefs and attempts to help candidates take on new beliefs, the research overall is rather dour about the prospects of changing candidates' beliefs in the long run. One argument that is advanced compellingly in this collection of essays is that equipping candidates with the "right" beliefs, be it constructivist philosophy or the importance of subject matter in teaching, may not be a necessary condition for effective professional practice. Focusing instead on the acquisition of effective practices may be the best route to good teaching—and hopefully beliefs would change as a result of successful practice. One could argue that it wouldn't make a difference if a Skinnerian implemented constructivist pedagogy, if the constructivist model were implemented well. Is it the belief that counts in teacher education, or is the bottom line what teachers actually do?

Why is the topic of teacher beliefs so contentious when the role beliefs play in teacher education and in teaching is so palpable? First, there is the question of what beliefs to teach and who decides?

Take the case of constructivism. Constructivist learning theories have been around for quite some time—perhaps first as embedded in the philosophy and the practice of progressive education, 1916-1945. But in the 1980s, the National Council of Teachers of Mathematics wrote standards that associated good teaching in mathematics with the constructivist view. Other disciplines quickly followed—science, English, and social studies. Do these leaders have it right? Should teacher educators work hard to change the beliefs of their candidates so that the mandates of constructivism are more likely to be practiced in the classroom? What should happen to candidates who hold atavistic views about learning? Should such candidates be dropped from programs? Or should teacher educators adopt some sort of relativistic view, such as, "Some people believe in constructivism, some do not. That's ok!" Further, the ethical issue of grading or assessment poses a challenge to teacher educators. What happens if a student, in spite of all the faculty interventions, still retains beliefs that are counter to the premises of professional standards? Should the candidate be dropped from the program? Should a recommendation for licensure be withheld for this student? Are there academic freedom issues here?

In sum, the topic of "teacher beliefs" is rife with intellectual conflict and ethical issues. As editors, we invited authors who might speak to the following principal questions:

1. Should teacher educators take on the goal of changing selected candidate beliefs?
2. Do teacher educators have available to them effective mechanisms for changing the beliefs of teacher candidates?
3. Does the profession hold a general consensus regarding what counts as "better beliefs"?
4. Is there a serious ethical issue involved in attempting to change the beliefs of teacher candidates?
5. Do emotions account for the difficulty in changing beliefs?
6. Are measures of beliefs that are essentially self-reports sufficiently precise to study teacher beliefs?
7. Are teacher beliefs shaped or influenced significantly by those of the school to which they are assigned?

For obvious reasons, it was not our intention to have each author address each one of these questions. The authors were invited to participate in this project because of their research programs in the problem area of "teacher beliefs." Each author approaches the problem area with different methodologies, different epistemologies, and different assumptions about teacher education. We wanted to take advantage of this diversity, and leave it essentially up to the reader to find how the essays related to the overall topic and these specific questions.

In her chapter, "Preservice Teachers Beliefs," Virginia Richardson provides an overview of the research on teacher beliefs and discusses the challenges teacher educators face in attempting to change them. Richardson argues for the importance of focusing on beliefs and believes that their development and refinement is an important goal of teacher education. The research literature cited here supports the idea that beliefs are very difficult to change, particularly within the confines of the traditional preservice program; however, Richardson point out that there is also a basis for optimism in these studies.

Mary Lundeberg and Barbara Levin share their insights into the means of changing teacher beliefs in "Prompting the Development of Preservice Teachers' Beliefs through Cases, Action Research, Problem-based Learning and Technology." The authors systematically review the literature on each type of instruction, as well as share the findings of their own classroom research. These methodologies, according to Lundeberg and Levin, are advocated on the basis of the values inherent in them (collaboration, learner choice and responsibility, among others) and also in light of the failure of traditional pedagogies to have a lasting impact on beliefs. The authors provide a very useful springboard for further research into specific pedagogical practices that hold promise for deepening the impact of teacher education. They conclude that a single experience or a single course which utilizes these methods is probably not sufficient to have a lasting effect on teacher belief, but rather multiple opportunities over time are necessary for lasting change.

In "Teacher Beliefs, Performance and Proficiency in Diversity-Oriented Teacher Education Programs," Peter Murrell Jr. and Michèle Foster address the issue of teacher candidates beliefs about race and culture. Murrell and Foster discuss the growing "culture gap" between the predominantly white, middle class teaching force and the increasingly diverse public schools. They describe two approaches for addressing the gap. The first strategy is the recruitment of a more diverse population into the teaching profession. The second is to attempt to transform teacher beliefs toward greater cultural competence, typically through coursework on cultural and linguistic diversity. Such coursework is frequently aimed at reducing cultural and racial bias. Murrell and Foster reject the latter approach as skirting the more important issue of actually promoting dispositions associated with effective practice in diverse settings. In other words, focusing on improving beliefs has diverted efforts away from assisting candidates in the acquisition of sound practices. Regardless of candidates' beliefs, they aver, the bottom line is what they actually do in diverse classrooms. Their chapter offers several recommendations for teacher education programs with respect to the preparation of teachers for diverse settings.

Richard Prawat, in "Is Realism a Better Belief that Nominalism? Reopening the Ancient Debate," recounts a philosophical debate that extends back to Medieval times, yet is relevant to classroom practices today. The debate between realists, who believe that some form of reality exists "out there" independent of our perception of it, versus nominalists, who believe that knowledge of the world is really knowledge of our own ideas and sense experience, is explicated and linked to contemporary educational theory. Prawat argues that the persistence of the influence of nominalism in educational theory serves to keep us swinging on a pendulum between didactic methods on the one hand and progressive, experiential methods on the other. In his view, realist constructivism provides a way out of this false dichotomy and can provide a significant advance in pedagogical practices.

Patricia Ashton and Michele Gregoire provide an analysis of the role of emotion in belief change, a subject that they assert has been understudied and/or dismissed in error in the literature on conceptual change. As they note, the "failure to incorporate an understanding of the instrinsic relationship between emotion and cognition in educational and psychological research has severely limited the development of our understanding of teachers' thinking and action." In their view, researchers need to take a close look at the role of emotions as the "energizers" of belief change and their role in the development and continuity of beliefs. For Ashton and Gregoire, it is an error to separate emotions from cognition in models of conceptual change. The model of belief change they advance in this chapter is an integrative one which holds much promise over previous models which focus on cognition alone.

Also from the discipline of educational psychology, Maria Teresa Tatto and Daniel Coupland study the problem of how beliefs are taught and measured in teacher education. In their review of the literature on attempts to change entering teachers' beliefs, Tatto and Coupland also note that teacher beliefs tend to be trenchant, yet few interventions aimed at changing teacher beliefs have been programmatic. They describe efforts at Michigan State University to develop a coherent, programmatic approach to belief change and a corresponding research agenda. Focusing on the fields of literacy and mathematics, Tatto and Coupland report that their teacher candidates and faculty show significant agreement regarding the teaching and learning of subject matter at the conclusion of the candidates' programs.

Roger Goddard focuses on the construct of "collective efficacy," which refers to teacher beliefs regarding the capability or capacity of a school faculty to develop and execute a systematic plan to positively impact students' learning. In this framework, high collective efficacy is a form of social capital that can function to induce individuals' actions in the pursuit of organizational goals. Goddard's chapter focuses on the relationship between collective efficacy and the self-efficacy beliefs of teachers. After exploring the relationship between several context variables, such as socioeconomic status, proportion of minority students, and collective efficacy, among others, and teachers' sense of personal efficacy, Goddard concludes that collective efficacy is the most important contextual variable impacting teachers' personal efficacy beliefs. Schools with low collective efficacy "debilitate" the personal efficacy beliefs of teachers, while high collective efficacy has the opposite effect. He concludes that collective efficacy is a powerful way of depicting school cultures and calls for longitudinal studies which might reveal how these perceptions change over time.

In sum, there are important insights, findings, and propositions advanced in this text related to teacher beliefs and teaching beliefs.

Amy C. McAninch
Rockhurst University

James Raths
University of Delaware

October 2002

REFERENCES

Doyle, W., & Ponder, G. A. (1977-1978). The practicality ethic in teacher decision-making. *Interchange, 8*(3), 1-12.

Kennedy, M. M. (1997). Defining an ideal teacher education program. Unpublished manuscript.

Wells, A. S., & Crain, R. L. (1997). *Stepping over the color line*. New Haven, CT: Yale University Press.

CHAPTER 1

PRESERVICE TEACHERS' BELIEFS

Virginia Richardson
University of Michigan

The cognitive revolution has greatly altered our way of thinking about teaching, and the methods of conducting teacher education and professional development. No longer do we focus entirely on classroom behaviors, skills, and activities. Instead, teacher education has become highly cognitive in focus. Teachers in professional development programs and candidates in teacher education programs discuss the understandings they bring into their programs, and their beliefs are challenged through classroom readings, dialogue, and classroom experimentation. These changes in approach to teacher education and professional development accompany a very different vision of teaching in which the teacher, as facilitator, helps pupils create meaning around the topic of interest. Implementation of this vision relies on strong and complex thought processes on the part of teachers. Thus, the new ways of thinking about the teaching side of the teacher/learner relationship focus on what goes on in the minds of teachers and teacher education candidates as they engage in learning to teach, planning, classroom action, reflection, and assessment. The research related to this vision addresses descriptions of and methods for determining teacher cognitions, the relationship between cognitions and classroom actions, and ways of affecting changes in both. This chap-

Advances in Teacher Education, pages 1–22
Copyright © 2003 by Information Age Publishing
All rights of reproduction in any form reserved.

ter focuses on a particular form of cognition—beliefs—in preservice teacher education students (referred to in this chapter as teacher candidates).

One form of cognition that has received considerable attention in the research and practice literature is beliefs. The strong beliefs that teacher candidates bring with them to the teacher education classroom are thought to be stumbling blocks in the reform of K-12 classroom instruction. As will be pointed out, the experiential judgment among teacher educators that teacher candidates' beliefs about teaching, learning, content, and instruction are very strong, at times misguided, and difficult to change is supported by research. The difficulty in changing beliefs of teacher candidates is particularly problematic at this point as the national standards movement and other large-scale improvement efforts attempt to reform classroom teaching from the transmission model to a more constructivist approach. The beliefs that teacher candidates bring with them into their teacher education programs relate strongly to the form of teaching they have experienced. Thus, many students have an understanding of teaching that suggests that the role of the teacher is to place knowledge into the heads of their students. Further, they view teaching from the standpoint of an individual student—that student being themselves.

The purpose of this chapter is to review the literature on teacher candidates' beliefs to uncover (1) the relationship between beliefs and actions, and (2) the changeability of these beliefs. In so doing, I will first develop a definition of beliefs, suggesting how this construct differs from knowledge. I will then explore what we know about teacher candidates' beliefs on a variety of topics, and where these beliefs may have come from. Finally, research on change in beliefs will be summarized in the third section.

WHAT ARE BELIEFS?

Beliefs have been explored by philosophers, social psychologists, anthropologists, sociologists, and researchers in the "derivative" fields of study such as education, organizational theory, business, and nursing. There is considerable agreement on the definition of beliefs as psychologically held understandings, premises, or propositions about the world that are felt to be true.

There is also considerable agreement that these systems are not necessarily logically structured. Rokeach (1968), for example, suggested that there are some beliefs that are more central than others and that the central beliefs are more difficult to change. In Green's (1971) philosophical treatise on the nature of teaching, he proposed that an individual may hold beliefs that are incompatible or inconsistent. This occurs because beliefs are held in clusters, and there is little cross-fertilization among belief systems. Thus, incompatible beliefs may be held in different clusters. Green proposed that the incompatibility may remain until the beliefs are set side by side and examined for consistency. As suggested, later, this process of investigation has become a component in teacher education and professional development programs that attempt to develop and change beliefs.

Beliefs, however, are just one form of cognition that have been investigated in relation to teaching and teacher education. We also find the terms attitude, values, perceptions, theories, and images, all of which Pajares (1992) suggested are beliefs in disguise. However, the conceptual question that creates considerable confusion and disagreement in teacher cognition studies is the differentiation (or lack thereof) between the concepts of beliefs and knowledge.

In the traditional philosophical literature, knowledge is thought to depend on a "truth condition" or warrant that compels its acceptance as true by a community (Green, 1971; Lehrer, 1990). Propositional knowledge, then, requires epistemic standing; that is, some evidence to back up the claim. Beliefs, however, do not require a truth condition. Feiman-Nemser and Floden (1986) agree with this differentiation between beliefs and knowledge: "It does not follow that everything a teacher believes or is willing to act on merits the label 'knowledge'" (p. 515).

On the other hand, within the educational psychological literature that examines teachers' knowledge and beliefs, there is often no distinction made.[1] For example, Alexander, Schallert, and Hare (1991) equated beliefs and knowledge: "*knowledge* encompasses all that a person knows or believes to be true, whether or not it is verified as true in some sort of objective or external way" (p. 317). In a review of the literature on preservice teacher learning, Kagan (1990) agreed. She suggested that since teachers' knowledge is subjective, it is much like beliefs.

In this chapter, I use the more philosophical distinction between beliefs and knowledge as derived from Green (1971). Beliefs are propositions that are accepted as true by the individual holding the belief, but they do not require epistemic warrant. Knowledge, however, does. The reason I make this distinction is because of the need for warrant in the conception of knowledge. If propositions that are not warranted may be held by an individual, how can they be called "knowledge," particularly if there is evidence that the proposition is false? Is an incorrect knowledge proposition to be called incorrect knowledge? Untrue knowledge? Thus, analytically, I find that it is better to differentiate between beliefs and knowledge—knowledge being a set of warranted propositions held by a community of experts. This also means that the major goal of education is to develop, modify, and transform students' beliefs and belief systems (Green, 1971), and this may happen, in part, through asking students to question their beliefs and bringing students in contact with knowledge.

WHY ARE BELIEFS IMPORTANT IN TEACHER EDUCATION?

The importance of beliefs has been considered within teacher education in two ways, one within a philosophical approach, and the other within a psychological frame. First, beliefs, in large part, are thought of as the focus of change in the teacher education program, particularly within the more philosophical views. Second, preservice teacher education candidates bring with them strong, and perhaps central beliefs about teaching into their teacher education programs. Within a constructivist conception of learning, beliefs are thought of as critical in terms of what and how the candidates make sense of what they are studying. They are also thought to guide teaching action.

The philosophical view focuses on the development of beliefs as one of the main goals of education. For Green (1971), teaching involves the formation of beliefs in students, and one teaching goal is to help students develop belief systems that consist of a large proportion of beliefs based on evidence and reason.

> Teaching has to do, in part at least, with the formation of beliefs, and that means that it has to do not simply with *what* we shall believe, but with *how* we shall believe it. Teaching is an activity which has to do, among other things, with the modification and formation of belief systems. (p. 48)

This view of the purpose of education was extended by Fenstermacher (1979) to teaching and teacher education. His view brings together the cognitive with the philosophical. He argued that one goal of teacher education is to help teachers transform tacit or unexamined beliefs about teaching, learning, and the curriculum into objectively reasonable or evidentiary beliefs. He suggested that an important function of teacher education programs is to ask teacher candidates to identify and assess their beliefs in relation to classroom action.

The psychological frame of current cognitive theory suggests that learning is an active and meaning-making process that is influenced by an individual's existing understanding, beliefs, attitudes, and preconceptions (Resnick, 1989). These theories of learning have also been used to understand how teacher candidates learn to teach. They come into their programs with strong theories of and beliefs about teaching and learning that have been acquired over the years from their experiences of schooling. These unsubstantiated theories or beliefs have been shown to affect what they learn from teacher education and how they learn it (for summaries, see Borko & Putnam, 1996; Calderhead & Robson, 1991). Smylie (1988) conducted a path analysis of data on 56 teachers who were undergoing a staff development process. The data included organizational contexts, nature of student population, and interactions teachers had with their colleagues. He concluded that "teachers' perceptions and beliefs are the most significant predictors of individual change" (p. 23).

The relationship between beliefs and actions in teaching has been well documented (Richardson & Placier, 2001). However, the question is still open as to whether beliefs guide action, actions—and particularly the results of action—guide beliefs, or that they interact such that beliefs or action may be dominant and affect the other depending on many factors. Quite recently, Tillema (2000) conducted a study with teacher candidates, and examined the relationship between beliefs and classroom performance. He concluded:

> From this study, it would be more appropriate to envisage beliefs as being concommitant to behaviour or intermingled with it. This is not to say that performance or action in teaching can do without beliefs…. But one cannot contend that they guide action. (p. 587)

Where Do the Beliefs Come From?

Several years ago, in a chapter on teacher beliefs and attitudes, I suggested three major sources for teacher beliefs: personal experience, experience with schooling and instruction, and experience with formal knowledge—both school subjects and pedagogical knowledge (Richardson, 1996). Perhaps the most important of these sources for teacher candidates' beliefs about teaching and learning is the second—experience with schooling and instruction. In comparison with neophytes in other professions, novices entering teaching have had considerable experience with the nature of the work. They have been students in formal schools for many years. Lortie (1975) described this phenomenon as the "apprenticeship of experience." Thus, teacher candidates bring with them a set of deep-seated and often tacit beliefs about the nature of teaching, learning, and schooling. For the profession of teaching, however, these preexisting beliefs and understandings may be somewhat distorted for purposes of considering the teaching role since the teacher candidates experienced teaching as students, not as teachers. These particular views of teaching, which were set within a framework of studenting, may be narcissistic, idiosyncratic, and somewhat simplistic. It is speculated that these strong beliefs, gained over a long period of time and combined with the salience of the real world of teaching, create conditions that make it difficult for preservice teacher education programs to have an impact on beliefs within the very short time that the teacher candidates participate in them.

Beliefs of Teacher Education Candidates

Most published empirical studies of professional development or teacher education, today, feature beliefs/conceptions/images/perceptions as significant elements of the study. For example, five out of six of the articles in a recent *Teaching and Teacher Education* (Vol. 17, no. 8) focus on beliefs, use beliefs as central data, and/or focus on cognitions that often may be described as beliefs—such as perceptions. Thus, summarizing all of this literature in one chapter would be difficult, if not impossible. I will therefore focus on examples of such work in an organization scheme describing the foci of the literature on preservice teachers' beliefs that I used in Richardson (1996): Entering beliefs of preservice students; entering beliefs by categories of students; and influence of beliefs in learning to teach.

Entering Beliefs of Teacher Education Candidates
The entering beliefs of teacher candidates have been characterized as highly idealistic, loosely formulated, deeply seated, and traditional. In the United States and other countries, teachers enter the profession for purposes of helping children, engaging in public service, and improving teaching (Ben-Peretz, 1990; Book & Freeman, 1986; Kam, 1990; Pigge & Marso, 1997). There is little evidence that they enter teaching for extrinsic rewards such as salary (Mitchell, Ortiz, & Mitchell, 1987). However, during this period of economic uncertainty, it might be interesting to approach this question once again. Applications for positions in teacher education are expected to increase as students see teaching as a relatively stable occupation as compared, for example, to the dot-com occupations.

A number of studies have identified a relatively simplistic and loosely formulated set of beliefs held by teacher education candidates, particularly in the area of diversity. This is not surprising given the demographics of those entering teacher education (Dilworth & Brown, 2001). These largely white, middle-class students may enter the teacher education program with little experience in culturally, ethnically, and SES-diverse classrooms. Zimpher and Ashburn's (1992) survey indicates the amazingly little contact candidates have had with minorities and other cultures. Avery and Walker (1993) found candidates' explanations for ethnic differences in achievement to be "simplistic" in nature, and the results of the Teacher Education and Learning to Teach (TELT) study indicated that candidates do not feel that differences among K-12 students make a difference in teaching, except in the area of personality (National Center for Research on Teacher Education, 1991). However, more recent research indicates that these views of the effects of ethnic, cultural, and gender differences on classroom social systems and particularly the inability to perceive the positive opportunities of classroom diversity are not held solely by white teacher education students, but appear more universal among a diverse population (Agee, 1998; Ladson-Billings, 1996; Reyes, Capella-Santana, & Kristy, 1998).

While teacher candidates' beliefs about diversity may be viewed as simplistic, they hold strong images of teaching, both positive and negative. These beliefs influence how they approach their teacher education program (Britzman, 1991; Calderhead & Robson, 1991). Perhaps because of the strength of their images of good and bad teaching, these students express confidence in their knowledge of teaching and in their own abilities to teach (Book & Freeman 1986). Weinstein (1989) suggested that these students are "unrealistically optimistic." They believe that there is not much that they can learn in their academic preservice courses, except in student teaching.

While the constructivist revolution has been described in the social science literature and practiced in some classrooms for a number of years, we still have a large group of preservice teacher education students who believe in the transmission model of teaching. This would perhaps have been expected in the 1990s since the reforms based on constructivist learning theory were just beginning to be implemented. This was, in fact, determined to be the case (Black & Ammon, 1992; McDiarmid, 1990). Further, there was a positivist view of science, as described in Erickson and MacKinnon (1991), and of mathematics in Civil's (1993) study. This view suggests that there is one right answer, and the teacher's goal is to make sure that children learn the correct answer. More recent studies indicate that many teacher education students still appear to hold transmission beliefs about the role of the teacher (Dana, McLoughlin, & Freeman, 1998; Mallette, Kyle, Smith, McKinney, & Readance, 2000), perhaps because there are large numbers of educators and segments of society—parents, for example—who still hold transmission beliefs.

However, anecdotal experience in my own teacher education classroom suggests that a growing number of teacher candidates now hold strong, constructivist beliefs about teaching and learning. And we are beginning to see what the issues are with these strong beliefs. For example, they often hold these beliefs dogmatically, in a way similar to those who preceded them in the transmission model. They also may focus too much on the process elements of constructivist pedagogies. MacKinnon and Scarff-Seatter (1997) introduced a case study of a student teacher in science who viewed the constructivist process as the important element of the teaching, with little concern for the science content of the classroom discussion. In a similar case study, Holt-Reynolds's (2000) prospective English teacher viewed constructivist pedagogies as ends in themselves, losing sight of the content and purpose of the particular teaching activities. Perhaps our biggest challenge for all teacher candidates regardless of their entering beliefs, is to help them become somewhat skeptical about their own beliefs and allow for the consideration of alternative conceptions of teaching and learning.

Entering Beliefs by Categories of Students

Brookhart and Freeman (1992) reported that entering preservice students should not be considered an undifferentiated group, but that attention should be paid to individual and group differences in beliefs, goals, and development levels. A number of studies have examined differences in the beliefs of teacher candidates depending on their elementary or secondary level of interest, ethnicity, gender, or traditional/ nontraditional status. Book and Freeman (1986), for example, reported that elementary teacher candidates were more child-oriented than secondary majors who are more interested in subject matter content (see, also, Kile, 1993). Differences have been found in the cognitive developmental level between elementary and secondary majors in their views of mathematics. In Avery and Walker's (1993) study of differences between elementary and secondary students, they concluded that secondary majors' rationale for ethnic and gender differences in achievement were more complex, and framed in a larger societal context.

Of particular interest in this literature, given the varying structures of preservice teacher education programs, are the differences in entering beliefs between traditional and nontraditional students. Nontraditional students are those who have had a gap in their formal education, either from working in another career or in the home. These students often have their BA/BSs in fields other than Education, and are attracted to the short and intense certification, Masters in Teaching, or Masters/Certification programs. Powell and Birrell (1992) reported that many nontraditional students' beliefs about teaching and learning were grounded in their role as parents, and in their former work experiences. Novak and Knowles (1992) found that the beliefs of nontraditional students who had successfully pursued another career were strongly affected by their past occupational experiences. Traditional students, however, frame their beliefs within their former schooling experiences. Kile's (1995) study of differences between the beliefs of nontraditional and traditional students in the same program cited differences in understandings of the complexities of the classroom. For example, he found that traditional students believed they could determine whether students were learning the content on the basis of whether they seemed to enjoy the activity. On the other hand, the nontraditional students believed that student learning could only be determined by examining student work.

Studies of the differences in beliefs between traditional and nontraditional students seem to back up Haberman's (1996) view that teacher candidates for urban teaching should be at least 30 years old. However, there is a differentiation among different groups of nontraditional students as well. For example, Crow, Levine, and Nager (1990) divided a sample of nontraditional students into three groups. The "homemakers" had always been interested in teaching but ended up doing something else. The "converted" had successful careers, but entered teaching because of a life-change such as the birth of a child. And the third group, "unconverted," had achieved high status in another occupation but became unsatisfied with it and expressed a vague interest in education. The first two groups made a satisfactory transition into teaching, but the third group did not, and tended to grow less interested in teaching as the program progressed.

The Importance of Beliefs in Preservice Teacher Education

There is considerable evidence that the entering beliefs of teacher candidates strongly affect what and how they learn, and eventually how they approach teaching in the classroom. For example, Ross, Johnson, and Smith (1991) examined teacher candidates' perspectives and learning in their teacher education program at the University of Florida. They reported a number of factors that influenced how and what their students learned in the preservice course, but the most important factor was their entering perspectives on teaching and learning.

Many of these studies examine what happens when teacher candidates enter their constructivist-oriented programs with traditional views about the transmission of knowledge. Holt-Reynolds (1992) found that a number of teacher candidates' beliefs on the processing of material in a content-area reading course contradicted the constructivist approaches that were being promoted by the professor. This disparity reduced the students' receptiveness to the professor's ideas. In a case study of a student teacher, MacKinnon and Erickson (1992) concluded that her positivist views about scientific knowledge led to her strong verbal domination of the classroom. She had great difficult understanding her cooperating teacher's critique of her classroom. Bryan (1998) examined a science student teacher's beliefs and her practice in attempting to implement a constructivist approach in science teaching. The case study documents the difficulties faced by the student teacher, difficulties that were attributed, in part, to her more traditional beliefs about teaching and learning.

Beliefs about self also affect teacher candidates' teaching and learning. In a collaborative study of two student teachers, Clift, Meng, and Eggerding (1994) described how one student teacher's image of self as a superior student interfered with her communication with the cooperating teacher. Calderhead (1988) found that the 27 students he studied learned very different things from their teaching experience, depending, in part, on their conceptions of professional learning and their own roles as student teachers.

One area that is quite well covered in the research is the nature of belief changes that occur during the course of student teaching, and how initial beliefs affect these changes. Some time ago, a significant study examined the way in which student teachers move from the humanistic beliefs about teaching and learning to more custodial beliefs about their role as someone who is there to control the students (Hoy, 1967). Cochran-Smith (1991) postulated that teacher candidates enter their teacher education programs with preexisting beliefs that match the custodial view, and may be swayed by the academic elements of the teacher education program, but move back to their preexisting beliefs during student teaching. Tillema (2000) suggested that the beliefs developed in academic courses are not personally validated or experienced ways of dealing with and interpreting practice, and thus may not hold through practice teaching. Zeichner, Tabachnick, and Densmore (1987) used classroom vignettes before and after reflective student-teaching experience, and found that the students tended to solidify their initial beliefs rather than change them. Smith (1997) examined the beliefs of two groups of student teachers about their beliefs about developmentally appropriate practice. One group had elementary education preparation, and the other had early childhood and elementary preparation. There were initial differences between the two groups in terms of developmentally appropriate practice. These differences did not change over the course of the student teaching experience. Smith concluded that there was strong continuity in beliefs across student teaching, and these beliefs were not affected, significantly, by those of the cooperating teachers.

In summary, the literature describes the strength of preexisting beliefs that teacher candidates bring into the program with them and their potential inappropriateness in learning to teach and educational reform. These beliefs have been acquired in large part through the experience of being a student in formal education, and they appear to affect what the teacher candidates learn and how they learn it. The next section looks specifically at research on belief change.

Changing Beliefs

It has been assumed for some time that changing beliefs of teacher candidates is difficult, although not impossible. Studies have focused on changes within three elements of teacher education programs: one class, the academic element of a teacher education program, and student teaching (see Wideen, Mayer-Smith, & Moon, 1998, for an excellent summary of this work). At the class level, Feiman-Nemser, McDiarmid, Melnick, and Parker (1989) examined teacher candidates in an introductory course, and found that a number of conceptions changed, such as believing that teaching was more complex than they had originally thought, and beliefs about teacher knowledge expanded considerably. However, while some change may occur, change is not always found in all students depending considerably on the beliefs that they bring into the classroom with them. For example, Richardson and Kile (1999) examined changes in beliefs of traditional and nontraditional students enrolled in a first semester teacher education course. They found that teacher candidates' orientations toward teaching shifted from traditional (teachers as knowledge givers) to a more constructivist theory of learning. There were also, however, differences in the responses between the traditional and nontraditional students. At the beginning of the class, the nontraditional teacher candidates brought views of teaching that focused on the teacher's role, and the traditional teacher candidates focused on the student role. By the end of the class, the nontraditional teacher candidates had strengthened their focus, and the traditional students had changed their focus from student to teacher.

Other researchers/teacher educators have examined changes in their teacher candidates during a course, and found that many students' beliefs and conceptions did **not** change (Ball, 1990; Civil, 1993; McDiarmid, 1992; Simon & Mazza, 1993). By and large, changes in beliefs during one academic class that is not accompanied by significant and structured involvement in a field experience either do not happen, or if they do, may be somewhat suspect because of measurement problems with the change measure. Students may be providing their instructors with the answers they believe the instructors want. These researchers question the possibility of changing teacher candidates' beliefs in one class or even one program.

There is also considerable research that indicates that changing prospective teacher candidates' beliefs in their academic programs, taken as a whole, is remarkably difficult. For example, Olson (1993) found that students did not change their beliefs and assumptions about good teaching during the course of their teacher education programs. Tillema and Knoll (1997) examined action and belief change in teacher candidates who were engaged in a conceptual change process, and found that while they changed some teaching behaviors, they did not change beliefs. They suggested that without changes in beliefs, changes in performance will be superficial. Researchers have also examined changes in beliefs after one year, or during student teaching. Anderson, Smith, and Peasley (2000) examined three teacher candidates' changes in conception of the learner after one year in a program with a major theme being the development of an integrated view of learner and learning outcomes. They reported that two of the students finished the year with an integrated conception, although their ways of getting there differed considerably, in part on the basis of their beliefs when they entered the program. However, the third prospective student, who held traditionalist beliefs about the role of the teacher at the beginning of the program, had not integrated the two elements, and was prepared to give up on content goals if his students appeared unenthusiastic. Borko and Mayfield (1995) also found limited change in four student teachers' practices or beliefs, but did find that the cooperating teacher was the most influential factor in affecting change in these students.

Two hypotheses are suggested and have been investigated as to why these prospective students' beliefs are difficult to change during the more academic elements of the teacher education program. One, as suggested by Weber and Mitchell (1996) and others, is that certain of these beliefs and images are so powerful as to be impossible to change during the short teacher education program. Weber and Mitchell made this suggestion on the basis of a study that asked teacher candidates and elementary teachers to draw a picture of an elementary school teacher. The overwhelming image was one of a pleasant, traditional, female teacher who points and explains.

The second suggestion is that programs designed to change teacher candidates' beliefs probably should involve them in field work in classrooms—in fact in some form of student teaching—such that they experience the classroom and therefore develop beliefs on the basis of procedural and practical knowledge. This theory of change suggests that the teacher candidates experience dissonance in their understandings and beliefs as they enter the role of teacher that challenges their beliefs about teaching acquired in the student role. Recall that one of the strongest influences on their entering beliefs is experience as students in the classroom. Thus, these students have developed a form of procedural beliefs over the period of up to 14 to 16 years. How would it be possible to change these beliefs in three to six academic courses?[2]

These two hypotheses are not in conflict. The beliefs and images of teaching held by the teacher candidates are strong and have developed over years of experience in schools in their role as students. The preservice teacher education program is quite short, and a significant element of it consists of academic courses with propositional knowledge and theory being presented to the students within the context of an academic setting. Since the preservice teachers' beliefs were acquired in a practice/action setting and are often tacit, it would be difficult for academic, propositional knowledge to be used to adjust the beliefs about teaching acquired in an action setting.

These hypotheses concerning the rationale for the difficulties in changing and developing teacher candidates' beliefs about teaching and learning suggests two approaches to change in teacher education classes:

1. Encouraging students to make less tacit and examine their existing beliefs and understandings about teaching and learning;

2. Engaging the preservice teachers in a structured practice situation such that the construct and propositional knowledge presented in the academic classes may be observed in practice and examined in relation to their own beliefs.

The next section will examine examples in the recent literature of research on programs that attempt one or both of these approaches.

Approaches to Belief Change

The first approach described above suggests that a reflective emphasis on an examination of beliefs in the academic element of teacher education affect belief change in teacher candidates. However, as mentioned above, the results have been discouraging (Korthagen, 1988; Bolin, 1990; Zeichner, Tabachnick, & Densmore, 1987). As suggested by Cochran-Smith (1991), superficial belief change may come about in the academic element of the program, but experience in student teaching may send teacher candidates back to preexisting beliefs about teaching and learning. One problem may be our conceptualization of teacher education as separating procedural and practical knowledge, structurally. Wideen, Mayer-Smith, and Moon (1998) described the typical teacher education program model:

> the implicit theory underlying traditional teacher education was based on a training model in which the university provides the theory, methods, and skills; the schools provide the setting in which that knowledge is practiced; and the beginning teacher provides the individual effort to apply such knowledge. In this model, propositional knowledge has formed the basis of university input. (p. 167)

They suggested that this model does not work in changing teacher candidates' beliefs.

However, it would appear that several of the studies reported at least some belief change after one class or at the completion of the academic element of the program. Elements that seem to make a difference in affecting beliefs in these classes include various attempts at bringing propositional and practical knowledge together through such elements as an accompanying practicum (field experience) that is well coordinated with the class, use of cases, particularly videocases that bring K-12 classrooms visually into the university classroom (Lampert & Ball, 1999; Richardson & Kile, 1999); and conceptual coordination of program across classes (Feiman-Nemser, McDiarmid, Melnik, Parker, 1989). Without these or similar program elements, it is doubtful that belief change will occur in the academic elements of teacher education programs.

Dana, McLaughlin, and Freeman (1998) describe a second approach, suggesting that creating dissonance in prospective teachers' beliefs about teaching and learning science helps to change their beliefs. They were able to successfully do this through a process of plan-teach-assess-reflect cycles in the field. They were interested in helping the prospective teachers develop the beliefs and actions required for teaching science for understanding, and found that dissonance between initial beliefs and results (and nonresults) in a structured field experience created dissonance that compelled students to examine and change their beliefs. Zanting, Verloop, and Vermunt (2001) also developed a way of combining a reflective approach to practice teaching by engaging the teacher candidates in an inquiry concerning their own beliefs, their cooperating teachers' practical knowledge, and the propositional knowledge that they were learning in their classes. This process helped the teacher candidates to develop and change their beliefs within a structured student-teaching framework.

It would appear, then, that a combination of the two approaches listed above would be helpful in belief change. Evidence of this comes from Tillema (2000) who conducted a study that compared belief change in two groups of teacher candidates: one engaged in a comprehensive reflective seminar prior to engaging in a reflective practice teaching experience, and the second group was immersed in a reflective practice teaching experience prior to the reflective seminar. While the first group changed beliefs quite dramatically in the first seminar, they moved back toward their original understandings and beliefs during the immersion period. The second group, however, changed beliefs somewhat during the immersion period, and continued the change in the desired direction during the seminar. Tillema (2000) concludes that reflection after practice has a positive effect on belief change; however, reflection prior to practice does not ground belief change in practice, thereby making them unstable.

A radical approach to teacher education supports the Tillema view. Fenstermacher (1993) suggested that schools of education are best suited to helping teachers understand the educative function of schooling—those functions that help students to become autonomous, enlightened, and virtuous human beings. He suggested that these college of education aspects should be developed *after* students have been engaged, through internships in professional development schools, in the systemics of schooling, and have developed practical knowledge about classroom management, scheduling, curriculum, and so forth. Tom (1995) also made a strong case for this approach.

This approach was attempted at Queen's University, Canada, and was developed as a case study (Upitis, Luce-Kapler, & Munby, 2000). Russell (1995) examined the differences between two groups of students' approaches to their science methods courses. One was a typical fifth-year group, and the other a group that had started their teacher education program with nine weeks of student teaching. The differences in beliefs, approaches and understandings were strong. For example, those who had been in the classroom for nine weeks had more of a need to know than those who had not experienced classroom teaching. Russell (1999) also poignantly described how difficult it was institutionally to develop, and particularly maintain such a radical change in the teacher education program.

SUMMARY

Beliefs are an important construct in education, and therefore in preservice teacher education. When differentiated from knowledge in a philosophical sense, they are remarkably important since beliefs include what those using a more psychological approach often think of as knowledge. Changing, developing, and refining beliefs are thought of as a primary goal of education; entering beliefs affect the ways in which teacher candidates approach the teacher education program and what they learn; and beliefs are also studied as anticipated or unanticipated outcomes of the educational process.

As a consequence of the constructivist revolution, teacher and student cognitions dominate the research literature, beliefs probably being the most studied. In fact, the topic that has dominated the preservice and inservice teacher education literature is changes in belief from those that accompany a more traditional method of teaching to those that surround a constructivist approach. For research suggests that beliefs accompany, if not influence, classroom strategies and action (Richardson, 1996). Thus, it is thought that changes in approaches to teaching requires considerably more than training in behaviors, but also demands a consideration of the beliefs of the participants in relation to the underlying framework of any new strategy or teaching approach.

The focus in the preservice teacher education literature has been on the very strong beliefs about teaching and learning that students bring into their programs with them based on 12 or more years as students in formal education. In particular, the questions concentrate on whether or how these initial, and often thought to be simplistic, misdirected, incorrect, and/or ineffectual beliefs may be changed during the teacher education program.

The literature suggests that changes in beliefs are difficult at the preservice teacher education stage. The various rationale for this difficulty as expressed in the literature include: the very short time-period in which students are actually engaged in preservice teacher education; the disconnect between the academic program of teacher education and practice in the field; the lack of time and experience in which the students can develop a sense of "need to know" such that they realize the importance of the academic and skill preparation material in their academic classes. Thus, while seeming changes in beliefs may take place during the academic elements of teacher education (usually experienced prior to practice in the field), these beliefs can change back to their prior state when they enter the field. This may also lead to the sense that teachers teach as they were taught.

All of the rationale mentioned above that were developed to explain the difficulty in changing beliefs of teacher education candidates undoubtedly contribute to the problem, and have lead to a sense of the importance of the connection between the academic programs and observation, inquiry and practice in the field. When one considers that the beliefs and understanding of the field were acquired by students in action and through experience rather than through academic study, it may be that changes in these beliefs may best be accomplished with attention paid to real life or at least visual displays of teaching action (e.g., videocases). Thus, the call for structured field practica that accompany the academic courses. These practica, however, must be structured such that the constructs and propositions discussed in the academic classes become visual and experienced in the classroom, and the experiences in the classrooms become an element of the academic classes.

An alternative to the efforts of bringing together the academic and practice is to consider the Fenstermacher (1979) process of placing students in a structured situation in the field such that they can develop a framework of practice as a teacher to use when they subsequently take academic classes. This latter suggestion also relates to the sense that change in teacher's beliefs seems easier to accomplish in inservice rather than preservice teacher education (Richardson & Placier, 2001).

In sum, it is suggested in this chapter that beliefs are important in the education of teacher education candidates, that their change and development should be a goal of teacher education programs, and that, while difficult to change and develop at this stage, research indicates that it is possible. Focusing on existing research, however, leaves out an important element of consideration, and that is the ethical issues of how one makes a decision as to which beliefs should be changed. Recently, many of us have ideologically embraced constructivist pedagogy, and are convinced that this provides a better education for the young. This entails changing from traditional to constructivist beliefs and understandings about the nature of learning and teaching and the goals of education. Are these changes warranted? Might we be developing a group of teachers who ideologically cling to constructivist beliefs at such point as another, perhaps more worthy, approach is developed? It is certainly important that teacher educators consider, carefully, the nature of their curriculum, the beliefs they are asking their students to acquire and develop, and the ways in which they are acquiring them.

NOTES

1. The educational psychologists locate both knowledge and beliefs in the individual's head. This is a quite different stance from philosophers who may locate beliefs within the individual's head, but have a much more social sense of knowledge.

2. Academic course suggestions are Introduction to Teaching, Educational Foundations, Educational Psychology, literacy, and various methods depending on whether the student is in elementary or secondary education.

REFERENCES

Agee, J. (1998). Confronting issues of race and power in the culture of schools: A case study of a preservice teacher. In M. E. Dilworth (Ed.), *Being responsive to cultural differences: How teachers learn* (pp. 21-38). Thousand Oaks, CA: Corwin Press.

Alexander, P. A., Schallert, D. L., & Hare, V. (1991). Coming to terms: How researchers in learning and literacy talk about knowledge. *Review of Educational Research, 61*(3), 315-343.

Anderson, L., Smith, D., & Peasley, K. (2000). Integrating learner and learning concerns: Prospective elementary scheice teachers' paths and progress. *Teaching and Teacher Education, 16*(5-6), 547-574.

Avery, P. G., & Walker, C. (1993). Prospective teachers' perceptions of ethnic and gender differences in academic achievement. *Journal of Teacher Education, 44*(1), 27-37.

Ball, D. (1990). Reflections and deflections of policy: The case of Carol Turner. *Educational Evaluation and Policy Analysis, 12*, 241-245.

Ben-Peretz, M. (1990). Research on teacher education in Israel: Topics, methods and findings. In R. P. Tisher & M. F. Wideen (Eds.), *Research in teacher education* (pp. 207-225). London: Falmer.

Black, A., & Ammon, P. (1992). A developmental-constructivist approach to teacher education. *Journal of Teacher Education, 43*(5), 323-335.

Bolin, F. (1990). Helping student teachers think about teaching: Another look at Lou. *Journal of Teacher Education, 41*(1), 10-19.

Book, C., & Freeman, D. (1986). Differences in entry characteristics of elementary and secondary teacher candidates. *Journal of Teacher Education, 37*(2), 47-51.

Borko, H., & Mayfield, V. (1995). The roles of the cooperating teacher and universitysupervisor in learning to teach. *Teaching and Teacher Education, 11*(5), 501-518.

Borko, H., & Putnam, R. (1996). Learning to teach. In R. C. Calfee & D. C. Berliner (Eds.), *Handbook of educational psychology* (pp. 673-708). New York: Macmillan.

Britzman, D. (1991). *Practice makes perfect: A critical study of learning to teach.* Albany: State University of New York Press.

Brookhart, S. M., & Freeman, D. (1992). Characteristics of entering teacher candidates. *Review of Educational Research, 62*(1), 37-60.

Bryan, L.A. (April, 1998). Learning to teach elementary science: A case study of teacher beliefs about science teaching and learning. Paper presented at the annual meeting of the National Association for Research in Science Teaching, San Diego.

Calderhead, J. (1988). Learning from introductory school experience. *Journal of Education for Teaching, 14*(1), 75-83.

Calderhead, J., & Robson, M. (1991). Images of teaching: Student teachers' early conceptions of classroom practice. *Teaching and Teacher Education, 7*, 1-8.

Civil, M. (1993). Prospective elementary teachers' thinking about teaching mathematics. *Journal of Mathematical Behavior, 12*, 79-109.

Clift, R., Meng, L., & Eggerding, S. (1994). Mixed messages in learning to teach English. *Teaching and Teacher Education, 19*(3), 265-279.

Cochran-Smith, M. (1991). Reinventing student teaching. *Journal of Teacher Education, 42*(2), 104-118.

Crow, G. M., Levine, L., & Nager, N. (1990). No more business as usual: Career changers who become teachers. *American Journal of Education, 98*(3), 197-223.

Dana, T., McLaughlin, A. S., & Freeman, T. B. (April, 1998). Creating dissonance in prospective teachers' conceptions of teaching and learning science. Paper presented at the annual meeting of the National Association for research in Science Teaching, San Diego.

Dilworth, M., & Brown, C. (2001). Consider the difference: Teaching and learning in culturally rich schools. In V. Richardson (Ed.), *Handbook of research on teaching* (4th ed., pp. 643-667). Washington, DC: American Educational Research Association.

Erickson, G., & MacKinnon, A. (1991). Seeing classrooms in new ways: On becoming a science teacher. In D. Schön (Ed.), *The reflective turn: Case studies in and on educational practice* (pp. 15-37). New York: Teachers College Press.

Feiman-Nemser, S., & Floden, R. E. (1986). The cultures of teaching. In M. C. Wittrock (Ed.), *Handbook of research on teaching* (3rd ed., pp. 505-526). New York: Macmillan.

Feiman-Nemser, S., McDiarmid, G. W., Melnick, S. L., & Parker, M. (1989). *Changing beginning teachers' conceptions: A description of an introductory teacher education course* [Research Report 89-1]. East Lansing, MI: National Center for Research on Teacher Education, College of Education, Michigan State University.

Fenstermacher, G. D. (1979). A philosophical consideration of recent research on teacher effectiveness. In L. S. Shulman (Ed.), *Review of research in education* (Vol. 6, pp. 157-185). Itasca, IL: Peacock.

Fenstermacher, G. D. (1993). *Where are we going? Who will lead us there?*. Washington, DC: American Association of Colleges of Teacher Education.

Green, T. (1971). *The activities of teaching*. New York: McGraw-Hill.

Haberman, M. (1996). Selecting and preparing culturally competent teachers for urban schools. In J. Sikula (Ed.), *Handbook for research on teacher education* (2nd ed., pp. 747-760). New York: Macmillan.

Holt-Reynolds, D. (1992). Personal history-based beliefs as relevant prior knowledge in course work. *American Educational Research Journal, 29*(2), 325-349.

Holt-Reynolds, D. (2000). What does the teacher do? Constructivist pedagogies and prospective teachers' beliefs about the role of a teach. *Teaching and Teacher Education, 16*(1), 21-32.

Hoy, W. (1967). Organizational socialization: The student teacher and pupil control ideology. *The Journal of Educational Research, 61,* 153-259.

Kagan, D. (1990). Ways of evaluating teacher cognition: Inferences concerning the Goldilocks principle. *Review of Educational Research, 60*(3), 419-469.

Kam, H. W. (1990). Research on teacher education in Singapore. In R. P. Tisher & M. F. Wideen (Eds.), *Research in teacher education* (pp. 105-120). London: Falmer.

Kile, R. S. (1993). *Preconceptions of elementary and secondary preservice teachers* Unpublished doctoral dissertation, University of Arizona, Tucson.

Korthagen, F. A. J. (1988). The influence of learning orientations on the development of reflective teaching. In J. Calderhead (Ed.), *Teachers' professional learning* (pp. 35-50). Philadelphia: Falmer.

Ladson-Billings, G. (1996). Silences as weapons: Challenges of a Black professor teaching White students. *Theory into Practice, 35*(2), 79-85.

Lampert, M., & Ball, D. (1999). *Investigating teaching: New pedagogies and new technologies for teacher education*. New York: Teachers College Press.

Lehrer, K. (1990). *Theory of knowledge*. Boulder, CO: Westview Press.

Lortie, D. (1975). *Schoolteacher: A sociological study.* Chicago: University of Chicago Press.

MacKinnon, A., & Erickson, G. (1992). The roles of reflective practice and foundational disciplines in teacher education. In T. Russell & H. Munby (Eds.), *Teachers and teaching: From classroom to reflection* (pp. 192-210). London: Falmer.

MacKinnon, A., & Scarff-Seatter, C. (1997). Constructivism: Contradictions and confusions in teacher education. In V. Richardson (Ed.), *Constructivist teacher education: Building new understandings* (pp. 38-56). London: Falmer.

Mallette, M. H., Kyle, S., Smith, M. M., McKinney, M., & Readance, J. E. (2000). Constructing meaning about literacy difficulties. Preservice teachers beginning to think about pedagogy. *Teaching and Teacher Education, 16*(5-6), 593-612.

McDiarmid, G. W. (1990). Tilting at webs: Early field experiences as an occasion for breaking with experience. *Journal of Teacher Education, 41*(3), 12-20.

McDiarmid, G. W. (1992). What to do about differences? A study of multicultural education for teacher trainees in the Los Angeles Unified School District. *Journal of Teacher Education, 43*(2), 83-93.

Mitchell, D., Ortiz, F., & Mitchell, T. (1987). *Work orientation and job performance: The cultural basis of teaching rewards and incentives.* Albany: State University of New York Press.

National Center for Research on Teacher Education. (1991). *Final report: The teacher education and learning to teach study.* East Lansing: College of Education. Michigan State University.

Novak, D., & Knowles, J. G. (1992). *Life histories and the transition to teaching as a second career.* Paper presented at the annual meeting of the American Educational Research Association], Chicago, IL.

Olson, M. R. (1993). *Knowing what counts in teacher education.* Paper presented at the Canadian Association of Teacher Educators, Canadian Society of Studies in Education, Ottawa, CA.

Pajares, M. F. (1992). Teachers' beliefs and educational research: Cleaning up a messy construct. *Review of Educational Research, 62*(3), 307-332.

Pigge, F., & Marso, R. (1997). A seven-year longitudinal multi-factor assessment of teaching concerns development through preparation and early years of teaching. *Teaching and Teacher Education, 12*(2), 225-236.

Powell, R., & Birrell, J. (1992). *The influence of prior experiences on pedagogical constructs of traditional and nontraditional preservice teachers.* Paper presented at the annual meeting of the American Educational Research Association, San Francisco.

Resnick, L. B. (Ed.). (1989). Introduction. In *Knowing, learning, and instruction: Essays in honor of Robert Glaser* (pp. 1-24). Hillsdale, NJ: Erlbaum.

Reyes, S., Capella-Santana, N., & Kristy, L. (1998). Prospective teachers constructing their own knowledge in multicultural education. In M. E. Dilworth (Ed.), *Being responsive to cultural differences: How teachers learn* (pp. 110-125). Thousand Oakes, CA: Corwin Press.

Richardson, V. (1996). The role of attitudes and beliefs in learning to teach. In J. Sikula (Ed.), *Handbook of research on teacher education* (2nd ed., pp. 102-119). New York: Macmillan.

Richardson, V., & Kile, R. S. (1999). *The use of videocases in teacher education*. In M. Lundberg, B. Levin, & H. Harrington (Eds.), *Who learns from cases and how? The research base for teaching with cases* (pp. 121-136). Hillsdale: NJ: Erlbaum.

Richardson, V., & Placier, P. (2001). Teacher change. In V. Richardson (Ed.), *Handbook of research on teaching* (4th ed., pp. 905-947). Washington, DC: American Educational Research Association.

Rokeach, M. (1968). *Beliefs, attitudes and values: A theory of organization and change.* San Francisco: Jossey-Bass.

Ross, D., Johnson, M., & Smith, W. (1991). *Developing a professional teacher at the University of Florida.* Paper presented at the annual meeting of the American Educational Research Association, Chicago.

Russell, T. (1995). Returning to the physics classroom to re-think how one learns to teach physics. In T. Russell & F. Korthagen (Eds.), *Teachers who teach teachers* (pp. 95-112). London: Falmer.

Russell, T. (1999). The challenge of change in teaching and teacher education. In J. Baird (Ed.), *Reflecting, teaching, learning: Perspectives on educational improvement* (pp. 219-238). Cheltenham, Victoria, Australia: Hawker Brownlow Education.

Simon, M., & Mazza, W. (1993). *From learning mathematics to teaching mathematics: A case study of a prospective teacher in a reform-oriented program.* Paper presented at the annual meeting of the North American Chapter of the International Group for the Psychology of Mathematics Education, Monterey, CA.

Smith, K. E. (1997). Student teachers' beliefs about developmentally appropriate practices: Pattern, stability, and the influence of locus of control. *Early Childhood Research Quarterly, 12,* 221-242.

Smylie, M. (1988). The enhancement function of staff development: Organizational and psychological antecedents to individual teacher change. *American Educational Research Journal, 25*(1), 1-30.

Tillema, H. (2000). Belief change towards self-directed learning in student teachers immersion in practice or reflection on action. *Teaching and Teacher Education, 16*(5-6), 575-591.

Tillema, H., & Knoll, W. (1997). Promoting student teacher learning through conceptual change or direct instruction. *Teaching and teacher Education, 13*(6), 579-595.

Tom, A. (1984). *Teaching as a moral craft.* New York: Longman.

Upitis, R., Luce-Kapler, R., & Munby, H. (Eds.). (2000). *Who will teach: A case study of teacher education reform.* San Francisco: Caddo Gap Press.

Weber, S., & Mitchell, C. (1996). Using drawings to interrogate professional identity and the popular culture of teaching. In I. Goodson & A. Hargreaves (Eds.), *Teachers' professional lives* (pp. 109-126). London: Falmer.

Weinstein, C. S. (1989). Teacher education students' preconceptions of teaching. *Journal of Teacher Education, 40*(2), 53-60.

Wideen, M., Mayer-Smith, J., & Moon, B. (1998). A critical analysis of the research on learning to teach: Making the case for an ecological perspective on inquiry. *Review of Educational Research, 68*(2), 130-178.

Zanting, A., Verloop, N., & Vermunt, J. (2001). Student teachers eliciting mentors' practical knowledge and comparing it to their own beliefs. *Teaching and Teacher Education, 17*(6), 725-740.

Zeichner, K., Tabacknick, R., & Densmore, K. (1987). Individual, institutional, and cultural influences on the development of teachers' craft knowledge. In J. Calderhead (Ed.), *Exploring teachers' thinking* (pp. 21-59). London: Cassell.

Zimpher, N. L., & Ashburn, E. A. (1992). Countering parochialism in teacher candidates. In M. E. Dilworth (Ed.), *Diversity in teacher education: New expectations* (pp. 40-62). San Francisco: Jossey-Bass.

CHAPTER 2

PROMPTING THE DEVELOPMENT OF PRESERVICE TEACHERS' BELIEFS THROUGH CASES, ACTION RESEARCH, PROBLEM-BASED LEARNING, AND TECHNOLOGY

Mary Anna Lundeberg
Michigan State University

Barbara B. Levin
University of North Carolina–Greensboro

Because the beliefs teachers hold influence their classroom judgments and actions, understanding more about the beliefs of teachers is essential to improving teaching practices (Pajares, 1992; Richardson, 1996). Because the beliefs preservice teachers hold influence what and how they learn, beliefs are also important in learning to teach (Richardson, 1996). The beliefs of preservice teachers act as a filter through which preservice teachers acquire and interpret knowledge (Pajares, 1992). For example,

Advances in Teacher Education 23–42
Copyright © 2003 by Information Age Publishing
All rights of reproduction in any form reserved.

one of our preservice teachers, Megan, initially held the belief that teachers should answer questions from students directly, rather than use thought-provoking questions to enable students to discover answers for themselves. Consequently, Megan initially dismissed the idea that teachers should act as facilitators, reasoning that this pedagogical approach would frustrate students, and ignored much of the pedagogy taught in a teacher education course that focused on using questions and probing responses to facilitate student thinking. Thus, her initial belief that teaching is a process of dispensing information filtered the knowledge she acquired in that course.

Distinguishing between beliefs and knowledge is messy, because beliefs and knowledge are "inextricably intertwined" (Pajares, 1992, p. 325). Nonetheless, beliefs are a form of personal knowledge and have a stronger affective, evaluative, and episodic nature than does knowledge. Moreover, whereas beliefs represent an individual's personal judgment of the truth, knowledge implies a truth condition with a community of people agreeing on evidence to back up this knowledge (Richardson, 1996). In order to ascertain people's beliefs, researchers have asked teachers what they believe, or interpreted beliefs from what people say, say they intend to do, or do (Lundeberg & Fawver, 1993; Pajares, 1992; Richardson, 1996).

A decade has passed since Pajares (1992) argued that teachers' beliefs should become an important focus of educational inquiry. However, despite several calls for understanding more about teachers and preservice teachers' beliefs, relatively little research has emerged in this area (Pintrich, 1990; Pajares, 1992; Richardson, 1996). After discussing how traditional pedagogy has little influence on students' beliefs, this chapter focuses on what we know about changing beliefs based on research in science education and our research on using cases, action research, problem based learning, and technology. Both our experiences in using these approaches in teacher education courses and our values influence our pedagogy. Values are inextricably intertwined with beliefs, and in this chapter we do not usually distinguish between values, attitudes, and beliefs. For example, the student I mentioned earlier, Megan, held the value that teachers should never do anything to embarrass or frustrate a student, particularly an underachiever. This value supported Megan's belief that teachers should just answer students' questions, rather than engage them in thinking through an answer using interaction. However, while doing action research in a classroom situation, when Megan observed that an underachiever did not get frustrated by not being given the answer, she altered her belief about this. She realized that questions could enable the underachiever to get to the answer himself, and eventually came to understand and appreciate the role of teacher as a facilitator

The methods we are advocating in this chapter—cases, action research, problem-based learning and on-line discussions—are based on ideas we value in teaching, such as collaboration, learner choice, and responsibility, communication, community, constructivism, multiple perspectives, and anchored instruction. Our own beliefs are a manifestation of our values as instructors. As teacher educators, we try to promote the above values in our teaching and influence preservice teachers to use similar methods themselves in their future K-12 classrooms. Furthermore, because we understand that our attitudes and values are foundational to our beliefs, we use these terms interchangeably in this chapter (Pajares, 1992).

PROBLEMS WITH CONVENTIONAL PEDAGOGY

We know, from research in science education, that conventional pedagogy has little influence on changing beliefs, particularly misconceptions of students. Conventional pedagogy has been characterized as "teaching is telling; knowledge is facts, and learning is recall." Conventional pedagogy has several limitations. Students are treated as spectators in the learning process who are focused on solutions and answers already known; theories are presented out of context (or within limited contexts) and the teacher plays the role of a sage on the stage. Foundations courses in teacher education typically take an encyclopedic approach that sacrifices depth for breadth. Preservice teachers are bombarded with hundreds of terms, definitions, concepts, and theories that they have difficulty conceptualizing into a whole. This approach does little to involve, much less challenge, preservice teachers' beliefs about students, schools, the process of learning, or their vision of themselves as a future teacher.

PROMISING PEDAGOGY

On the other hand, we believe that the pedagogical approaches discussed in this chapter offer the potential for changing the beliefs of preservice and experienced teachers, if they are used in systematic ways during teaching education and in professional development settings. We have found that using cases, problem-based learning, action research, and on-line discussions can influence teachers' beliefs because they offer opportunities and challenges for teachers to consider and articulate their own attitudes, values, and beliefs, hear the perspectives of others, and defend challenges to their beliefs that come on the form of new experiences, new perspectives, and new knowledge they gain from engaging in these forms of pedagogy. In the following pages we describe our experiences with cases, problem-based learning, action research, and on-line discussions and share the results of our research into what is learned from these pedagogical practices.

Cases

Dilemma-based cases provide a real-world classroom context in which to foster discoveries about teaching and learning in future teachers (Lundeberg, 1999). These discoveries include theoretical and practical understandings; metacognition; reflection on social, ethical and epistemological growth; reasoning, and beliefs (Lundeberg, 1999). Employing dilemma-based cases in teacher education offers prospective teachers opportunities to confront some of their attitudes and values; hence, the use of cases has the potential to change preservice teachers' beliefs.

Learning from Cases

When Lundeberg asked students what they thought they learned from case analysis, they reported being able to anchor theories to real situations, and see the practical, story component of the theories and concepts.

> I think case analysis has given me the opportunity to apply concepts/theories in a more practical sense. I have learned that recognizing issues will come in the form of listening to and researching a student's life. As a teacher I will be much more likely to remember Ed Psych concepts from story situations than from textbook reading. (Lundeberg & Scheurman, 1997, p. 793)

Students also reported developing flexibility in their thinking and multiple perspectives:

> It (case analysis) has taught me to take in all views. To see not only from a teacher's view but from a student's, principal's and other faculty. (Lundeberg & Fawver, 1994)

With regard to their epistemlogical beliefs, students reported that case discussions initiated their development from dichotomous thinking to multiple perspectives:

> I find in our case study discussions, I am always interested in how everyone handles the situation. I tend to see things in black and white. I realize now there are many answers to one problem. (Lundeberg & Fawver, 1994, p. 295)

Types of Cases

There are a variety of cases available for teacher educators to use in class, from short cases designed to illustrate theoretical principles often included in foundations textbooks (e.g., Good & Brophy, 1994) to open-ended, more complex dilemma-based cases located in case books such as Greenwood and Fillmer (1999). Video-based cases of exemplary teachers can be used to provide rich contexts for students to develop "pictures" of teaching. Cases are also available on the Internet and on CD-ROMs, such as those offered by the Vanderbilt group (e.g., http://www.casenex.com). Finally, preservice teachers can be taught to develop their own cases based on field experiences with students and teachers in the schools (Hammerness, Darling-Hammond, & Shulman, 2002; Lundeberg, Bergland, Klyczek, & Hoffman, 2002). A central question to keep in mind when choosing a case for a particular course is Lee Shulman's question: What is this a case of? (Shulman, 2001).

Although we use a variety of cases in our courses, we tend to prefer dilemma-based cases because they engender deeper social interaction among our students. Cases do not teach themselves. Indeed, without appropriate facilitation, student discussion of cases may lead to misconceptions and stereotypes. Most casebooks include ideas on facilitating the case and some cases include questions for students to consider as they read the case. We prefer to have students use a heuristic to analyze cases. We hope that by providing a framework for students to consider potential dilemmas in school, they can improve and transfer their reasoning to future classroom situations. This heuristic for problem solving is described in the next section.

A heuristic for Guiding Case Discussions

This is a description of how we generally use case discussions in class. Students are expected to read cases at home and take written notes on them, noting issues/problems, evidence as to why they perceive those problems, theories/concepts related to the case, potential solutions (including likely consequences for those solutions), and a reflection on their values and experiences related to the case.

In class, we sit in a circle (or U shape) for discussion. Until students learn one another's names, we use name cards to encourage direct response to one another and to encourage people to call one another by name. Disagreement is encouraged, as is building on one another's ideas. Usually the discussion begins with the question: "What are the issues in this case?" If students do not provide a reason for citing something as an issue, the instructor asks, "What leads you to think that was a problem?" Thus students refer to evidence from the case in framing the issues and often even read sentences from the case to support their ideas.

When appropriate, the instructor asks about the beliefs or assumptions of the people in the case, and tries to help students differentiate between evidence and assumptions. If students define the issue from only one perspective (e.g., the teacher's point of view), we might ask, "If you were a student in this class, what might you think?" Or, "If you were a principal observing this class, what might you say?" After eliciting several issues from a variety of perspectives, the instructor then moves on to a discussion of the concepts/theories relevant to the case, decisions/ solutions they would suggest, potential consequences of those decisions and finally, values, beliefs and experiences related to the case. Students are also encouraged to think about the case issues and solutions from the perspective of their future teaching situation. We try to encourage perspective taking, especially on ideas involving beliefs and values by asking questions such as, "Does everyone agree with that? Does anyone have a different point of view?" The emphasis is on reasoning and multiple forms of thinking, not on "correct" solutions to any given case.

While case-based pedagogy can be used as a catalyst to challenge the participants' prior beliefs, help them understand different perspectives than their own, and encourage them to articulate, defend or change current beliefs about their practice, problem-based learning (PBL) experiences often serve the same purposes. In fact, cases can serve as the foundation for PBL and offer a vehicle for presenting the problem(s) to be solved.

Problem-based Learning (PBL)

Problem-based learning (PBL) is an instructional method that encourages students to acquire and then apply content knowledge, critical thinking, and problem solving skills to real-world problems and issues. The instructor's role in PBL is to develop rich problems to be solved, offer guidance and instruction as needed, and to suggest resources that will help students acquire necessary content knowledge and use problem-solving skills. Students engaged in PBL take considerable responsibility for their own learning by locating much of the information they need to solve the problem(s) posed. PBL usually involves groups of students in discussion, reflection, research, projects, and presentations, although individuals can tackle problems on their own. The learning that occurs during PBL experiences is active rather than passive, integrated rather than fragmented, cumulative rather than finite, collaborative rather than isolated, and connected rather than disjointed (Levin, 2001). Evaluation of PBL should be authentic, performance-based, and on going. Problem-based learning usually begins with a real-world issue presented as a case or a problem to be solved. As with case-based pedagogy, there may be many solution paths and several good answers to the problems because there is not always just one "right" answer to a PBL experience.

Learning from PBL in Medical Education

Research conducted during the past few decades in medical schools that use PBL (Norman & Schmidt, 1992) along with findings from two meta-analyses indicates that medical students using a PBL curriculum demonstrate positive motivational characteristics including intrinsic motivation, self-regulation, and goal orientation to learning for understanding (Albanese & Mitchell, 1993; Vernon & Blake, 1993). In other studies set in medical colleges, PBL students were found to study for deeper understanding (Coles, 1985; Newble & Clark, 1986), retain information longer (Norman & Schmidt, 1992), and were more likely to apply scientific information appropriately (Allen, Duch, & Groh, 1996). While PBL has been used in medical schools for a number of years, it has also become a part of the curriculum in several disciplines in colleges and universities (Bridges, 1992; Camp, 1996). PBL has also been used to teach most subjects in K-12 schools (Delisle, 1997; Gallagher, Stepien, & Rosenthal, 1992; Stepien, Gallagher, & Workman, 1993; Torp & Sage, 1999).

Learning from PBL in Teacher Education

Levin used PBL with preservice elementary teachers in several courses offered at different points during their teacher education program (Levin, 2001). In evaluating students' learning following a semester-long PBL experience with undergraduates preservice teachers learning how to work with children with disabilities in an inclusion classroom, Levin and her colleagues (Hibbard, Levin, & Rock, 2001; Levin, Hibbard, & Rock, 2002) administered a pre- and postsurvey (Bailey & Winton, 1987) to assess their beliefs about the practice of inclusion. Students also completed the same survey of beliefs about inclusion one year later. The immediate post-PBL survey results indicated statistically significant increases in positive beliefs about including children with disabilities in the general education classroom. Furthermore, preservice teachers who continued to have internship experiences in inclusive settings after the PBL semester showed additional increases in their positive beliefs about inclusion in a follow-up survey one year later (Hibbard, 1998). Preservice teachers who did not have additional opportunities to intern in inclusive classrooms showed a decrease from their post-PBL scores, although their scores remained higher than their pre-PBL scores (Hibbard, 1998).

Analyses of written responses to the PBL activities (Hibbard, Levin, & Rock, 2001; Levin, Hibbard, & Rock, 2002) indicated that two experiences during the PBL semester were cited most often as contributing to changes in their beliefs, sense of efficacy, and willingness to teach exceptional children in inclusion settings: (1) their own research and study about the specific disabilities they chose to learn more about, and (2) observations or internships they had in inclusion classrooms.

Typical responses of students about working in inclusion classrooms before the PBL unit included comments such as this: "I have no idea how to organize or manage a classroom with such diversity in order to meet students' needs. I will have to gain a lot of knowledge before I would feel capable of such an endeavor" (Levin et. al, 1998, p. 15). Although only 19 of 44 participants indicated that they would accept a job teaching an inclusion classroom at the start of the PBL unit, by the end of the PBL unit 32 said they would teach in an inclusion classroom. The following comment is representative of the participants' who displayed positive dispositions about working with students with disabilities after the PBL experience:

> No two children are alike and therefore the same strategy might not work for every child, but the strategies that I learned through my research and from my peers would give me a jumping off point in beginning to work with these children.
> All of my thoughts began to change when I had the chance to see this working first hand and from being able to hear the inclusion teacher talk. The research did help because it gave me information that before I did not have, but the true help was the actual experience of seeing the class. (Levin et. al, 1998, p. 19)

Although participation in PBL activities appeared to enhance the knowledge base and influence the beliefs and attitudes of preservice teachers about working with students with disabilities in inclusion settings, Levin and her colleagues (1998, 2001, 2002) realized that other factors also contributed to apparent changes in student's beliefs. Nevertheless, they concluded that PBL can provide a catalyst for shifting beliefs by motivating and engaging prospective teachers to confront their beliefs through acquiring new knowledge, engaging in problem solving and critical thinking, collaborating, and making decision, which are a part of PBL. Collecting pre- and postdata from students helped document changes in student attitudes, which is a necessary prerequisite for changes in beliefs—although often not sufficient (Pajares, 1993; Richardson, 1996).

Other Research on PBL with Teachers

There are a limited number of empirical studies about the effectiveness of PBL as a learning tool in teacher education settings and the research base on PBL in undergraduate teacher education is sparse (Thomas,

2000). Furthermore, the evidence about knowledge retention and transfer is mixed. For example, Shumow (1999) found that teacher education students in her educational psychology classes performed significantly better on objective and essay tests when the PBL unit came during the second half of the semester. Shumow's students also rated the individualized research they conducted as the most educational aspect of PBL and indicated that engagement in PBL was valuable for their professional identity development as teachers. Shumow (1999) also reported that 84% of her students rated the PBL portion of the class as more motivating than the traditional, didactic method of learning used during the first half of the semester. However, Pyke and Porchet (1997) found that students in their educational psychology class enjoyed PBL but did not learn as much about motivational theory as the instructors believe they would in a more traditional class. Pierce (1999) found that undergraduate educational psychology students who experienced PBL rated their professors as more learner-centered, and Sage (1999) reported that engagement in PBL changed teachers' beliefs about the value of building classroom community and proved to be a good match for instructors and students who have constructivist views of learning.

In summary, the research that is available about using PBL with prospective teachers and medical professionals offers evidence that PBL can impact the motivation, beliefs, and self-directed learning of adult learners. Pajares (1993) defines beliefs as the attitudes and values that preservice teachers bring to their teacher education about teaching (p. 46). Our own research indicates that engagement in PBL experiences engenders more positive attitudes about working with students with disabilities, inclusion, and collaboration (Levin et. al, 1998, 2002), which may have a positive influence on beliefs about individual differences. More research needs to be done on the influence of PBL in changing beliefs.

In PBL, already-crafted, real-world problems are generally presented to students. An extension of PBL is to have teacher researchers pose problems that need to be solved in their own classrooms or schools. In the next section we describe a collaborative approach to link preservice teachers with action research in schools.

Action Research

Action research is systematic inquiry or problem posing by teachers, usually focused on promoting changes in practice (Cochran-Smith & Lytle, 1999; Henson, 1996). Action research is a valuable method of examining teachers' practices in Great Britian, Australia and the United

States (Cochran-Smith & Lytle, 1993, 1999; Elliott, 1990, 1991; Nixon, 1981).

In the past decade, action research has been advocated for both preservice and inservice teacher education as a means of improving teaching and learning through critical reflection on problems in practice (Gore & Zeichner, 1991; Lieberman, 1986). In the context of school-university partnerships, teacher action research has contributed to inquiry about pedagogical changes teachers are implementing (Catelli, 1995; Lundeberg et. al, 1995), as well as reform efforts (Lampert, 1990). The reflection involved in writing about classroom problems interwoven with the social interaction and multiple perspectives of other researchers may have a powerful influence on the development of preservice teachers' beliefs, knowledge and confidence.

Learning from Action Research

Lundeberg has used action research in several of her courses, including a research methods course, educational psychology, and most recently a seminar in science education. The primary purpose of the science education seminar was to investigate whether involving preservice science teachers in evaluating a case-based multimedia collaborative learning project altered their beliefs about technology integration, developed their pedagogical content knowledge about using technology, and/or enhanced their confidence in using technology (Lundeberg, Bergland, Klyczek, & Hoffman, 2002).

Preservice science teachers participated in a weekly seminar in which they read literature about multimedia simulations in science, gained experience with the Case It! software and then observed and collected data in a high school classroom. On the first and last days of the seminar preservice teachers completed a questionnaire assessing their confidence and knowledge in understanding biotechnology content and in using interactive multimedia in science. In addition, they wrote pre- and post-essays, giving advice to a science teacher who was considering using a multimedia internet project. Beliefs can be inferred by what preservice teachers say, intend and do (Pajares, 1992), and have been investigated using questionnaires as well as qualitative measures (Richardson, 1999).

In both years of the seminar these preservice teacher/researchers participated in designing the instruments used in the study, including the interview questions, and the rubrics used to assess the web posters and the quality of Internet conferences. In the seminar, as a group, they analyzed data collected from the previous year to gain experience with coding interview data, rating web posters, and coding interactions from web conferencing. In the first year these preservice science teachers collected and analyzed data after the project was completed, analyzing 30 web posters, interactions during the web conferencing of 60 students and interviews with 49 high school and college students. In the second year of the project, we decided to focus our research on the high school students, who included 8 groups of 17 students ranging from sophomores to seniors (Lundeberg, Bergland, Klyczek, & Hoffman, 2002).

We expanded data collection in the second year to include pre- and postcase-analysis assessments of the high school students and daily observations by at least two researchers who recorded their observations and reflections electronically on a Blackboard discussion site. The discussion site included a forum for observations of the class as a whole with a focus on what the teacher (and student teacher) were doing during class. There were eight forums for observations of each of the eight high school groups within the class as they were engaged in working on this multimedia project, and a forum for research assistants to discuss reflections, concerns, and questions. Each preservice teacher observed and wrote two case studies about 4 high school students (2 groups) over a month-long observation period. The case study included what high school students did (and did not) learn, the challenges and difficulties high school students and the high school teachers faced, and whether this multimedia project was effective in enhancing student construction of knowledge. Cases included excerpts from interviews with the high schools students, excerpts from students' Internet posters and conferencing sessions and observations of the students' working process as recorded in the Blackboard observations. Finally, preservice teacher/researchers reflected on what they learned as a research assistant in this project.

Being a research assistant involved in an action research project with a high school science teacher prompted thinking, writing, and conversations about some of the challenges and benefits of using case-based learning with high school students. These preservice teachers also thought and wrote much about their beliefs regarding the implementation of complex, involved multimedia projects into their future science classrooms and some of the technological pedagogical content knowledge they gained by their observations and study of students in this classroom (Lundeberg, Bergland, Klyczek, & Hoffman, 2002). For example, a misconception regarding interaction that was initially held by one preservice teacher (Megan) was that teachers should answer questions directly, rather than act as facilitators. As this preservice teacher reported:

> While at the school, I learned that when students have a question, it is more effective to give them direction in looking up the answers, rather than just giving it to them. Although we were told this in Educational Psychology, I thought this wouldn't work because students would just get more frustrated but as it turned out, this was completely the opposite. They didn't complain

when they didn't get the answer directly; they were thankful that they had an alternative to finding the answer. I most certainly will use this in my teaching.

This above example shows that students' personal beliefs/misconceptions are not necessarily changed just by information presented in an earlier foundations course or by the modeling that occurs in the foundations course. This student needed to see the concept illustrated in the context of a teacher working with students in her own discipline for her to believe that it would "work" and alter her initial conception of teacher as answer giver.

The on-line discussions these preservice teachers engaged in during their action research was a helpful tool in promoting discussion about their classroom observations. As one preservice teacher reported, she would have thought very differently about the inferences she made from her observations if it hadn't been for the Blackboard discussions in which other preservice teachers reported on the groups of students they observed and interviewed. In the next section, we describe how on-line discussions can be used to encourage reflection on beliefs.

On-line Discussions

On-line discussions, whether in the form of structured, moderated, asynchronous threaded discussions, e-mail exchanges, or synchronous and unmoderated chatrooms, all make use of computer-based technologies to extend opportunities for peer-to-peer interaction beyond the four walls of the university classroom. In the past decade many teacher educators have used various forms of on-line communication, including on-line discussions, as an integral part of their teaching (Levin, 1999; Thomas, Clift, & Sugimoto, 1996). One of our propositions in this chapter is that on-line discussions, like cases, problem-based learning, and action research may have the potential to influence and even change teacher beliefs because they provide alternative perspectives that prospective teachers may not be exposed to in other ways and require participants to articulate and often defend their own beliefs about topics under discussion.

Purposes of Electronic Communicatons
Today, more and more on-line courses are available to preservice and inservice teachers as a part of their professional development, and on-line discussions are often a major component of teacher preparation courses. Sometimes the goal of on-line discussion is to enhance communication

between instructors and students and to increase communication and support among students as a peer group around course content. The actual content of postings and exchanges in on-line discussions may range from personal to professional, from private to public, from to disconnected to essential, and from peripheral to substantive. Among the purposes that on-line exchanges can serve include reflection, feedback, support, evaluation, questioning, and problem solving (Levin, 1999). However, it should be noted that the content and the purposes of most on-line discussions in teacher education are influenced by the goals and purposes of course, which are provided either implicitly or explicitly by an instructor (Levin, 1999; Schlagal, Trathen, & Blanton, 1996).

Although the same goals and purposes for on-line discussions can be accomplished off-line through the exchange of dialogue journals and face-to-face during class discussions, we believe electronic communications will be used more and more in teacher education in the coming years. Therefore, we must note that while Clark (1983, 1985, 1994) wrote as a result of his research on teaching with technology that the medium is *not* the message, his research runs counter to our own experiences with technology-based learning, including on-line discussions. While we acknowledge that technology like the Internet is just a delivery system, and that similar outcomes may be achieved from face-to-face discussion, in today's world most preservice teachers are very comfortable engaging in on-line communication via email, chat rooms, and facilitated or unfacilitated discussion forums. Furthermore, most colleges and universities provide teacher candidates with e-mail accounts and free access to the Internet and the World Wid Web. Telecommunications makes accessing, sending, and sharing information almost instantaneous, and more and more instructors are taking advantage of digital formats for both synchronous and asynchronous communication. Therefore, the use of on-line discussions as a pedagogical tool deserves serious analysis.

Learning with Electronic Communications

Levin's experience with asynchronous on-line discussions and other forms of electronic communication over the past eight years prompted her to study the content and purposes of several different types of electronic communication used with one cohort of preservice teachers over a two-year period (Levin, 1999): (a) student-to-peer e-mail journals exchanged between self-selected pairs of preservice teachers within a cohort group; (b) student-to-keypal e-mail exchanges with teacher candidates in another state; (c) e-mail exchanges between students and their university instructor and supervisor; and (d) student-to-group messages exchanged during asynchronous, web-based threaded discussions. Levin's purpose in conducting this study was to identify the content and purposes of these four forms of electronic communications. One of the findings from this study was that the peer-to-group exchanges during on-line discussions during a semester-long, asynchronous, threaded discussion fostered more reflective exchanges than in any of the other forms of one-to-one electronic communication studied. Findings reveal that for 13 out of 14 topics discussed during the on-line discussions, between 86% and 100% of the exchanges were reflective in nature. Students articulated their values and beliefs about teaching and learning in these reflections.

These results contrasted sharply with the other types of electronic communication in which reflection served as the purpose for only 26% of student-to-peer exchanges, 14% of student-to-keypal exchanges, and 13% of the student-to-instructor messages. Other purposes the on-line discussions served (depending on the content of the topic being discussed) included "support" of another student's ideas expressed during the discussion (15%-75%), and "requests for feedback" from peers about particular situations in their field experiences (6%-67%). An example of the kinds of belief statements coded as "support" were: "I very much agree with Jennifer. Students do need the opportunity to discuss and share knowledge. I think Sherri made a good point about respect." An example of the types of statements coded as "requests for feedback" were: "If you could teach children what you think they should know, what would you teach?" Comments coded as "reflective" included belief statements such as "I have seen myself grow in the areas of communication with other people and also in the area of what my expectations may be for other people."

In this same study (Levin, 1999), more than half the student-to-peer e-mail was about individual or personal concerns, although nearly a third of these exchanges focused on teaching issues including beliefs expressed about curriculum, instruction, and planning. This finding contrasts with other published studies about e-mail exchanges among peers, which showed that the major purpose student-to-peer email served was social, emotional, and moral support (Anderson & Lee, 1995; Merseth, 1991; Souviney, Saferstein, & Chambers, 1995; Thomas et. al, 1996).

In trying to understand why the peer-to-group on-line discussions in this study contained so many reflective statements about curriculum, teaching, and planning, Levin analyzed the content of the participants' final written reflections about their on-line discussions. Two of the participants expressed their thinking about these discussions this way:

> Using TopClass was an interesting and educational experience because I was able to voice my opinion and read how other people felt about the same issue. This, in my opinion, is more beneficial than just receiving one other person's feedback. Just to hear what other people are thinking and feeling

really helps.
  I felt the on-line discussions were more valuable that the journal writing because I got to think about different kinds of questions. Plus, it was presented in a forum. I got to hear other people's ideas of different issues. I also go to hear from other people who never speak up in seminar.

Based on the participants' written reflections about their experiences with four kinds of electronic communications, several possible reasons emerged as to why the on-line peer-to-group discussions elicited more reflective thinking about the participants' beliefs than the other three types of exchanges including: (a) novelty, (b) appreciation of the chance to learn from others, (c) a sense of validation and belonging because their feelings, beliefs, and experiences were confirmed by others, and (d) preferring feedback from an audience of many peers rather than from one person. Apparently, these on-line discussions prompted social construction of knowledge and validation of beliefs about a variety of topics (Vygotsky, 1987). Furthermore, this occurred in a context with peers who had different perspectives to share, were at different stages of development, and who could provide alternative points of view and even scaffold the learning of others about a particular topic.

Learning from On-line Discussions
  Over the years, Levin has continued to use on-line threaded discussions with other cohort groups of preservice teachers and in her teacher education courses. Most recently, she used on-line discussions to exchange perspectives on how the content of the chapters in an educational psychology textbook (Ormrod, 2001) can be applied in the classroom. She also used on-line discussions as a pedagogical tool with the same cohort of students taking a course about the interaction of classroom management and instruction during a subsequent semester. In both of these large classes, students were divided into groups of 9-12 students who remained together in the same on-line discussion groups for an entire semester. In the educational psychology class, one pair of students was responsible for (a) preparing two discussion questions about an assigned chapter, (b) moderating and facilitating the on-line discussions among all the groups for that week, (c) summarizing and posting a written summary of the discussion, and finally (d) presenting their summary to the class and guiding any additional discussion about their chapter's content. In essence, their experiences with on-line discussions in this course were as a participant and as a moderator or facilitator. In the classroom management course, the on-line discussions were held every other week and the class did not meet face-to-face during those weeks. Final written reflections from some of these students reiterates some of Levin's

earlier findings about how and why on-line discussions may influence pre-service teachers' prior beliefs:

> Last year I was a fan of our TopClass discussions, and this semester I enjoyed Blackboard discussions even more. In each case the class was given the immensely important opportunity to hear the opinions of a diverse group of teachers who find themselves in uniquely different situations. Having this opportunity allowed us to not only hear the opinions of our professor and discuss issues with her, but also hear those of our colleagues and discuss issues with them. As a result the class discussions were always taken much further than would have ever been possible—and issues that would never have been brought up in class were able to be addressed on-line (WW, 11/18/01).

> I particularly enjoyed the on-line discussion component of this course. It was an invaluable opportunity for me to read many ideas and experiences of other preservice and inservice teachers.... I was most interested in the discussions that involved the participation of many inservice teachers. It is helpful that my cohort has an internship experience to base opinions on, but I find that I value the inservice teachers' opinions more.... Overall I enjoyed the experience of on-line discussions. It was not only a convenient learning experience for students with very busy schedules, but it was valuable in that it lasted longer than any one class could ever be held. I could participate in several different discussions at one time and continue to reply for an entire week. The amount of knowledge that I acquired from the experience was more than I ever could have gained from reading any textbook [JW, 11/15/01].

These students appeared to enjoy participating in on-line discussions and perceived that they learned from others—both their peers and more experienced others. This adds to earlier research evidence that indicates that participation in on-line discussions fosters reflection in preservice teachers (Levin, 1999). On-line discussions also appear to be useful tools for allowing multiple perspectives to emerge and be shared. If positive attitudes, reflective thinking, and exposure to different points of view are important precursors to changes in beliefs, as we and others believe that they are (Pajares, 1992; 1993; Richardson, 1996), then participation in well-structured on-line discussions may be a valuable pedagogical tool for influencing teachers' beliefs. In this instructional scenario, the importance of hearing from others, often more experienced teachers who teach in different contexts and have differing perspectives, seems to be important in fostering changes in beliefs, although these assertions need to be tested empirically as on-line discussions become more and more popular pedagogical tools.

CONCLUSIONS

We have described four pedagogical approaches to initiating preservice teachers' reflection on their beliefs: cases, problem-based learning, action research, and on-line discussions. Our own pedagogical beliefs and the results of our research have led us to believe that these teaching strategies are effective for prompting preservice and inservice teachers to articulate and clarify their beliefs. We believe that pedagogy that offers opportunities for collaboration, choice, communication, community, constructivism, understanding multiple perspectives, and anchored instruction has the potential to change our students' prior beliefs. However, we also understand that beliefs are difficult to change and that engaging in a few case discussions, having on-line discussions in one course, participating in one round of action research or in one PBL unit is not likely to change a person's beliefs. More than likely, it takes multiple opportunities to engage in and reflect on these kinds of learning activities that help our students confront their beliefs. Beliefs may be idiosyncratic and this may make measuring them through questionnaires difficult. Moreover, other problems with measurement, such as the biases inherent in self-report research, particularly when students are studied within a professor's courses, make us cautious about interpreting such research. More research in these areas, especially longitudinal qualitative research that shows changes over time, will allow us to better understand the contributions of each approach to developing or changing preservice teachers' beliefs. Nevertheless, we are cautiously optimistic, based on the results of the research shared in this chapter, that some forms of pedagogy are more likely to change teacher beliefs than others—especially compared to more conventional forms of pedagogy.

REFERENCES

Albanese, M. A., & Mitchell, S. (1993). Problem-based learning: A review of the literature on its outcomes and implementation issues. *Academic Medicine, 68*, 52-81.

Allen, D. E., Duch, B. J., & Groh, S. E. (1996). The power of problem-based learning in teaching introductory science courses. *New Directions for Teaching and Learning, 68*, 43-52.

Anderson, J., & Lee, A. (1995). Literacy teachers learning a new literacy: A study of the use of e-mail in a reading instruction class. *Reading Research and Instruction, 34*, 222-238.

Bailey, D., & Winton, P. (1987). *Benefits and drawbacks of early childhood inclusion.* Chapel Hill, NC: Frank Porter Graham Child Development Center.

Bridges, E. M., with P. Halinger. (1992). *Problem-based learning for administrators*. University of Oregon: ERIC Clearinghouse on Educational Management.

Camp, G. (1996). Problem-based learning: A paradigm shift or a passing fad? *Medical Education Online, 1: 2*. Available: MEO@utmb.edu.

Catelli, L. A. (1995). Action research and collaborative inquiry in a school-university partnership. *Action in Teacher Education, 16*(4). 25-38.

Clark, R. E. (1983). Reconsidering research on learning from media. *Review of Educational Research, 53*, 445-459.

Clark, R. E. (1985). Confounding in educational computing research. *Journal of Educational Computing Research, 1*, 137-148.

Clark, R. E. (1994). Media will never influence learning. *Educational Technology Research and Development, 42*(2), 7-19.

Cochran-Smith, M., & Lytle, S. (1993). *Inside/outside: Teacher research and knowledge*. New York: Teachers College Press.

Cochran-Smith, M., & Lytle, S. (1999). The teacher research movement: A decade later. *Educational Researcher, 28*, 15-25.

Coles, C. R. (1985). Differences between conventional and problem-based curricula in their students' approaches to studying. *Medical Education, 19*, 308-309.

Delisle, R. (1997). *How to use problem-based learning in the classroom*. Alexandria, VA: Association for Supervision and Curriculum Development.

Elliott, J. (1990). Teachers as researchers: Implications for Supervisions and for teacher education. *Teaching & Teacher Education, 6*(1), 1-26.

Elliott, J. (1991). *Action research for educational change*. Milton Keynes: Open University Press.

Gallagher, S., Stepien, W., & Rosenthal, H. (1992). The effects of problem-based learning on problem solving. *Gifted Child Quarterly, 36*, 195-200.

Good, T. L., & Brophy, J. E. (1994). *Educational Psychology* (5th ed.). New York: Longman.

Gore, J. M., & Zeichner, K. M. (1991). Action research and reflective teaching in preservice teacher education: A case study from the United States. *Teaching and Teacher Education, 7*, 119-136.

Greenwood, G. E., & Fillmen, H. T. (1999). *Educational psychology cases for teacher decision-making*. Upper Saddle River, NJ: Merrill

Hammerness, K., Darling-Hammond, L., & Shulman, L. (2002). Toward expert thinking: How curriculum case-writing prompts the development of theory-based professional knowledge in student-teachers. *Teaching Education, 13*, 219-243.

Henson, K. T. (1996). Teachers as researchers. In J. Sikula, T. Buttery, & E. Guyton (Eds.), *Handbook of research on teacher education* (2nd ed., pp. 53-64). New York: Macmillan. Washington, DC: American Educational Research Association.

Hibbard, K. L. (1998). *Preservice teachers' beliefs about including children with special needs in the general education classroom: Can change happen?* Unpublished manuscript, University of North Carolina at Greensboro.

Hibbard, K., Levin, B., & Rock, T. (2001). The inclusion classroom problem: Learning about students with disabilities. In B. B. Levin (Ed.), *Energizing teacher education and professional development with problem-based learning* (pp. 56-72). Alexandria, VA: ASCD.

Lampert, M. (1990). When the problem is not the question and the solution is not the answer: Mathematical knowing and teaching. *American Educational Research Journal, 27,* 29-63.

Levin, B. B. (1999). Analysis of the content and purpose of four different kinds of electronic communications among preservice teachers. *Journal of Research on Computing in Education, 32,* 139-156.

Levin, B. B. (Ed.). (2001). *Using problem-based learning in teacher education.* Alexandria, VA: ASCD.

Levin, B. B., Hibbard, K. L., & Rock, T. T. (1998, October). *Exploring problem-based learning with undergraduate preservice teachers: A vehicle for instruction about inclusion.* Paper presented at the annual meeting of the American Association for Teaching and Curriculum, Orlando, FL.

Levin, B. B., Hibbard, K. L., & Rock, T. T. (2002). Using problem-based learning as a tool for learning to teach students with special needs. *Teacher Education and Special Education, 25*(3), 69-81.

Lieberman, A. (1986). *Rethinking school improvement.* New York: Teachers College Press.

Lundeberg, M. A. (1999). Discovering teaching and learning through cases. In M. A. Lundeberg, B. B. Levin, & H. Harrington (Eds.), *Who learns what from cases and how: The research base for teaching and learning with cases* (pp. 3-23) Mahwah, NJ: Lawrence Erlbaum.

Lundeberg, M. A., Bergland, M., Klyczek, K., & Hoffman, D. (2002). Using action research to develop preservice teachers' confidence, knowledge and beliefs about technology. *Journal of Interactive Online Learning.* Available: http://ncolr.uidaho.com/journal/jounal.asp.

Lundeberg. M. A., Coballes-Vega, C., Daly, K. Bowman, G., Uhren, P., & Greenberg, D. (1995). Wandering around the world: Building multicultural perspectives through K-12 telecommunications projects. *Journal of Technology and Teacher Education, 3*(4), 301-321.

Lundeberg, M. A. & Fawver, J. E. (1993, April). Cognitive growth in case analysis. Paper presented at American Educational Research Association, Atlanta, GA.

Lundeberg, M. A. & Fawver, J. E. (1994). Thinking like a teacher: Encouraging cognitive growth in case analysis. *Journal of Teacher Education, 45*(4), 289-297.

Lundeberg, M. A. & Scheurman, G. (1997). Looking twice means seeing more: developing pedagogical knowledge through case analysis. *Teaching and Teacher Education, 13*(8), 783-797.

Merseth, K. K. (1991). Supporting beginning teachers with computer networks. *Journal of Teacher Education, 42,* 140-147.

Newble, D. I., & Clark, R. M. (1986). The approaches to learning of students in a traditional and in an innovative problem-based medical school. *Medical Education, 20,* 267-273.

Nixon, J. (Ed.). (1981). *A teacher's guide to action research.* London: Grant McIntyre.

Norman, G. R., & Schmidt, H. G. (1992). The psychological basis of problem-based learning: A review of the evidence. *Academic Medicine, 67,* 557-65.

Ormrod, J. E. (2000). *Educational psychology: Developing learners* (3rd ed.). Upper Saddle River, NJ: Merrill.

Pajares, M. F. (1992). Teachers' beliefs and educational research: Cleaning up a messy construct. *Journal of Educational Research, 62*(3), 307-332.

Pajares, F. (1993). Preservice teachers' beliefs: A focus for teacher education. *Action in Teacher Education, 15*, 45-54.

Pierce, J. W. (1999). *Problem-based learning: A learner-centered tool for higher education.* Paper presented at the annual meeting of the American Educational Association, Montreal, Canada.

Pintrich, P. R. (1990). Implications of psychological research on student learning and college teaching for teacher education. In W. R. Houston (Ed.), *Handbook of research on teacher education* (pp. 826-857).

Pyke, S., & Pourchet, T. (1997). *Development and assessment of a problem-based learning curriculum for the teaching of educational psychology.* Paper presented at the annual meeting of the American Educational Research Association, Chicago, IL.

Richardson, V. (1996). The role of attitudes and beliefs in learning to teach. In J. Sikula (Ed.), *Handbook of research on teacher education* (pp. 102-119). New York: Simon & Schuster/Macmillan.

Sage, S. (1999). *What does a mobile home park have to do with it anyway? Using problem-based learning to teach problem-based learning in graduate teacher education.* Paper presented at the annual meeting of the American Educational Association, Montreal, Canada.

Schlagal, B., Trathen, W., & Blanton, W. (1996). Structuring telecommunications to create instructional conversations about student teaching. *Journal of Teacher Education, 47*, 175-183.

Shulman, L. (2001). Learning from cases: Closing the "Theory-Practice" gap? Symposium presented at the annual meeting of the American Educational Association, Seattle, Washington.

Shumow, L. (1999). *Problem-based learning in undergraduate Educational Psychology: Contributor to student learning and motivations?* Paper presented at the annual meeting of the American Educational Association, Montreal, Canada.

Souviney, R., Saferstein, B., & Chambers, E. (1995). Internet: Network communication and teacher development. *Journal of Computing in Teacher Education, 11*(4), 5-15.

Stepien, W. J., Gallagher, S. A., & Workman, D. (1993). Problem-based learning for traditional interdisciplinary classrooms. *Journal for the Education of the Gifted, 16*, 338-357.

Thomas, J. (2000). *A review of research on project-based learning.* [On-line]. Available at http://www.autodesk.com/foundations. [8/1/00].

Thomas, L., Clift, R.T., & Sugimoto, T. (1996). Telecommunications, student teaching, and methods instruction: An exploratory investigation. *Journal of Teacher Education, 46*, 165-174.

Torp, L. & Sage, S. (1998). *Problems as possibilities: Problem-based learning for K-12 education.* Alexandria, VA: Association for Supervision and Curriculum Development.

Vernon, D. T. A., & Blake, R. L. (1993). Does problem-based learning work? A meta-analysis of evaluative research. *Academic Medicine, 68*, 550-563.

Vygotsky, L. (1987). *Thought and language.* Cambridge, MA: MIT Press.

CHAPTER 3

TEACHER BELIEFS, PERFORMANCE AND PROFICIENCY IN DIVERSITY-ORIENTED TEACHER PREPARATION

Peter C. Murrell, Jr. and Michèle Foster

One of the most prominent and frequently discussed issues in the literature on teacher preparation of great concern to researchers, teacher educators, and policy makers is the demographic imbalance between the proportion of students of color and the proportion of teachers of color in American public schools. Already overwhelmingly populated by White, culturally mainstreamed females, the teaching force is becoming even more so, in contrast to a student population that is increasingly culturally, linguistically, and racially diverse. This is a trend expected to increase in the coming decades. According to statistics of the National Center for Education Statistics (1997), in 1994 the teaching force was 87% White with only 13% teachers of color, whereas the student population of color was approaching 50% nationwide.

One consequence of this demographic imbalance has been the considerable attention and effort marshaled toward preparing White teachers to

Advances in Teacher Education 43–64
Copyright © 2003 by Information Age Publishing

"teach to diversity." In the policy arena, for example, the National Council for the Accreditation of Teacher Education (NCATE), one of the major national accrediting agencies for teacher education, includes diversity among its five required program standards that teacher preparation institutions must meet to become accredited. The diversity standard reads:

> That the unit designs, implements, and evaluates curriculum and experiences for candidates to acquire and apply the knowledge, skills, and dispositions necessary to help all students learn. These experiences include working with diverse higher education and school faculty, diverse candidates, and diverse students in P-12 schools. (NCATE, 2002, p. 29)

In similar fashion, most state departments of education include at least one diversity standard among the professional teaching standards they require of all teacher education programs.

An added dimension to the imperative for greater cultural responsiveness is the fact that national and state policy are increasingly requiring performance assessment in the evaluation of teachers, teacher candidates, and teacher education programs. Program approval by state departments of education and oversight of the state approval process by the federal government (i.e., the Title II report card) are based on performance standards. National accreditation evaluations administered by professional organizations such as NCATE are all based on performance standards as well. In fact, the new accreditation standards of NCATE require the demonstration of a candidate's proficiency in terms of *P-12 pupil* achievement performance.

This national movement toward performance-based accountability ups the ante considerably regarding the preparation of preservice teachers for diversity. The implication for teacher preparation is that no longer will *the mere exposure* to diverse experiences (e.g., field experiences in diverse settings, multicultural education courses) be acceptable as evidence for candidate readiness and program quality. Increasingly, successful "diversity training," for instance, in teacher preparation will need to be evidenced by teachers' demonstrations of achievement of children of diverse backgrounds.

Teacher preparation programs have generally responded to these accountability imperatives regarding diversity by creating preservice teacher curricula aimed at transforming candidates' belief systems with regard to race and culture. This is so that teacher candidates become less "culturally encapsulated" with regard to the cultural, racial, and linguistic diversity they are likely to encounter in public schools. Requiring that future teachers be equipped for successful work in racially and culturally diverse settings has meant contesting their racial bias and sense of race privilege. These efforts range from merely "raising awareness" to experiences that seriously challenge dispositions of racial privilege and White supremacy (Cooney & Akintunde, 1999; Melnick & Zeichner, 1997). For example, some states require that prospective teachers take course work in multicultural issues. Both Wisconsin and California have multicultural components to licensure. California offers a Cross-cultural Language and Academic Development (CLAD) endorsement for multiple subject and single subject credentials, which typically includes some combination of courses such as Foundations for Multicultural Education, Multicultural & CLAD Perspective, and/or Observation/Participation in Multicultural Settings.

The concern frequently articulated in the teacher education literature (e.g., Sleeter, 2001b; Zeichner, 1996) is that the increasingly White, culturally mainstreamed, and middle class teaching force will continue to be ill-prepared to teach in increasingly diverse public schools. This "cultural gap," (to use Sleeter's term) accounts for a predominance of the professional and scholarly literature on multicultural education. Sleeter (2001b, p. 93) notes the broad recognition of this cultural gap in the literature, as well as the challenge it presents to teaching, teacher research, and teacher preparation.

The current theory and practice regarding teachers' beliefs with respect to race and class are driven by the concern that, as a whole, this large cohort of White preservice teachers possesses very little cultural knowledge or experience with which to develop productive and effective teaching practices when they move into culturally, racially, and linguistically diverse settings (Barry & Lechner, 1995; Grant, 1997; Sleeter, 2001b; Smith, Moallem, & Sherrill, 1997; Zeichner & Gore, 1990; Zeichner & Melnick, 1996).

TWO APPROACHES TO CLOSING THE CULTURAL GAP

Presently, preservice teacher education programs use two main approaches to address the "cultural gap." The first attempts to bring individuals from culturally, racially, and linguistically diverse communities into the teaching profession. The second tries to shape ethnically and culturally congruent dispositions and multicultural competence among the predominantly White cohorts of preservice candidates (Sleeter, 2001b, p. 96). We will refer to these two approaches as IMT (increasing minority teachers) and the TTB (transforming teacher beliefs), respectively.

The TTB method is the prevalent approach to the cultural gap, evidenced by the preponderance of research literature that focuses on changing beliefs toward greater multicultural competence in teacher education (cf. Ladson-Billings, 1999; Sleeter, 2001b) An unfortunate consequence of employing the TTB approach to address the cultural gap has been that teacher education programs now focus more on preparing the predominantly White prospective teaching force than on figuring out how to produce more teachers of color. This priority continues to be the case despite recent research that provides evidence that having the same race teachers may have a greater impact on the performance of children of color than previously thought (Dee, 2001).

CHANGING TEACHER BELIEFS: AN INSUFFICIENT TACTIC?

The concern that future teachers are inadequately prepared to teach students from diverse backgrounds has found its way into the research on teacher beliefs. For better or worse, the focus on beliefs and attitudes has been more reactive than proactive. A proactive approach would have focused more on the dispositions underlying accomplished practice among diverse learners. The present reactive approach tends to focus on reducing teacher candidates' resistance to values of social justice, and eliminating racial bias and stereotypical thinking regarding learners of color. Although not inconsistent with the NCTAF (National Commission on Teaching and America's Future) formulation of what teachers should know (cultural knowledge), be able to do (be culturally competent in crossing cultural borders), and be disposed to do (orientation toward anti-racist, social justice practice), this TTB approach is limited. Specifically, the approach is not producing multicultural competent teachers. Despite its good intention, this approach, consisting mainly of changing preservice candidates' beliefs and attitudes so that they are less "culturally encapsulated" regarding issues of diversity, does not guarantee that teacher candidates improve their ability to work successfully and effectively with diverse learners. The mere elimination of bias is not tantamount to elevating the quality of one's practice.

Unless teacher programs demonstrably improve preservice teachers' ability to be effective in diverse settings, it will not matter whether or not their beliefs and attitudes are changed. The remainder of this chapter will examine some of the problems inherent in the current approaches to teacher preparation for diversity that address of teacher beliefs and attitudes. We conclude with recommendations for research, practice, and policy concerning teacher beliefs in teacher education.

DEFINING TERMS

It will be useful to define several terms. The common use of the terms *beliefs* and *dispositions* need to be contrasted with their use in the teacher education community. In every day use, *belief* (American Heritage Dictionary, Fourth Edition, 2000), is defined as the mental acceptance of and conviction in the truth, actuality, or validity of something; or something believed or accepted as true, especially a particular tenet or a body of tenets accepted by a group of persons. An attitude is an opinion or general feeling about something.

In contrast to *beliefs* and *attitudes* the term *disposition* connotes enactment of one's beliefs or one's attitudes. It would be pointless to set professional standards like "teachers must *believe* children of color are no less capable than White children" or "teachers must have positive *attitudes* about diversity" because there simply is no way to verify them in teaching performance. However, it is vitally important to set practice standards that require that teachers not inadvertently degrade the quality of learning for their students of color or perpetuate structural inequality in their practice and pedagogy. For example, a teacher might enact as a disposition the stereotypic belief that Black children come from disorganized and undisciplined homes by requiring the Black children in her classroom to do comparatively more individual seat work, perhaps pedagogically justifying the practice as an effort to provide discipline through more focused individual effort for those children. In this example, the disposition is the regular, consistent requirement the teacher sets over time for her Black students. It is based on a belief concerning the home lives her students experience.

Where the distinction between a belief and disposition becomes important is when we consider how to assist or assess the practice of a teacher or teacher candidate whom we observe carrying out this potentially destructive practice. Beliefs and attitudes that degrade the teacher's credibility and effectiveness with her African American students should be noted and so that this practice can be modified. However, we might only note negative beliefs as errors of commission—such as when a teacher is observed expressing a racial stereotype, is overheard making a racial slur, or is seen giving differential treatment to Black and White students. The teacher or teacher candidate who learns not to do these things—or at least, learns *not to be observed doing these things*—has in neither case become more effective with her African American students. We, as teacher educators must also be concerned with the errors of omission—namely, what it is that teachers are disposed to do and fail to do with regard to their African American students. It is for this reason that dispositions, not beliefs, are what we key on to assist or assess teachers' performances with regard to improving their practice in diverse contexts.

In the literature on teacher education and the language of professional teaching standards, the term *disposition* is used to specify the attitudinal components of what candidates are expected "to know and be able to do" by indicating what, in addition, they *should be disposed to do*. There are, therefore, severe limitations to any approach in teacher education that seeks to merely instill attitudes or change the beliefs of candidates with regard to issues of diversity, structural inequality, and institutional racism. Beliefs and attitudes are terms that express subjective states with regard to something—how an individual feels or thinks about another person, idea, pedagogy, principle, or system of ideas. The problem is that beliefs and attitudes are not changed independently of an individual's world-view and epistemology. There can be no accountability for teacher performance if the focus is only on internal states of mind. If we want to change and improve teachers' practice, we have to focus on what teachers actually do in practice, not on their states of mind independent of the context of meaningful activity. This is the reason and necessity for working with dispositions that account for attitudes and beliefs as they are manifested in behavior and professional activity.

Standards for teacher performance set forth by national professional organizations such as NCATE and INTASC (Interstate New Teachers Assessment and Support Consortium, 2001) as well as state departments of education adopt the term *disposition* as a performance-based proxy for professional beliefs and attitudes. The added value in adopting the term disposition over beliefs as the focus of teacher education programs is that *dispositions* can be assessed in performance as the *enactment* of the individual's beliefs and attitudes In short, beliefs and attitudes are what candidates bring to their teacher preparation; dispositions are the expectations we place on a teacher candidate's practice given those beliefs and attitudes as they are reflected in professional or instructional activity.

In summary, *a belief is the conviction that something is true* and a *disposition* is a *belief* given *action*. As such, only *dispositions* can be assessed directly through performance with respect to professional teaching standards. Dispositions are simply the expectations we place on teacher candidates to be more effective in diverse contexts.

PROBLEMS WITH THE CURRENT TTB APPROACH

Is a program of changing candidates' beliefs tantamount to candidates embodying particular dispositions? The answer is clearly "no" since a belief implies nothing about practice, or what a candidate is disposed to do when facing real challenges of effective work in culturally, racially, and linguistically diverse settings. Herein lies the crux of the problem for addressing the cultural gap. Typically, teacher preparation programs, including those where equity and diversity are focal issues, assume that changing beliefs through teacher education curriculum is a precursor to changing dispositions and altering practice (Wideen, Mayer-Smith, & Moon, 1998, pp. 160-161).

The major theme in diversity focused teacher preparation over the last 10 to 15 years has been that of developing a greater multicultural sensitivity—including values of social justice, culturally responsive practice, and ethical practice in diverse settings by challenging teacher candidates' belief systems regarding racial privilege (see Hayman & King, 1997; Irvine, 1996; for two edited volumes). The predominant approach to diversity development has been to "educate" prospective teachers out of their stereotypical thinking, racial and cultural bias, and socialized sense of privilege, and to encourage them to embrace the values of social justice and ethical practice.

As the work of Tatum (1992) shows, however, changing teacher candidates' belief systems regarding race and racism is more than a matter of providing the "right" educational experience. It is also a developmental process requiring considerable time and committed engagement on the part of the candidates' themselves to interrogate their beliefs. Beliefs about children and communities of color and attitudes of racial privilege and superiority are not easily changed because they are so deeply embedded in the world views of preservice teachers' cultural and social reference group (e.g., King, 1991). Consequently, when asked to interrogate their racial privilege and assumptions about race, not only do culturally mainstreamed, White teachers struggle with concepts that challenge their own system of ideas and taken-for-granted assumptions, they frequently experience the inquiry as an assault on their identity.

Changing the ideologies and tenets espoused by White, culturally mainstreamed students requires more than their merely learning about culture, increasing tolerance, and increasing understanding of other groups. Beliefs of racial superiority and their subsequent attitudes toward people of color constitute at least a part of the racial identity that many teacher candidates seek to protect in the course of experiences that interrogate whiteness and explore institutional racism. Even if these individuals' beliefs were sufficiently malleable to be changed in the context of a course experience, the reality is that these beliefs and attitudes are enmeshed in, and sustained by, the larger context of their lives so that they re-emerge in their practice. Racial privilege exists not just in individuals' belief systems, but also as a dominant ideology embedded in their social networks and the cultural fabric that supports and sustains them.

Diversity courses do not merely challenge isolated beliefs or attitudes, but candidates' entire belief systems or world views.

Changing prospective teachers' attitudes does not occur merely by being told about or being exposed to examples of culturally relevant practice. We have evidence, in fact, that teacher candidates who are merely exposed to issues of multicultural teaching and learning often become more firmly entrenched in their own beliefs. As such, multicultural courses can "backfire" in that students emerge with more negative attitudes toward ethical practice in diverse settings than when they began (Haberman & Post, 1992; McFalls & Cobb-Roberts, 2001; Reed, 1993).

Despite being the most common recommendation of policy makers in teacher education, the TTB option also generates at least two unsettling consequences as an approach to addressing the cultural gap. First, it has led to a disproportionate focus on challenging beliefs and instilling attitudes toward diversity held by the predominantly White prospective teaching force, which then diminishes efforts to produce more teachers of color by bringing into teaching those who are proven, accomplished practitioners in diverse settings. Second, contrary to the national movement toward accountability and the demonstration of proficiency in diversity-related professional teaching standards, the TTB approach redirects the focus of diversity training toward changing beliefs and instilling about race, class, and ethnicity, and away from actually developing dispositions associated with the teaching proficiencies necessary for effective work in diverse settings. The result is a misalignment of agendas—the efforts to transform preservice teacher beliefs in diversity preparation may actually be at odds with the aim of holding teachers, candidates, and programs accountable for improving teaching practice in diverse contexts.

The impact of the TTB approach in teacher education is questionable because there is little evidence indicating that changing the beliefs of beginning teachers has any effect on improving their practice with respect to children of color (Wideen et. al, 1998, pp. 160-161). Based on the available evidence it is doubtful whether providing knowledge is sufficient to change beliefs and whether changed beliefs trigger, or translate into, appropriate practice in this area. Sleeter (2001a, 2001b) reviewed the multicultural education literature with regard to transforming the belief systems of White preservice teachers and concluded that there is little to guide current practice in the preparation of culturally competent teachers and concludes that it provides no clear guidance as to what do (Sleeter, 2001b, p. 96).

FIVE PROBLEMS WITH THE TTB APPROACH

There is little in the educational research literature to suggest that programmatic efforts to transform individual teacher candidates' beliefs regarding diversity improves their teaching practice. Why has the TTB approach had so little impact on closing the cultural gap? If we are to refit effective teacher preparation so as to close the cultural gap and meet the new demands of professional teaching standards, we need to know the answer to this question. We believe there are five reasons, summarized in Table 3.1 and discussed in this section. In the following section we will detail recommendations and solutions to these issues (Table 3.2) from the respective contexts of our current work.

One reason why the TTB approach has had little impact is that most White preservice candidates bring to teacher education too little cultural awareness, cross-cultural experience, or understanding of discrimination, racism, or structural inequality in education (Su, 1996, 1997; King, 1991; Melnick & Zeichner, 1997). They are simply too naïve about the lives,

Table 3.1. Five Reasons for Limited Impact of the TTB Approach

Reason for Scant Impact	Evidence Source
Most White preservice candidates bring too little awareness, cross-cultural experience, or understanding of discrimination, racism, or structural inequality in education. Most White preservice teachers are naïve about the lives, experiences, and culture of children in diverse communities, and bring biases.	Cochran-Smith (1997) Irvine (1996) King (1991) Melnick & Zeichner (1997) Schultz, Neyhart, & Reck (1996) Su (1996, 1997)
The relatively modest gains in moving White preservice teachers from their entrenched belief systems seem to require an enormous investment of time, energy, and curricular activity.	McIntyre (1997) Valli (1995) Tatum (1992) Sheets (2000)
Few preservice programs articulate effective performance indicators for "multicultural competence" that are appropriate and necessary for effective work in culturally, linguistically and racial diverse urban schools.	Haberman (1995) Murrell (2001)
There is little evidence to suggest, even when dispositional changes were accomplished with respect to preservice teachers beliefs and attitudes about practice in diverse settings, that these changes are reflected in teaching practice.	Cook & Flay (1978)
There is evidence suggesting that candidates of color are dissatisfied with, turned-off by, and turned away from "multicultural" components of their teacher education program.	Murrell (1991) Parker & Hood (1995)

experiences, and cultures of children in diverse communities, and bring biases that are difficult to dislodge (Schultz, Neyhart, & Reck, 1996; Murrell, 1991). Changing candidates' beliefs is made more difficult because there is so much ground to cover in simply appreciating different cultural forms. To make matters worse, many White students often experience this kind of inquiry as a threat to their own identity (McIntyre, 1997; Valli, 1995; Tatum, 1992). They experience these diversity-related topics as personally threatening and inconsistent with their own views of good teaching (McFalls & Cobb-Roberts, 2001; Vavrus, 1994). For example, McIntyre (1997) noted how her student teachers invoked colorblindness as a way of avoiding the confrontation of their own fear in the process of interrogating their beliefs.

We contend that beliefs do not matter if they are not instantiated in behavior or action, nor are they changed without a context of professional interaction and reflective interpretation of practice. We recommend that the experience of preservice teachers incorporate active engagement with people, problems, and positions in contexts in which those beliefs matter. We further contend that transforming beliefs is not the issue, but rather the development of dispositions that is of central importance, particularly where the focus is on how teacher candidates interpret culturally unfamiliar situations. Dispositions are best developed and strengthened through an immersion in diverse contexts in which candidates become participants in the successful and effective instructional practice of practitioners with proven capability teaching children of diverse backgrounds.

The second reason that the TTB approach has had little impact is related to the first. Efforts to change candidates' beliefs regarding diversity have had only modest impacts because, even when it occurs, the transformation of White preservice teachers' entrenched belief systems requires enormous investments of time, energy, and curricular effort. Teacher candidates rarely alter their core beliefs about race and class privilege without difficult conversations in which there is an interrogation of their White privilege—something that rarely occurs regularly or systematically in teacher education programs. Tatum's (1992) research for example, documented how difficult and slow this process can be, and testified to the improbability that a single course can produce substantial changes in this important area.

In some cases the curricular effort takes the form of courses focused on "Whiteness studies" and "White racial identity" that, while of potential interest and value, encroaches on the time and activity that would otherwise be devoted to candidates' learning how to teach their children to read, write, and think in diverse classrooms. Sheets (2000) illustrated how easily identity work can become equated with "multicultural competence" or readiness to teach to diversity even though no evidence exists to that effect.

We have argued to this point that a change in beliefs regarding people of color is not itself an achievement of teaching proficiency, but rather a development that *could* enable the dispositions required for effective work in diverse settings. Theoretically, our argument is for understanding the situated nature of attitudes, beliefs, and dispositions. By this we mean that it is vitally important to take account of how the context of human goals, relationships, and purposeful activity of a given instructional setting determines what and how dispositions are expressed. Pragmatically, our argument is for immersion experiences that place White, culturally mainstreamed students in contexts that require they critically examine and confront their racial privilege through educational activity with people of color who present powerful counter examples to their stereotypes.

A third reason that the TTB approach has had scant impact on multicultural competence is that it offers few performance indicators for what multicultural competence should look like in practice. As previously noted, surveys and reflective inventories of candidates' beliefs are insufficient as assessments of multicultural proficiency. Candidates respond to such surveys motivated by social acceptance, and therefore are more apt to adopt a persona of political correctness and edit their responses according to what they think they are expected to say. In these instances, there is very little correspondence between what is expressed and what is demonstrated in actual practice, and this lack of correspondence is even greater with respect to racial attitudes and behaviors (Dovidio & Fazio, 1992; Fazio, Jackson, Dunton, & Williams, 1995).

Indicators of multicultural competence, if they are to be tied to the achievement of children, must be derived from actual practice as well as by research—and ought to be done in collaboration with educators and scholars of color whose knowledge and experience with children of color have already been proven. On this account, it would be important to draw upon research that brings to light accomplished practice of teachers of color (e.g., Foster, 1997, 1999, 2001) already dedicated to, and successful in, elevating the academic achievement and personal development of children of color (e.g., Murrell, 2001, 2002). The development of actual instructional practice with, and among, successful teachers of color is an important research endeavor—and more fruitful in the development of multiculturally competent White candidates than academic investigations of "Whiteness."

Multicultural competence is not merely a bag of pedagogical tricks that will "work" with urban children of color in linguistically, culturally, and racially diverse settings. Rather, multicultural competence consists of qualities that go beyond a teacher's pedagogical repertoire. Multicultural competence includes, but is not limited to, how a teacher values, understands, and inquires into the varied and overlapping contexts of the lives of urban children of color. This competence is not completely explicable or visible unless a teacher's practice is appraised in the context of real activity among, and in collaboration with, educators of color engaged in the work of educating Black and Brown children.

This brings us to the fourth reason for limited impact of the TTB approach—that there are too few programmatic experiences that promote *change in practice*. The critical identity work that preservice teachers need to do to develop critical understandings of race, ethnicity, racial privilege, class, and culture requires more than just reading about them or taking a number of multicultural education courses. This type of *culturally situated learning* must involve activity—action, reflection, and/or discursive examination. Few teacher preparation programs provide the contexts for candidates to do the necessary and difficult 'identity work' to change their dispositions. The importance of actual engagement in real social situations is crucial. This point is supported by the work of developmental theorists Thomas Cook and Brian Flay (1978) who remark that we are more likely to *act ourselves into new ways of thinking than think ourselves into new ways of acting*.

The fifth and perhaps most critically important reason for the limitation of the TTB approach concerns candidates of color. In addition to drawing attention away from the IMT approach, there is evidence that curricular efforts designed to address diversity by transforming teacher beliefs actually frustrate and discourage candidates of color. For example, Parker and Hood (1995) found that students of color were dissatisfied with programs in which the multicultural pedagogy not only failed to draw on and extend what they already knew, but was disjointed and superficial. Our own data suggest that African American candidates find "diversity education," even in strong programs, to be trivial, shallow, insulting, and burdensome (as they tend to become "authorities for their race").

FIVE RECOMMENDATIONS FOR
DIVERSITY TEACHER PREPARATION

In this section we describe two work contexts that provide, for each of us, vantage points to articulate recommendations for diversity relevant teacher preparation in light of the shortcomings to the current TTB approach. These are summarized in Table 3.2. The recommendations reveal how "diversity development" can be articulated, assessed, and infused within the pedagogical training at the entry point of teacher preparation as well as in the first years of teaching. These recommenda-

Table 3.2.   Five Recommendations for Diversity Teacher Education

Reason for Scant Impact	*Recommendations*
Most White preservice candidates bring too little awareness, cross-cultural experience, or understanding of discrimination, racism, or structural inequality in education. Most White preservice teachers are naïve about the lives, experiences, and culture of children in diverse communities, and bring biases.	Dispositions are best developed through an immersion in diverse contexts in which candidates become participant observers (no matter how peripheral) in successful and effective instructional practice with children of diverse backgrounds is under the supervision of (and collaboration with) educators of color.
The relatively modest gains in moving White preservice teachers from their entrenched belief systems seem to require an enormous investment of time, energy, and curricular activity.	There is no better way to assess how White mainstream candidates are disposed to work productively and collaboratively with, say African Americans, than to have them attempt to work productively and collaboratively with African Americans.
Few preservice programs articulate effective performance indicators for "multicultural competence" that are appropriate and necessary for effective work in culturally, linguistically, and racial diverse urban schools.	Programs should develop the criteria for successful teaching with diverse learners from actual situations of successful teaching with diverse learners. That is, develop the indicators for good multicultural teaching based on what diverse instructional settings require of mainstream, White candidates.
There is little evidence to suggest that, even when dispositional changes were accomplished with respect to preservice teachers beliefs and attitudes about teaching in diverse settings, these changes are reflected in teaching practice.	Let candidates confront their issues and biases early, learn what is expected of them as good practitioners, and let them determine for themselves whether they can make the necessary changes in dispositions to become multiculturally competent teachers.
There is evidence suggesting that candidates of color are dissatisfied with, turned-off by, and turned away from "multicultural" components of their teacher education program.	Dramatically increase our emphasis on the IMT (increasing the number of minority teachers) approach. For the continuing TTB approach, let's not make people of color the ambassadors for their race and culture, as if using their participation or input can provide a program with the necessary "dose of diversity"; nor assume the participation of candidates of color addresses the requirements of accomplished teaching for children of color.

tions offer ways in which the requirements for effective teaching in culturally, linguistically, and ethnically diverse contexts can be made more explicit for, and developed among White, culturally-mainstreamed preservice teachers.

First, it will be necessary to describe briefly the contexts of our work. One of us (P. Murrell, Jr.) is working in the context of a newly evolving urban-focused, community-dedicated, and practice-oriented teacher education program that is hallmarked by an early immersion of college students into urban community-based sites run by people of color. The anchoring enterprises in the reconstruction of the new school of urban education include a course and field experience called the Introduction to Education for the undergraduates, and a Community Teacher Institute for postbaccalaureate participants. The undergraduate Introduction to Education course is a prerequisite for all students applying to the School of Education, but open college-wide to those wishing to fulfill distribution requirements. The course includes a thematic survey of critical issues in urban schooling, a 20-hour field experience in an urban community site teaching or tutoring African American children in a variety of academic after-school programs, and a one-hour per week cadre group debriefing. The core concepts of the experience are "culture," "race," "ethnicity," "community," and "schooling" are critically examined and deconstructed through a readings, discussions, and reflective papers and through a focus on the role and place of education in America today.

This community teacher immersion experience is premised on the idea that students' first experience should be a community setting with African American and Latino teachers, parents, and youth workers, rather than a school. This experience provides the context for students to develop a community-centered perspective on education, so that they might better interrogate the critical distinction between education and schooling (e.g., Shujaa, 1994), and see the connection to culturally and ethnically constituted traditions of education in diverse settings. At the post-baccalaureate level, graduate students are placed in a teaching experience in the form of a yearlong, intensive, immersion-in-practice teacher preparation program and a leadership-focused whole-school new teacher induction system that runs concurrently with the teacher preparation program. The Institute is the joint enterprise of the School of Education and an urban high school composed of 80% students of color. The goal is to produce accomplished urban teachers, ready to assume a position in under-resourced urban public schools. The development of accomplished urban teachers is the core aim of the Institute. The Institute consists of an integrated program of co-teaching, guided practice and systematic inquiry into teaching and learning.

One of us (M. Foster) is the organizer and principal investigator of a study of Learning Through Teaching in an After School Pedagogical Laboratory (L-TAPL), a professional development project in two of the largest urban California school districts funded by the National Science Foundation (NSF) and the Office of Educational Research and Improvement (OERI). These after-school programs serve as pedagogical laboratories and professional development community sites for new teachers. The pedagogical laboratories operate from the assumption that teachers learn to teach best by working under the guidance of skilled practitioners who have demonstrated expertise working with urban African American children and other children from diverse cultural backgrounds. L-TAPL integrates teacher learning with the student learning that occurs in the pedagogical laboratories. Participating teachers spend one day per week working in the after school pedagogical lab where in exchange for their participation they receive 6 graduate credits at a California State University and a stipend to purchase instructional supplies for their classrooms.

In the pedagogical laboratories in-service teachers come to understand the role of motivation in learning, specifically how the expert teachers create conditions in the classroom including but not limited to utilizing students' identities, interests background, and cultural knowledge to entice student and draw them into self-regulated, disciplined study. The in-service teachers learn the importance of paying attention not only to the cognitive dimensions of learning but to the behavioral, affective and social dimensions that serve as a foundation for cognitive learning.

The most significant change observed in teachers who participated in the L-TAPL is a definite shift in their views of the problems in their classrooms from one of child-centered deficits to one of deficits in their practices (see Foster, Lewis, & Onafowora, 2002; NEA Foundation for the Improvement of Education, 2003a, 2003b). Additional information about the program may be located at the following addresses: http://www.nfie.org/usingdata.htm and www.theeditors.com/review/ltapl.

The first recommendation addresses the concern that most White preservice teachers bring little cultural awareness or understanding of structural inequality to their teacher preparation program. Our recommendation is to immerse them in contexts in which they have to work with, collaborate with, and be supervised by more capable educators of color in the enterprise of working successfully and effectively with children of color. For students in the community teacher immersion experience, intense interrogation of issues through the course reading and self-reflection produced some dramatic development, as evidenced by this male freshman (Krasnow & Spurlock, 2001, p. 7):

I see now that had I been born in Harlem or El Paso to low-income parents with no college experience, the odds are that I would not be where I am now. For many people, this is difficult to admit, because it means that you don't necessarily deserve to be where you are because you are the smartest or the most capable. It means that you were lucky, that you were in the right place at the right time and were able to succeed. It means giving up what Peggy McIntosh refers to as the "myth of meritocracy," and privileged Americans cling to this myth because to let go would be to turn their whole world upside down. Perhaps this is exactly what we need—to turn all of society upside down and as a result the world of education will be transformed as well.

The second recommendation addresses the slow and tenuous change in candidate beliefs. There is no better way to assess how White mainstream candidates are disposed to work productively and collaboratively with people of color—both adults and children—than to actually have them do so in a setting where their progress can be assisted and assessed. Immersion in community sites in African American social settings creates opportunities for insight and dispositional growth that are difficult to produce in a regular course of study. For example, a second male freshman, wrote (Krasnow & Spurlock, p. 8):

> My first day at the tutoring site proved to be one of the most useful in implementing all of the things that I had learned in class and bringing them together in the real world. I had missed the initial orientation day, so I called up the site coordinator, Ms. [coordinators name], and we decided that I would come to the [Church's name] Church that Thursday to talk to her. This wasn't going to be my regular day, but simply a quick visit so we could meet and sort out what day I would actually be doing the tutoring. Even as I walked up the stairs into the Ruggles T-Stop, I wasn't quite prepared for what I was about to encounter. During class, when each of the representatives from the sites came in, they had discussed the issue of race to some extent. The in-class readings had also prepared me somewhat, but none of it truly sank in until I walked up the steps of the bus and took a seat. As I looked around, I realized that I was the only White person on the bus. I felt completely out of place. Then I realized that this is often the type of thing that Black people must go through every day. I had been on buses many times when there was only one Black person, and I thought nothing of it. Finally, I got to see things from a different perspective. This was different from simply reading about race relations in a book, this was truly experiencing it. (p. 8)

The third recommendation is that programs should develop the criteria for successful teaching with diverse learners from actual situations of successful teaching with diverse learners. That is, develop the indicators for good multicultural teaching based upon what diverse instructional settings require of mainstream, White candidates. Rather than reading about culturally relevant pedagogy, it is possible for students to develop understandings and practices first hand. From his community teacher immersion experience, a White sophomore male wrote (Krasnow & Spurlock, 2001, p. 10):

> The reason I think I've learned so much is because of where I grew up. I'm sure that this is the case for most people would say they have learned a lot in

this class. Growing up in a White, middle class, fairly small neighborhood, may have given me more of a certain kind of social capital, but it never showed me what was going on outside of my school system. I had many, many assumptions and theories for something that I had no experience with. I was never exposed to this different type of reality until this class. I never even had a real concept of what urban schooling was like, or how to even begin to handle these differences. For example, I would have never thought about something as simple as cultural differences (like how a Black child may tend to answer a question with clever phrases, rather than a straight answer) to be behind "behavior issues." I may have classified this as a behavior problem or labeled that child in a way that I now know would have no relevance. Creating at least somewhat of a concept of this reality was a very important thing for me, and one of the biggest general things that I learned from the class.

The Community Teacher Institute has developed a number of practice standards based on the requirements and key elements of effective practice culled from systematic observations of accomplished teachers of color.

The fourth recommendation addresses the critique that we do not know what candidates are really disposed to do in practice in a diverse context presenting challenges to culturally mainstream teacher candidates. Early on in the teacher preparation sequence of most programs, candidates are never really certain whether they are up to the rigors and challenges of meeting diversity-related performance standards. Our recommendation is to situate, through intense immersion, candidates in practice-oriented and issues-rich experiences so that they can assess for themselves their continued interest in teaching. A White female freshman in the community teacher immersion experience writes:

After considering my options here at [university name] I have decided to enter my sophomore year with an undecided major, not sociology major with a minor in education, which I initially sought after. This decision resulted from many mornings when I left the course angered and frustrated at the discussions held that particular day. Initially, I held that the discussion would become educational centered and less racially/ethnically centered, but to my dismay such discussions never subsided. I realize that race plays a gigantic part in the quality of education in America, and with such prominent conflicts and constant unfairness with issues such as "White privilege" and financial status determining a child's chances at a quality education, I do not feel that I am prepared to take on such a career. I understand that my anger concerning these issues should drive me to further research and perhaps alleviate them but at the current time I am no longer interested in doing so. I have not completely discarded my love of teaching and children nor have I forgotten the rewards associated with being an educator but I would like to say that I am "taking a break," and venture onto other areas perhaps.

The fifth recommendation relates directly to our point early in this chapter about the two approaches to diversity teacher preparation. Designed as it is primarily for White teacher candidates, the TTB approach tends to divert attention from increasing the number of minority teachers. We need, perhaps in equal measure, the IMT (increasing minority teachers) approach to address the culture gap. It is important to not underestimate the importance of alternative teacher preparation and professional development settings where White people are not in the majority—as these do make a difference (Foster, 2001).

Finally, the TTB approach needs to reduce its reliance on people of color to provide the "dose of diversity." Students of color in the community teacher immersion experience do not share White students' appreciation of the course as a "transformative experience." They do, however, articulate an appreciation that their White, culturally mainstream peers are addressing issues of diversity. A Black female third-year student writes (Krasnow & Spurlock, 2001, p. 7):

> I greatly appreciated the cultural aspect of the class. It is important to know where the kids and families that we will be working with come from. Throughout my educational process I have been appalled at the lack of diversity in the instruction that we receive…. As a minority in America, I will not thrive unless I am bi-cultural. I am forced to adhere to "mainstream" social and cultural norms once I walk outside of the nurturing arms of my community. Yet many of my White counterparts have no knowledge of my culture and social norms (aside from what they extract from the media: the hardcore hoodlum or the crossed-over tom). Generally, they don't have to "get down with my people" to survive. I've had to conform and adjust—wear different makes and costumes—more times than anyone who is not in a costume show should. I greatly appreciate the fact that we read the "White privilege" article. This aspect of the class is so overwhelmingly important as many of us will be dealing with disenfranchised people who have—through circumstances and force—concocted a culture of poverty that many times cannot be dissolved into the "mainstream." We will be faced with situations and people who to us (college graduates and fledgling middle class people) may be quick to judge and say, "Why don't these people just do 'right' and help themselves?" You cannot teach in an urban environment without understanding the origin of the circumstances of the families and children that we are working with.

It is important that people of color not be cast in the role of ambassadors for their racial and cultural group. Their participation or input should not provide a program with the necessary "dose of diversity" nor should their participation be viewed as addressing the requirements of accomplished teaching for children of color.

CONCLUSION

Our perspective regarding the role of teacher beliefs in the preparation of teachers for effective work in diverse schools and communities departs from much of the prevailing teacher education research on teacher beliefs. Beliefs can neither be prescribed nor accurately assessed, but dispositions based in practice *can*. The dispositional changes that White teachers need to undergo in order to be effective with children of color can occur if programs change the mix of classroom and field experience. Placing candidates in practice-rich field experiences where multicultural competencies and dispositions are regularly acted out and where they have many opportunities to practice them may be an essential first step in moving a large segment of White teachers from *believing they are competent* to teach urban students from diverse cultural backgrounds to *actually being competent* to do so.

REFERENCES

Barry, N. H., & Lechner, J. V. (1995). Preservice teachers' attitudes about and awareness of multicultural teaching and learning. *Teaching and Teacher Education, 11*, 149-161.

Cochran Smith, M. (1997). Knowledge, skills, and experiences for teaching culturally diverse learners: A perspective for practicing teachers. In J. J. Irvine (Ed.), *Critical knowledge for diverse teachers and learners* (pp. 27-87). Washington, DC: American Association of Colleges of Teacher Education.

Cook, T., & Flay, B. (1978). The persistence of experimentally induced attitude change. In L. Berkowitz (Ed.), *Advances in experimental social psychology* (Vol. 11, pp. 2-50). New York: Academic Press.

Cooney, M., & Akintunde, O. (1999, Winter). Confronting White Privilege and color blind paradigm in a teacher education program. *Multicultural Education*, 9-14.

Dee, T. S. (2001). Teachers, race and student achievement in a randomized experiment. Working paper 8432. Cambridge, MA: National Bureau of Economic Research. Available: http://www.nber.org/papers/w8432

Dovidio, J. F. & Fazio, R. H. (1992). New technologies for the direct and indirect assessment of attitudes. In J. M. Tanur (Ed.), *Questions about questions: Inquiries into the cognitive bases of survey* (pp. 207-237). New York: Russell Sage.

Fazio, R. H., Jackson, J. R., Dunton, B. C., & Williams, C. J. (1995). Variability in automatic activation as an unobstrusive measure of racial attitudes: A bona fide pipeline? *Journal of Personality & Social Psychology, 69*(6), 1013-1027.

Foster, M. (1997). *Black teachers on teaching*. New York: New York Press.

Foster, M. (1999). Race, class, and gender in educational research: Mapping the educational terrain. *Educational Policy, 13*(1): 77-85.

Foster, M. (2001). *Learning through teaching in an after-school pedagogical laboratory.* Proposal submitted to The Office of Educational Research and Improvement, Field Initiated Studies Program.

Foster, M., Lewis, J., & Onafowora, L. (2003). Anthropology, culture and research on teaching and learning: Applying what we have learned to improve practice. *Teachers College Record, 105*(2), 261-277.

Grant, C. A. (1997). Critical knowledge, skills, and experiences for the instruction of culturally diverse students: A perspective for the preparation of preservice teachers. In J. J. Irvine (Ed.), *Critical knowledge for diverse teachers and learners* (pp. 1-26). Washington, DC: American Association of Colleges of Teacher Education.

Haberman, M. (1995). *STAR teachers of children of poverty.* West Lafayette, IN: Kappa Delta Pi.

Haberman, M., & Post, L. (1992). Does direct experience change education students' perceptions of low-income minority students? *Midwest Educational Researcher, 5*(2), 29-31.

Hayman, W., & King, J. (Eds.). (1997). *Meeting the challenge of diversity in teacher preparation.* New York: Teachers College Press.

Interstate New Teacher Assessment and Support Consortium, Council of Chief State School Officers. (2001). *Model standards for the review of accountability of teacher education programs.* Washington, DC: Author

Irvine, J. J. (Ed.). (1996). *Critical knowledge for diverse teachers and learners.* Washington, DC: American Association of Colleges of Teacher Education.

King, J. E. (1991). Dysconscious racism: Ideology, identity, and the miseducation of teachers. *Journal of Negro Education, 60*(2), 133-146.

Krasnow, J., & Spurlock, S. (2001). *Border crossings: An internal report of the development of students in community partnerships.* Boston: Northeastern University.

Ladson-Billings, G. (1999). Preparing teachers for diversity. In L. Darling-Hammond & G. Sykes (Eds.), *Teaching as the learning profession* (pp. 86-123). San Francisco: Jossey-Bass.

McFalls, E. L., & Cobb-Roberts, D. (2001). Reducing resistance to diversity through cognitive dissonance instruction: Implications for teacher education. *Journal of Teacher Education, 52*(2), 164-172.

McIntyre, A. (1997). *Making meaning of Whiteness.* Albany: State University of New York Press.

Melnick, S. L., & Zeichner, K. M. (1997). Enhancing the capacity of teacher education institutions to address diversity issues. In J. E. King, E. R. Hollins, & W. C. Hayman (Eds.), *Preparing teachers for cultural diversity* (pp. 23-39). New York: Teachers College Press.

Murrell, P. C., Jr. (1991). Cultural politics in teacher education: What's missing in the preparation of African-American teachers? In M. Foster (Ed.) *Readings on equal education* (Vol. 11, pp. 205-225). New York: AMS Press.

Murrell, P. C., Jr. (2001). *Community teachers: A conceptual framework for effective urban teaching.* New York: Teachers College Press.

Murrell, P. C., Jr. (2002). *African-centered pedagogy: Developing schools of achievement for African American children.* New York: SUNY Press.

The National Education Association Foundation for the Improvement of Education. (2003a). Learning through teaching in an after-school pedagogical laboratory. [On-line] Available: http://www.nfie.org/usingdata.htm

The National Education Association Foundation for the Improvement of Education. (2003b). Using data about classroom practice and student work to improve professional development for educators. *Establishing High-Quality Professional Development, 5,* 1-12.

National Council for Accreditation of Teacher Education. (2002). *Professional standards for the accreditation of schools, colleges, and departments of education, 2002 Edition.* New York: NCATE. National Commission on Teaching and America's Future.

Parker, L., & Hood, S. (1995). Minority students versus majority faculty and administrators in teacher education: Perspectives on the clash of cultures. *Urban Review, 27*(2), 159-174.

Reed, D. F. (1993). Multicultural education for pre-service students. *Action in teacher Education, 15*(3), 27-34.

Schultz, E., Neyhart, K., & Reck, U. M. (1996). Swimming against the tide: A study of prospective teacher's attitudes regarding cultural diversity and urban teaching. *The Western Journal of Black Studies, 20*(1), 1-7.

Sheets, R. H. (2000). Advancing the field or taking center stage: The White movement in multicultural education. *Educational Researcher, 29*(9), 15-21.

Sleeter, C. E. (2001a). Epistemological diversity in research on preservice teacher education for historically underserved children. In W. G. Secada (Ed.), *Review of research in education* (Vol. 6). Washington, DC: AERA.

Sleeter, C. E. (2001b). Preparing teachers for culturally diverse schools: Research and the overwhelming presence of whiteness. *Journal of Teacher Education, 52*(2), 94-106.

Smith, R., Moallem, M., & Sherrill, D. (1997). How preservice teachers think about cultural diversity. *Educational Foundations, 11*(2), 41-62.

Su, Z. (1996). Why teach: Profiles and entry perspectives of minority students as becoming teachers. *Journal of Research and Development in Education, 29*(3), 117-133.

Su, Z. (1997). Teaching as a profession and as a career: Minority candidates' perspectives. *Teaching and Teacher Education, 13,* 325-340.

Tatum, B. (1992). Talking about race, learning about racism: The implication of racial identity development in the classroom. *Harvard Educational Review, 62*(1), 1-24.

U.S. Department of Education. (1997). *America's teachers: Profile of a profession,* 1993-94. Washington, DC: National Center for Education Statistics.

Valli, L. (1995). The dilemma of race: Learning to be color blind and color conscious. *Journal of Education, 46*(2), 120-129.

Vavrus, M. (1994). A critical analysis of multicultural education infusion during student teaching. *Action in Teacher Education, 16*(3), 45-57.

Wideen, M., Mayer-Smith, J., & Moon, B. (1998). A critical analysis of the research on learning to teacher: Making the case for an ecological perspective on inquiry. *Review of Educational Research, 68*(2), 130-178.

Zeichner, K. (1996). Educating teachers for cultural diversity. In K. Zeichner, S. Melnick, & M. L. Gomez (Eds.), *Currents of reform in pre-service teacher education* (pp. 133-175). New York: Teachers College Press.

Zeichner, K., & Gore, J. (1990). Teacher socialization. In W. R. Houston (Ed.), *Handbook of research on teacher education* (pp. 320-348). New York: Macmillan.

Zeichner, K., & Melnick, S. (1996). The role of community-based field placements in preparing teachers for cultural diversity. In K. Zeichner, S. Melnick, & M. L. Gomez (Eds.), *Currents of reform in pre-service teacher education* (pp. 176-196). New York: Teachers College Press.

CHAPTER 4

IS REALISM A BETTER BELIEF THAN NOMINALISM?

Reopening the Ancient Debate

Richard S. Prawat
Michigan State University

It is reasonable to assume that some kinds of teacher beliefs may be more important for teaching and learning than others. If so, then the beliefs being considered in this chapter—which deal with the question of what constitutes knowledge and how that knowledge is acquired—should meet this criterion. The debate about the merits of one position or the other regarding the nature and origin of knowledge is of ancient vintage, of course, as the title of this chapter suggests. So heated, in fact, was this debate seven hundred years ago that the name of the loser, a thirteenth century scholastic scholar called John Duns Scotus, became synonymous with the term for slow-wittedness or stupidity (i.e., "dunce," derived from Duns). Although currently out of fashion, this term was widely used by teachers in the nineteenth and early twentieth century to punish and motivate students who evidenced what was considered at the time to be almost willful stupidity. In fact, mid-nineteenth century teachers, not content with the use of a verbal rebuke alone, decided to up the ante by add-

Advances in Teacher Education 65–97
Copyright © 2003 by Information Age Publishing
All rights of reproduction in any form reserved.

ing a tangible consequence—the conical shaped head fitting known as the "dunce cap."

How could a seemingly arcane medieval debate about the nature of knowledge have generated so much heat that fisticuffs often broke out between the two protagonists at prestigious, albeit recently established institutions of higher learning such as Oxford and the University of Paris? What was at issue, of course, turned out to be not so arcane after all: It is the question of the status of "universals" (i.e., regularities or laws like photosynthesis and gravity). One school insisted that universals are created in the head, the product that results from the process of individual sensemaking. The other school thought that universals, or "generals" as they have come to be called, are actually present *in* the world. Weinberg expresses this latter view well from the perspective of modern science when he writes, "The laws of physics are real ... in pretty much the same sense ... as the rocks in the fields" (1996, p. 14). As the Weinberg quote suggests, the importance of this issue, the ontological status of generals, has not diminished in the several hundred years since it was first formulated. In fact, it is at the core of what a number of philosophers have recently characterized as "the science wars" (Ashman & Baringer, 2001), an acrimonious debate that pits, as they are variously called, constructivists against nonconstructivists, postmodernists against modernists, nonscientists against scientists.

As I will argue, the labels that best capture the nature of this disagreement are those of "nominalist" and "realist." The story of this on-going debate is told in this chapter. It is one that continues to be relevant for teachers and philosophers because it has broad implications for how we view knowledge and learning. It is one that, periodically since the middleages, has occupied the finest minds in philosophy and education, including a brilliant but little known U.S. scholar named Charles Sanders Peirce. It was Peirce who coined the term "pragmatism" in the early 1870s and was given the enviable title of "the philosopher's philosopher" by none other than the great John Dewey himself (*LW* 6: 273).[1] In the second half of his long and illustrious career, Dewey came to accept Peirce's argument that Scotus had been wronged and that the view of knowledge that both of these scholars championed deserved a second chance. Unfortunately, neither philosophical heavy weight—Peirce or Dewey—succeeded in convincing philosophers and educators of the merit of what Dewey variously referred to as "logical realism" (MW 10: 340) or "pluralistic realism" (*LW* 17: 415). The reasons for each man's failure, however, differed dramatically.

Peirce's failure to advance Scotus's realist theory was a consequence of his precarious position in the community of scholars. Due both to his irascible personality and what many considered his questionable morals (he left his wife to take up with a French women), Peirce was unable to secure employment in the academy. He thus lacked a reputable platform from which to espouse his Scotish alternative to mainstream philosophy. Dewey's failure to advance the theory is the mirror image of Peirce's. Peirce's reputation hindered him in his efforts to resurrect Scotus's philosophy. Dewey's reputation hindered him as well, but in a totally different way. His early writings, especially in education, were so well received and widely disseminated that Dewey found it virtually impossible to convince his followers that he had undergone a profound change in his thinking at mid-career. It was at this point, around 1915, as I document elsewhere (Prawat, 2000, 2001), that Dewey picked up the Scotus-Peirce mantle.

Most recently, eminent philosophers such as Susan Haack (1998) have added their voices to that of Peirce and Dewey, arguing that nominalism—the winner in the great medieval debate—is responsible for the great conundrum that many educators and philosophers find themselves in today: If, as the nominalists in Scotus's time and since aver, knowledge construction (i.e., conceptual understanding) is a private, internal affair, a process that people engage in as they seek to make sense out of their own individual experience, how can we ever feel confident about the product of that process? Nominalists argue that the individual can point to only two known things in an attempt to describe what happens in the course of knowledge construction: First, the raw data that (apparently) represents a starting point for the individual and, second, the propositional language used to express meaning which signals an end point in the process.

Everything in between is a mystery for advocates of the anti-Dunce position, so much so that postmodern philosophers like Richard Rorty suggest that we ignore it altogether. "For all we know or should care," he writes, the great scientific discoveries of individuals like Galileo, Newton, or Darwin "were the results of cosmic rays scrambling the fine structure of some crucial neurons in their respective brains" (1989, p. 17). The best one can do is focus on propositions and the role that they play. Truth, Rorty is fond of saying, is nothing more than a successful move in the "language game." It is, he writes, "nothing more than what our peers will let us get away with saying" (1979, p. 176).

Rorty's notion may strike many as being cynical in the extreme. One goal in the present chapter is to convince the reader that this view is not extreme given the decision, seven hundred years ago, to reject Scotus's theory of knowledge in favor of the theory alluded to above, termed "nominalism," which has exerted a profound influence on our thinking from that time forward. This influence has not been felt in philosophy alone; it has strongly influenced how we think about education as well. Before delving into some of the history behind this idea and the counterview put forth by John Duns Scotus, it might be well to lay out nominalism's basic premises and contrast those with the ideas presented by the Dunce, John Scotus. In the third section of the paper, I will develop the educational implications of the great debate that sprung up in the middle ages, was reopened briefly at the turn of the last century, and that is showing signs of yet again having currency in the current debate between modernist and postmodernist views of knowledge and education (Rochberg-Halton, 1986).

NOMINALISM AND THE SENSE/MEANING DIVIDE

Nominalism is a profoundly skeptical view of knowledge. As Carre (1950, p. 122) explains, nominalists believe that there are only two things that we can know with any degree of certainty: The sensations we experience and, to a lesser degree, the process we go through when we create meaning out of this input. The best example of the latter occurs at the end of the knowledge generating process when logic is used to relate one term (e.g., "Socrates") to another ("human") in a proposition (e.g., "Socrates is human"). The notion that there are but two certainties—sensations and the logic expressed in language—became the foundation for all of modern philosophy according to Carre (p. 123). Empiricists fastened on sensory input, rationalists like Descartes took logic and language to be their purview. Carre is correct in saying that it was the developer of nominalism, a scholar known as William of Ockham (1288-1347), who first introduced this distinction.

Ockham argued that the distinction between experience, on the one hand, and language and logic on the other, is obvious when we turn our attention inward. The inward turn, in fact, became a key aspect of his philosophy; it represents Ockham's major contribution not only to philosophy, but I will argue, to education as well. "According to nominalism," Hemisoeth writes (1994), "when we know something we never know objects (or tiny images thereof) but only our own ideas as states or activities within ourselves" (1994, p. 135). "Knowledge of the world," he adds, "is fundamentally self-knowledge." This is a key notion, directly attributable to William of Ockham and his nominalist theory. It is worth quoting Hemisoeth at length here:

> Inner experience is not merely knowledge about existence that is more important and closest to the knowing subject (but which in the final analysis is still coordinated with external experience of nature that is given); on the contrary, the upshot of the matter is that all experience is originally inner experience and that inner experience is also the source of all so-called outer experience. In other words, knowledge of inner sense always lies at the basis of knowledge of outer sense. (p. 135)

This notion played a key role in early modernist thinking in science and philosophy, which dates from the sixteenth century. In fact, the hallmark of this way of thinking is the reliance on personal sense making. Trust the evidence of your own eyes, modernist philosophers insisted, and your ability to reason about that evidence. Shapin expresses this maxim well when he writes: "If you really want to secure truth about the natural world, forget tradition, ignore authority, be skeptical of what others say, and wander the fields alone with your eyes open" (1996, p. 69). Many historians of philosophy trace the origins of this view, known as "intellectual individualism," back to Ockham and the nominalists (Blumenberg, 1983). It is for this reason that Eugene Rochberg-Halton calls nominalism "the philosophical basis for Western thought and culture" (1998, p. 48).

Now that I have established the power and pervasiveness of the nominalist way of thinking, it is fair to ask what exactly is included under this rubric. What do nominalists believe? At the heart of the theory is the notion that *all* order or regularity is a creation of the human mind, fashioned out of the particular, individual sensation-experiences that work their way into our minds. The individual mind is like the alchemist that converts dross to gold. Even an everyday regularity like the notion of "horseness" represents the outcome of a protracted process, as has been suggested: First, we must attend to the experience of our senses as we interact with various animate objects; second, we must sort these experiences into those that are like and those that are unlike; third, we must search out a name from the myriad of names provided by one's culture which we think will describe the category of like experience. The name or label is called a concept.

Concepts play a key role in nominalist theory. They are the basic building blocks of understanding. Propositions like "Horses were the primary means of transportation prior to this century" are composed of concepts like "horses," "transportation," and "prior to this century." Absent this intermediate way of organizing raw experience, the concept, there can be no meaning or knowledge according to nominalist theory. No less a source than Merriam-Webster recognizes this basic fact about knowledge. Understanding depends upon concepts; in the 1984 edition of this best selling dictionary understanding is defined as "the power to make experience intelligible by applying concepts and categories;" an earlier edition (1958) makes this even more explicit. Understanding, according to this source, is "the power to render experience intelligible by *bringing perceived particulars under appropriate concepts*" [italics added]. This is the nub of the theory. Dewey, who embraced nominalism early in his career only to turn against it later, considered this key aspect of the theory as among its most suspect:

It would be difficult to imagine any doctrine more absurd than the theory that general ideas or meanings arise by the comparison of a number of particulars, eventuating in the recognition of something common to them all. (*LW* 1: 147)

A lot of baggage accompanies the assumption that we construct order from the ground up, as it were (i.e., by processing particular experiences). For one, there is the assumption that learning is hierarchical—that, in learning, we move from the single and concrete to the collective and abstract. Our senses are initially assailed by the qualities of objects and events, the pungent smell of sweat in the case of a horse, the brisk feel of its hair. Most are discarded as irrelevant as we begin to hone in on the specific features deemed most important in putting the individual objects together. These features, invariably, are those that seem uniquely important to the object in question: Having four legs would not qualify for horse-like objects but having a mane and being of a certain size would.

The understanding that emerges from the process of noting what is uniquely important about an individual object—the notion, for example, that each and every horse is an herbivore—is powerful. For this reason, it also must somehow be less "real," a notion that permeates modern psychology. Neisser expresses it well when he writes that, for psychologists, mental activity is thought to flow internally from the specific to the general, from "details of the input pattern to categories and abstractions" (p. 112). The concept, according to nominalists, is an outgrowth of the categorization process. This does not mean, however, that it is equivalent to a kind of composite image, at least in nominalist theory. The concept, according to nominalists, is more akin to a set of persisting mental notes one makes when observing individual objects or events. Thus, the individual may say, "This horse is brown, hairy, and has a mane." The first note (i.e., "brown") drops out when the person realizes that it does not apply to the next horse-like object. The second note (i.e., "hairy") goes by the boards a little later when the person realizes that this feature is widely shared by a host of four-footed creatures. This leaves only the attribute of maneness as a viable contender for the coveted role of defining feature.

While a composite image can be constructed from persisting mental notes, it is not the same as a concept, Ockham argued. To equate the two is to come perilously close to saying that defining qualities—be they size or maneness—actually do exist *as such* in the individual thing. As will become clear, the notion that common qualities exist in some specific form in each individual object was one that the nominalists could not accept. "No universal [i.e., no defining quality] is existent in any way whatsoever outside the mind of the knower," Ockham insisted (in Knowles, 1988, p. 294). As indicated, nominalists believe that order or regularity, be it horseness or something more profound like gravity, does not present itself to the human mind; it is, rather, *created* by the mind from particular experience.

Nominalist theory is reductionist in its insistence that settling on the "units" of experience (i.e., concepts like horseness or gravity) is a first step in the process of knowing. Most units can be defined by simply pointing at some specific set of experiences, but not all. In addition to concepts like "horse" that meet this criterion, there are other, more complex concepts like "cause" and "white" that do not. These concepts must, originally at least, be defined in terms of other concepts (Panaccio, 1999). A "cause," for example, is defined as "something upon the existence of which another thing follows" while "white" is defined in a seemingly more straightforward way as "something having a whiteness." The purpose here, however, is to get back, albeit in a circuitous way, to some point-at-able experiences or set of experiences (i.e., events that consistently follow other events in the first case, white objects in the second).

As the comments about propositions suggest, Ockham was also interested in the process that connects one concept to another. Language and logic play key roles here. The two work hand in hand, language expressing the logical relationship, logic telling us how to test that relationship against experience. The simplest type of relationship is the identity relationship. Not surprisingly, this finds expression in the simplest type of proposition, consisting of a subject, a predicate, and a verb that joins the two (e.g., "Every horse is an animal). The logic that underlies this proposition points to a simple two-part process of verfication: Search the "mental notes" that define the predicate first; if the notes that apply to the predicate (i.e., "is an animal") also apply to the subject (i.e., "horse"), the proposition is judged true.

Not all language and logic is this straightforward, however. According to Ockham, more complex type sentences like "This horse is running" are actually made up of two or more simple sentences. The key to determining the truth-value of this type of sentence is to break it down into each of its component sentences (i.e., "This is running; this is a horse") and check each against a category of experience (i.e., horseness and the act of running). I get into this level of complexity for one reason: To illustrate the extent to which nominalists value the role that logic plays in connecting language to experience. Propositions, which relate terms, must be tested against experience—in this case, the experience of what goes with what (e.g., Does one category subsume another? Does the current, complex state of affairs jibe with experience? Logic guides this process).

In nominalist theory, logic is more closely linked to language than to experience (Skorupski, 1998). The opposite is true in the alternative view put forth by Scotus, as I will soon explain. The fact that nominalists consider logic several steps removed from experience was a source of endless mischief in the post-medieval era, as indicated earlier. It became the basis, in modernist philosophy, for the schism between empiricists like Locke, Hume, and Mill who put their emphasis on experience and assigned a relatively passive role to mind, and rationalists like Descartes who emphasized language and logic and assigned a very active role to mind. Both extremes were fraught with peril, as Howe and Berv (2000) make clear. Empiricists had trouble explaining how experience, which comes to us unordered or unpatterned, organizes itself into elements like chairs, persons, and the like. Rationalists faced the opposite problem: If, as many rationalist aver, logic constitutes a set of fixed, a priori rules that are imposed on language, what prevents these rules from running roughshod over common sense? Howe and Berv present an example—one of Zeno's famous paradoxes:

> Reason tells us that Achilles cannot cross the stadium. He must first traverse half the distance, then half the remaining distance, then half the remaining distance, and so on, ad infinitum, such that there will always be some remainder. Viewed from the other end of the sequence, Achilles not only cannot cross the stadium, he cannot move at all! Zeno, the rationalist, took this to be a victory. For, in his view, it shows that motion is an illusion and experience cannot be trusted. (2000, p. 21)

The problem empiricists faced was how experience was even possible absent the existence of some set of a priori organizing principles. The problem rationalists faced—the disconnect between logic, which represents mind at its zenith, and the booming buzzing confusion that constitutes raw sensory input—was the result of the emphasis they placed on logic and language.

The dilemma that nominalism helped create in the mind of modernist philosophers had an impact on education as well. Like the rationalists and empiricists, educators in the modernist era were presented with two choices: Either place an emphasis on logic and language (i.e., words and definitions) in one's teaching or assign the highest priority to the students' personal experience. The first approach is associated with didactic or traditional instruction; the second with progressive, "hands on" instruction. Although the popularity of the hands on approach is justifiably considered to be of relatively recent vintage, it was championed early on by empiricists like John Locke, who warned educators not to fill the student's head with "perfectly useless trumpery" but rather to train them to use their powers of observation to gain first hand knowledge of the world (Porter, 2000, p. 341).

Given the fact that most enlightened educators now consider the hands on or experiential second approach to be the only viable one, it is tempting to overlook the extent to which didactic instruction itself represents a modernist construction not unlike that which occurred in science. Both didactics and science were late sixteenth, early seventeenth century inventions. The word "didactic" is derived from the Greek and stresses the role of presentation and clarification in instruction (Uljens, 1997, p. 44); this idea can be traced back to Ockham's emphasis on language and logic.

Montgomery, in his book on the role of language in science (1996), makes much of the fact that the beginning of science was correlated with language reform. Interestingly, the didactic movement in education was also correlated with language reform, as I point out below. What was being reformed in both domains, in the interest of connecting the spoken and written word more directly to the data of sense experience (the nominalist agenda), was the language associated with the middle ages, a way of talking and writing that Francis Bacon thought put words ahead of the things that the words represented. Language was too detached from the everyday world, he argued.

Words, if not carefully selected, can thus mislead as well as lead. The solution to language's tendency, in Bacon's words, to "snatch away" knowledge (Montgomery, 1996, p. 34) was a simple, unadorned form of speech—terminology that directly connects to objects and events. Montgomery describes the goal in science this way: The discourse of the scientist must be capable of conveying and reproducing the experiences upon which understanding is based. "Fitting words," using Bacon's terminology, straightforwardly connect the natural philosopher back to the experiential data upon which the scientific understanding is based (Montgomery, 1996, p. 76).

The move to clean up language was but one of two initiatives aimed at putting science on firmer footing. As in philosophy, there were those who preferred to focus on the other end of the nominalist process, emphasizing experiential input rather than language and logic output. Prior to the nominalism's influence on modernist thinking, little attention was devoted to the supposed "raw stuff" that forms the basis for understanding. In fact, the mere recollection of a happening, like the general sense that arrows shot straight up return to the spot where they are launched, was thought to constitute sufficient grounding for important principles, like Aristotle's notion that the earth is stationary (Shapin, 1996, p. 81). As with language, the new crop of scientists questioned this reliance on everyday or common sense experience. What was needed was a much more carefully catalogued and purified compilation of facts, they thought. This meant, Shapin explains, that accounts of experience had to be carefully monitored to ensure that they were authentic. "The experiential facts providing the foundations of a reformed natural philosophy were to be statements not 'of what happens in nature' but of 'what actually *happened* in nature,'" Shapin writes (pp. 89-90).

NOMINALISM APPLIED TO EDUCATION: DIDACTIC VERSUS EXPERIENTIAL LEARNING

While educators were influenced by efforts to reform language and experience in science, the converse also was true. In fact, it is fair to say that the effort to reform language in science was part of a broader agenda that relates to economics, education, and religion, as Montgomery points out (1996, p. 27). In England and in other European countries, important religious and social movements were underway throughout the 1600s. One of the most significant was the rise of a Protestant middle class, which began to question the relevance of the classic education, popular throughout the middle ages despite some misgivings expressed by the church (Lindberg, 1992). The classic education focused on literature, grammar, and rhetoric, the so-called "trivium," which was taught, not surprisingly, in Latin and Greek. The fact that the plural of trivium, the word "trivia," has come to signify unimportant matters is not happenstance. This was at the core of the problem in the seventeenth century when education was seen, more and more, as the vehicle for social advancement (Hale, 1993). The enterprise was becoming a serious business. The change in view about the great medieval practice of rhetoric is a case in point, as Nelson, Megill, and McCloskey explain (1987, p. 7).

Rhetoric is the art of persuasion. The fact that it relies on a host of beguiling techniques explains why the core of the word "persuasion," "suadere," shares a root with "suavis," which is Latin for "sweet." At any rate, as Nelson et al. point out (1987, p. 7), sweet reason gave way in the early modernist era to "convincere," which means "to defeat thoroughly." Knowledge, acquired through language, was thus no longer the plaything of the aristocratic class—an occasion for the wellborn to flex their intellectual muscles as it were. "The old, abstract, aristocratic, and 'useless' studies [were replaced] with the modern, concrete, popular, and useful" (in Montgomery, 1996, p. 81). Mathematics and science became important parts of the curriculum at all levels, elementary school through the university (Hale, 1993, p. 573). The latter was increasingly being taught in the vernacular, using the new technique of "didactics."

Nominalism, with its emphasis on language and logic, helped usher in the new approach to education. Because instruction in the two subjects places a premium on precise language, science and mathematics teaching was an ideal arena to test out the new approach. Given the association between nominalism and subject matter teaching, it is not surprising that the same two domains were, much later, associated with another "new" approach to education, this time based on the nominalist emphasis on *experience*. What perhaps is surprising is that it took so long. In science, as was pointed out, the reform of language and the recasting of experience set in motion by Ockham's theory (Gilson, 1937, p. 68) occurred at the same time. The fact that it took so long for educators to exploit the second key dimension in Ockham's theory, experiential input, is a testament to the effectiveness of the didactic system. Despite the early concerns expressed by scholars like Locke and Hume, an emphasis on language and logic remained central, so much so that the narrow range of ability associated with language and logic processing came to define the very essence of "intelligence" tests (cf., Jensen, 1969, p. 7).

It was not until the late nineteenth and early twentieth century that educators began to seriously question the efficacy of the didactic approach, which emphasized strengthening the powers of the mind (i.e., logic) and filling it with content (i.e., language and definition) (Kliebard, 1987, p. 5). The occasion, of course, was the decision to dramatically broaden the population of students served by education. In the United States alone, the percent of youth attending secondary school quadrupled between 1890, when only 7% of the 14 to 17 year olds were in high school, and 1920, when a third were in attendance (Kliebard, 1987). Given this diverse new population, many educators began to question the efficacy of the didactic approach. One self-professed nominalist philosopher, William James, entered the fray with dramatic results. Like Ockham centuries before, James made the recasting of personal experience the cornerstone of his approach to knowledge. We think in terms of concrete phenomena presented in experience, he argued, and in terms of the names we assign to the patterns detected in those phenomena. James was one of the first psychologists to explicitly link "names" or concepts to the process of induction. Induction is the process of putting the elements of experience together, of figuring out what goes with what. Particular experience lends itself to this process: "The same matters," James wrote, "can be thought of in successive portions of the mental stream, and some of these portions can know that they mean the same matters which the other portions meant" (1890/1950, p. 459).

As suggested, James was quick to see the educational implications of the nominalist focus on experience. Education, from a nominalist perspective, is about making sense of one's *own* experience. From this a number of things follow, or so James thought. The motivation for naming or re-naming personal experience must come from within—sparked, he surmised, by two things: The failure to achieve some important goal and, of equal importance, the perception that one's current lack of knowledge has contributed to this failure. Although the teacher plays an important role in ensuring that the child gets into the right kind of problematic situation, education at root, James wrote,

> is an affair that works itself out between the individual student and his opportunities. Methods of which we talk so much, play but a minor part. Offer the opportunities, leave the student to his natural reaction to them, and he will work out his personal destiny, be it a high one or a low one. (1906/1956, p. 362)

Although the early Dewey is typically associated with "child-centered," "hands-on," "activity-oriented" pedagogy, this great scholar took his cue from James, as I have pointed out elsewhere (Prawat, 2000).

Dewey, in the first part of his career, was a nominalist through and through. As they did for James, concepts played a key role in Dewey's epistemology. Concepts are arrived at inductively, he argued: "The mind attacks the mass of facts which it suspects not to be facts piece-meal," he wrote. "It picks out some one aspect or relation of these 'facts,' isolates it (technically the process of abstraction), and of this isolated relation it forms a hypothesis" (*EW* 3: 87). The most meaningful concepts, Dewey thought, following James's lead, are those the individual induces for him or herself. Induction is thus the cornerstone of what came to be known as Dewey's theory of progressive education. "After the conquests of the inductive method in all spheres of scientific inquiry," Dewey wrote in a passage he would later regret, "we are not called upon to defend its claims in pedagogy" (*EW* 5: 545). Like James, the early Dewey believed that the teacher ought to play an indirect role in education: It is the teacher's responsibility to subtly guide the process that results in students inducing the rules that connect seemingly disparate facts (*MW* 6: 246).

The 1930s in the United States witnessed the first, large-scale test of a nominalist inspired, experiential approach to education. As its critics pointed out, this reform waned largely because, although students were more engaged in the process of learning, they were not necessarily learning more, particularly in the vital subjects of mathematics and science (Kliebard, 1987, p. 268). Even Dewey joined the chorus of those saying that the experiential approach had been carried to an extreme: Much of the hands-on activity, he wrote, was "too trivial to be educative" (*LW* 6: 86). "What is needed in the new education," he emphasized, "is more attention, not less, to subject-matter" (1940, p. 294). This, it should be pointed out, was Dewey *after* he had made his mid-career shift, rejecting nominalism in favor of the realist alternative developed six hundred years before by the "Dunce," John Duns Scotus.

Dewey's major objection to nominalism was that it is inherently dualist: it draws an unbridgeable line between mind and world. The process of detecting patterns in sensory input, labeling those patterns, and relating the resulting concepts in propositions all occur far removed from the world of objects and events. This is evident when one contrasts mind with world. It is also evident within the mind in the hard and fast distinction between sense and meaning. The development of meaning in the mind mirrors the movement away from the concrete and toward the abstract. Nominalism is thus doubly dualist: Not only is the final product of the mind, the language that signals understanding, inherently distinct from the objects and events it supposedly references in the real world, that product is also inherently distinct from the sensory input from which it is derived. As argued earlier, the nominalist notion that experiential input and language output anchor two ends of a discontinuous process led directly to the great divide in philosophy between the rationalists and the empiricists (Carre, 1950, p. 123).

Dewey devoted his professional life to the effort to counter dualism in philosophy (*LW* 5: 153). He was originally attracted to James's theory precisely because it addressed two dualities that loomed large in his thinking at the time, that between science and religion and intellect and emotion (Prawat, 2000, p. 823). It was only belatedly that Dewey realized that James's version of nominalism left untouched the important sense versus meaning distinction mentioned above. Dewey devised an ingenious approach, known as instrumentalism, which addressed the outward manifestation of this distinction, which is identical to that between mind and world. Language, Dewey argued, connects us with the world the way our use of a tool, a hammer for instance, connects us with the nail. Symbolic statements *act on* but do not *mesh with* objects and events in the world, a subtle but important difference, as will be seen when nominalism is contrasted with realism.

No sooner had Dewey addressed the outward version of the mind/world divide then he began to realize that he was only half-way home. Instrumentalism leaves intact the internal version of this distinction. In fact, he soon concluded, the distinction between experience and language, sense and meaning *in* the human mind is part and parcel of nominalist thinking. Why does this matter from an educational as opposed to a philosophical standpoint? The either/or nature of the mental distinction as viewed by nominalists, Dewey began to suspect, would force educators to take sides. Some would fervently embrace traditional, didactic instruction with its emphasis on language and logic; others would, with equal fervor, embrace experiential learning. What could conceivably be viewed as complementary positions could also be viewed as antagonistic "sects" (*MW* 7: 153); there is evidence, of course, that this is precisely what happened.

Two more times this century, in the 1960s and again in the 1990s, didactic education came under attack. Like a redo of the great progressive reform of the 1930s, advocates touted the experiential, activity-based approach to education as the only viable antidote for the failings of abstract, language and definition oriented instruction. In the 1960's reform, the famous Swiss psychologist, Jean Piaget, provided the theoretical rationale for experiential learning; this scholar, it should be emphasized, was quick to point out the similarity he perceived between his approach and that advocated by the early (i.e., nominalist) Dewey (cf., Flavell, 1963). (As an aside, Piaget was also explicit about the nominalist nature of *his* theory [Furth, 1981, p. 111].)

The 1990s reform occurred against a slightly different backdrop. More so then in the past, a consensus had formed among psychologists and progressive educators that earlier ways of thinking about learning were seriously flawed. Learning, many academicians began to argue, is inherently "constructivist" in nature. Whether it involves playing the so-called "language game" or inducing order from rich experiential input, learning is not a spectator sport; meaningful learning requires an active agent. About this, there was common agreement. Even within the confines of a broad constructivist orientation, however, a serious, underlying difference could be detected between those who stressed the role of language (i.e., the interactionalist and sociocultural constructivists) and those who stressed the role of experience (Piagetian or radical constructivists). The former, as I have pointed out elsewhere (Prawat, 1995, 1999), adopted a postmodern stand toward knowledge. The philosophical patron saint of postmodernism, Richard Rorty, is explicit about his nominalist tendencies (see above). At any rate, the nominalist distinction between language and experience lives on in the current constructivist climate. Bresler and Davidson go so far as to say that the disagreement about this issue dwarfs all others in importance among constructivists. Cobb (1994) agrees, adding that each adherent tells "half of a good story" (p. 17). When one realizes that, in the midst of the 1990s *constructivist* reform which split along nominalist lines, there was a group of traditional educators waiting in the wings, as they had in the earlier two reforms, convinced that the experiential approach would self-destruct, Dewey's concerns seem more than justified.

Traditional education, then, with its emphasis on precise language and careful definition, and progressive education, with its emphasis on personal experience, are stepchildren of nominalist theory almost as much as the new sciences and the new philosophies that sprang up in the seventeenth century. The two-pronged emphasis on language and experience in education has been divisive historically; this divisiveness continues, in a serious way, even among the current crop of otherwise progressive educators who subscribe to the so-called "constructivist" view of learning. As has been pointed out, nominalism also had a divisive influence on philosophy, giving rise to warring camps of rationalists and empiricists (Peirce, *CP* 2).[2] This was not the case in science where the two processes nominalism set in motion—that of rethinking the role of language and of experience—played a complementary role in launching science on its way. Ultimately, however, nominalism has played a mischievous role in this endeavor as well, as Charles Sanders Peirce pointed out.

"Modern thought has been extravagantly Ockhamistic," Peirce wrote at the turn of the last century (*CP* 6: 348). Prior to the advent of science, this theory might be considered "respectable;" not so any more according to Peirce. "After physical science has discovered so many general principles in Nature," he declared, "nominalism has become a disgraceful habitude of thought" (*CP* 6: 175). This strong statement has been echoed recently by prominent historians and philosophers of science. A. I. Miller (1996, p. 154), for example, who was a working scientist before he became one of the leading historians of science, argues that he can "seriously entertain only scientific realism." The philosopher Susan Haack is even more explicit about the merits of Scotish-Peircean realism as it relates to science. "I have sketched an epistemology of science which is realistic," she writes at the end of one of her recent essays. "I conclude as I began, by quoting Charles Peirce, himself a working scientist as well as the greatest of American philosophers—'a man must be downright crazy to doubt that science has made many true discoveries.' Or a women," Haack adds (1998, p. 100). (As an aside, Haack's positive assessment of Peirce is widely shared; Max Fisch, an eminent Peice scholar, calls him "the most profound native intellect to have appeared in the United States" [in Ketner & Klosel, 1986, p. vii].)

Do nominalists really deny that there is such a thing as truth in science? Indeed they do. This key tenet, the belief that all order (and thus all scientific truth) is created in the head, along with the second key tenet of nominalism, the notion that the process of creating this order—the move from sense to meaning—is inherently discontinuous, have not been seriously challenged by educators and philosophers for seven hundred years, Peirce and Dewey notwithstanding. The irony in all this is that the alternative to nominalism put forth by John Duns Scotus, the "Dunce," had just as strong a claim on philosophical grounds and remains, to this day, much more consistent with our common-sense way of thinking about the world. I turn now to his theory, which involves delving a bit into medieval philosophy writ large. The starting point for all medieval philosophy is, of course, Aristotle.

SCOTISH REALISM:
AUTHOR/OBJECT "CO-CONSTRUCTION"

The great issue in the middle ages was how to reconcile the discoveries of the ancients, many of which were just becoming known, with the infallible teachings of the church (Cantor, 1993). This required nimble footedness; fortunately, the so-called "schoolmen," the scholastics, were more than up to the task. Naturally, with so much at stake, the debates were furious, often leading to physical as well as verbal assaults. As Charles Sanders Peirce explains, "The discussions of the learned doctors sometimes ended with black eyes and bloody noses; and even monarchs patronized one party or the other and protected it by the power of the state" (*CP* 1: 361). The most vehement argument of all centered on the nature of "generals" or "universals" as they were called: Is there really humanity in man, animality in animals, the scholastics asked. The nominalists, who prevailed in this argument as we have seen, maintained that there was not. Humanity, animality, they thought, are mere words that signal the end of a process that begins with the decision to put together specific experiences involving entities like individual people or pets, and then to assign a name to that collectivity. Why had this become such a red-hot issue?

Aristotle is chiefly to blame. Aristotle was at once tantalizing and extremely vexing to the scholastics. His works burst onto the scene in the late twelfth century, thanks largely to their rediscovery by Arab scholars. "The impact of Aristotle's thought on the late Middle Ages cannot be overestimated," Grant writes (1986, p. 52). Aristotle's writings quickly swept aside the works of other ancient philosophers, led by Plato. In fact, Aristotle's arguments were so compelling that they defied efforts by the church authorities to ban them on several occasions. It is important to point out that Aristotle did agree with Plato on one fundamental point: Only the universal, the pure form that makes a dog a dog or a man a man, is real. Every thing possesses an essential form (e.g., "rationality" in man).[3] Real (i.e., non man-made) objects can have *no* existence apart from this form. Aristotle parted company from Plato on one key point: He insisted that form cannot exist separate from matter. Aristotle, however, was not able to spell out the exact nature of the relationship between these two aspects of being. Form precedes and structures matter but the latter also plays an active role, he thought. The material that is to be shaped or molded according to the game plan provided by form can be more or less receptive to form's influence.

Another way of putting it is to say that matter, for Aristotle, was at best an imperfect receptacle for form; it is subject to "accidents" of various sorts. (Socrates's snub nose is an example; it clearly departs from the aquiline ideal that the creator of noses must have intended.) Form, for this reason, assuming it can be mentally "pulled out" of matter, provides the only true basis for knowing something. Fortunately, form has the ability to "impress" itself on the human mind the way, using Aristotle's metaphor, a signet ring impresses itself on a piece of wax. The rational mind, which is the form or essence that defines man, also possesses the portability attribute. Aristotle believed that the human mind, after death, leaves the body and impresses itself on the Great Mind—the universal intelligence known as God. The soul, in Aristotle's theory, plays an important role in this process as the key intermediary between the higher domain of pure intellect and the lower earthly domain, which shares attributes like sensibility with the animal domain.

There were many things in Aristotle's theory to which churchmen could take exception. Perhaps the most important was the image of God that emerged from the theory. Aristotle's deity, Durant (1953) says, was like a "do-nothing" English king. He was, at best, an inspirer and an idea generator. The Christian God was much more hands-on, at least that is what Thomas Aquinas thought. Aquinas took it upon himself to reconcile Aristotelian science and philosophy with Christian dogma. By all lights, he succeeded admirably. God was more than the final perfection toward which all things tend, Aquinas argued. God was the first cause, the creator of heaven and earth. He thus plays an active as opposed to a mere "theory generating" role in bringing things into being. In Aristotle's system, form comes first, activating existence. Aquinas turned this around: Existence is the act that initiates, that confers being. Form, or essence in Aquinas's terminology, was thus alleviated of the responsibility that God now assumed. Essence can thus play more of a definitional role, delineating what it is that makes a horse a horse or a man a man. Aristotle conflated form and existence. Aquinas, by separating the two, could argue that essence can exist separate from existence—or a least, *particular* existence.

Aquinas accomplished an important goal by separating essence and existence. A single existent, specifically a person's mind, any person's mind, can be a complex essence. The two constructs, in other words, can go their separate ways. Aquinas's belief that the human mind is a complex essence, half rational, half animal or sensible, represents a decided improvement over Aristotle's approach; the latter believed that the mind was an immaterial substance that is somehow attached to the body in an extrinsic and not intrinsic way. Aquinas was able to have his cake and eat it too. The human intellect could depend for its data on bodily (sensory) organs but it need not use the body in any way when it came to processing these data.

Unfortunately, Aquinas was not able to account for how the mind was able to abstract the gist of something (i.e., its form or essence) from the sensory image at its disposal. This was one of the major problems that

Aquinas passed on to Scotus and Ockham. The issue is: How does the mind derive form or essence from sensory representations? Ockham, using his famous razor, did away with both form and sensory representation: Objects, he argued, are apprehended directly; the mind searches through the resulting input and pulls out patterns or regularities. "Form" or "essence" (i.e., the "general" or "universal") is entirely a creation of the human mind.

Duns Scotus took a totally different tack, as we will see. First, however, it is necessary to understand the way Scotus differed from Aristotle and Aquinas on the issue of how the general (i.e., form or nature) interacts with the particular. How, in other words, does Socrates's humanity interact with the features (e.g., his snub-noseness) that make him an individual? Aristotle staked out an extreme position in this regard. Form was primary for Aristotle. It came first and "accidents" like snub-noseness were unfortunate events that got in the way of form's ideal instantiation. Aquinas rejected this view. Form and accident, universal and particular features, took shape at one and the same time. Again, Aquinas could take this position because he separated existence from form and, for that matter, from individuation. Owens (1994, p. 186) explains it this way: "Existence gives the thing its thoroughgoing individuation by synthesizing everything in the thing into a single unit, both on the essential and accidental levels."

Matter and form codetermine one another. Individuality is not something that happens to form so much as it is an inevitable feature of matter acquiring real-world features or dimensionality. Aquinas was not out of the woods yet, however, or so Scotus thought. Accidents, individual features, still take a backseat to form in Aquinas's theory. This creates a logical problem, Scotus decided: If snub-noseness and quick wit are two of the individual traits that help make Socrates what he is, how can they be secondary to essence in defining him?

Scotus turned the classic problem on its head, as Kretzmann, Kenny, and Pinborg (1982, p. 823) explain: Before Scotus the issue was, crudely put, "Given knowledge of universals [dogness, humanness], find the individuals. After Scotus, there was a new problem, "Given the knowledge of individuals, find the universals." Ockham's solution was to deny that regularities (universals) exist in nature. Scotus's solution was to assume that the particular precedes the universal. This way of casting the problem fits much better with modern sensibilities.

Philosophers of science today are comfortable with the notion that scientists tease out the general or universal from the particular. It was Scotus's brilliance to develop a theory that explains how this happens. The one thing Scotus insisted on is that the process of discovering the general in the particular is one of "co-construction." Here, Scotus strikes a very contemporary chord when we writes, "Both knower and object are active in producing cognition.... Thus, we avoid the incongruities associated with the assumption that the intellect is wholly passive, or that it is wholly active, so that the object would do nothing" (in Wolter, 1990, p. 169 n). This is a key tenet of any realist view of knowledge. Be it photosynthesis in a plant, the gravitational interaction between a falling body and earth, or—on a different level—equinity in a horse, regularity is presumed to be present in the particular phenomenon. It is palpably there in the individual object or event, and the mind's task is to figure out how to tease it out. Fortunately, the regularity plays a role in this regard. This requires some elaboration.

After Peirce initially and Dewey later adopted Scotus's view of the inquiry process, a philosopher named Stephen Pepper wrote a famous book entitled *World Hypotheses* which is still cited today, fifty years later. In that book he explained how pragmatic realists deal with the issue of regularity in the environment. Pepper explains how ideas or hypotheses, aimed at capturing regularities like photosynthesis, when valid, merge or mesh with the object or event that contains the regularity. In the quotation that follows, Pepper is emphasizing how, in true hypothesis, the individual's anticipations about the regularities to be found in the environment bear fruit, they "carry through" into the verifying event, which is the correspondence aspect of what can be viewed as a cognitive-perceptual process. Pepper also points out how the object or event in question "talks back," adding "texture" to the original idea in a process that Pepper describes as becoming more "coherent:"

> Thus, in a certain sense, a true hypothesis *corresponds* with the event that verifies it, for the references carry through continuously into the verifying event. In a certain sense a true hypothesis coheres with the event that verifies it, for its references are not blocked, but are integrated there [italic added]. (1942, p. 277).

A valid idea, Pepper argues, "does in its texture and quality give some insight into the texture and quality of the event it refers to for verification" (p. 277). This is especially true of ideas that capture important regularities in objects and events. The term that Pepper applies to this process is that of "qualitative confirmation."

The test of any idea relating to a regularity is its ability to open up a phenomenon in a believable way to reveal the regularity that lies beneath the surface of the phenomenon. If the plant really is a "food factory," the individual ought to be able to actually see food production going on in the plant, within the narrow confines of the leaf. Viewing the regularity through the lens of this metaphor would involve being able to "see" the food being "warehoused" somewhere else in the plant, either in the form of fruit above ground or in fleshy roots below, to "see" the waste products that are being given off, and so forth.

Dewey and, before that, Charles Sanders Peirce, presented exactly this argument when they wrote about the relationship between ideas and the regularities they seek to capture. The qualitative confirmation part of the idea development process in Peirce's theory was called the "indexical stage." Here the idea, in schematic or skeletonized form, is literally "laid" on the object or event as an initial and key reality check. Hausman (1993) describes the index-object or event interaction as a case of "fancy" (qualitative understanding) meeting "fact." John Duns Scotus, was the originator of Peirce and Dewey's revolutionary, "co-construction" approach to learning. Before elaborating further on how he arrived at his views, it is important to draw some further distinctions between Scotus and Aquinas.

The notion of "form" or "common nature" was the dominate concept in Aquinas's theory. Like Aristotle, Aquinas believed there was only one per customer; all entities of the same kind, all dogs, all humans, have one essential form. It is that essential form or common nature that gives the individual object or event its unity—that constitutes its whole reality. It and it alone is all that is worth knowing about a phenomenon. Scotus, again anticipating how the moderns would approach the subject, argued that the common nature is only part of the story. The common nature in his theory is not distinct or separate from the individual, by definition; it is, in reality, merged with the individual. The latter, in fact, is a positive as opposed to an accidental or negative factor in Scotus's theory. It is the qualities associated with individualization that ensure, for example, that Socrates is and remains distinct from Plato.

Scotus took this argument to its next logical level by maintaining that more than one common nature (or universal or general or regularity—there is a plethora of terms) can apply to an individual entity. In the case of a particular dog, it might be "dogness," "animalness," and even "living being-ness." When many universals can do the job, no one suffices, which is contrary to what Aquinas thought. It is the general attributes working *together* with the entity's unique features that accomplish this goal, Scotus believed. The conclusion he drew from this was profound from an epistemological perspective: The human intellect, in its effort to understand an object or event, must assign equal weight to its individuality and to its common nature. This is the gist of the Dunce's approach.

Unlike Ockham, who believed that universals are created in the human mind, Scotus believed that they are discovered in real things (Wolter, 1990, p. 51). This may sound like a minor distinction but it looms large in philosophy and education, as I will soon show. The process Scotus thought was involved in discovering the general in the particular—in "teasing" it out of a welter of confusing data, maps onto descriptions of the process contained in the notes of scientists generated two or more centuries later. It might be helpful to develop a sense of that process, as described by the experts themselves, before returning to Scotus's account. Darwin, at least implicitly, attributes his great insight about "nature selecting" to the fact that he was an English countryman, well steeped in the lore of animal, especially dog, breeding. If man can select to produce certain new and unique species, it suddenly occurred to him, then nature can do the same. This insight, plus a second idea he lifted from Malthus's influential new book on the population "explosion," the notion of survival of the fittest, were the two pieces he used to tease out the great regularity we call "evolution" (Ghiselin, 1969).

Galileo tells a similar tale. He was on a barge in the Gulf of Venice, troubled by his failure to find evidence to support his hypothesis that the earth moves, when he suddenly took note of the way the cargo of water was sloshing in response to changes in the boat's direction and speed. Galileo later reported that he immediately equated the barge with the earth and the sloshing water with the ebb and flow of tides in the Mediterranean (Sobel, 1999, p. 73). Countless examples of this sort can be found (Miller, 1996). As Darwin and Galileo's accounts demonstrate, discovering universals in nature typically begins with an insight, sparked more often than not by the sudden awareness of a likeness: This is like that, the scientist thinks. Dog breeding is like nature "breeding;" the movement of water in casks is like the movement of the tides, both caused by the movement of the earth (Galileo was wrong here, of course; the moon is responsible for the tides). Metaphor provides the initial insight. Peirce and Dewey recognized this in their elaboration of Scotus's basic scheme; Peirce, in fact, insisted that, "A pure idea without metaphor ... is like an onion without a peel" (in Rosenthal, 1994, p. 93).

Scotus assigned a key role in the discovery of regularity to metaphor as well, although he did not use that term. Had Scotus been alive six hundred years later, when Darwin made his discovery, he likely would have described the process this way: It began with Darwin's sense (intuition) that the phenomenon he found so puzzling, the incredible diversity in plant and animal life, might offer up a regularity or universal if he could but get deep enough into it. Fortunately for Darwin, the vague sense of an underlying order sparked a sudden insight—nature's creations are like man's animal breeding "creations." The sign or image that came to Darwin's mind Scotus called the "phantasm." It is similar to what Peirce terms the "iconic" metaphor (i.e., a metaphor like "food factory" in image form). The defining feature of the phantasm, according to Scotus, is its naturalness; the sudden imaginative likeness that is the phantasm suggests itself to the mind without seeming effort (Tachau, 1988, p. 63). From

here the process follows closely the one Peirce laid out in the late nineteenth century, which is not surprising given the fact that Peirce based it
on Scotus's scheme (*CP* 6: 593).

The phantasm, the concrete image that captures the generality
thought to exist in the object or event, must be tested against reality. The
construct to which Scotus assigns the testing role is the "concrete universal," a hybrid of sign and object (Almeder, 1980, p. 162). This is where the
rubber meets the road, so to speak, in the process described by Pepper
(see above). In the Darwin example, the concrete universal is constructed,
if that is the correct term, when the phantasm, the image of nature
"selecting" species, is used as a lens to open up the phenomenon of interest, in this case the incredible diversity of plant and animal life. The sign
is the metaphor, the object, the phenomenon that is the focus of the
inquiry. To further complicate matters, Scotus used a second term to
describe the concrete universal, referring to it in several of his writings as
the "intelligible species." Brehier, in his classic book on the middle ages,
describes the role of the intelligible species this way: "The intelligible species," he writes, "is necessary not for producing the act of understanding,
which derives solely from the possible [i.e., imaginative] intellect, but for
relating the act to this or that object" [italics added] (p. 68).

The hybrid sign-object (i.e., the concrete universal or intelligible species) is the key input in a complex act of intellect; this act, which Scotus
considers part intuition and part abstraction, results in the derivation of
the concept. The concept is a true mental entity. As such, it plays a key
mediating role in Scotus's theory between the highly contextualized
understanding epitomized by the hybrid sign-object and the partially
decontextualized understanding associated with a name or expression. In
the Darwin example, the concept that results from the further processing
of the concrete universal is that of "natural selection." This expression,
then, evokes the concept which, in turn, evokes the highly imaginal
understanding that gave rise to the idea in the first place.

The concept, as Tachau points out (1988, p. 66), has as its major function the responsibility of ensuring that regularity is, in fact, grounded in
reality. Terms or expressions like "natural selection," in Scotus's approach,
find symbolic expression in propositions. It is the proposition that is subject to further efforts at verification. Unlike Ockham's approach, the
proposition (e.g., "Natural selection and survival of the fittest are the twin
mechanisms that account for evolution") maintains an important connection with concrete reality, a notion that Peirce considered key in his version of Scotish realism: "It is remarkable," Peirce pointed out, "that,
among all the definitions of the proposition ... there is, perhaps, not one
in which the conception of reference to an object or correlate is not the
important one" (*CP* 1: 558).

Use of the Darwin example to illustrate what Scotus had in mind is, of course, taking liberties with the actual course of events. Scotus formulated his masterful realist account of the origin of ideas in the second half of the thirteenth century; Darwin went public with his earth-shattering account of evolution six hundred years later. Science as Darwin knew it was only a glimmer in Scotus's eye. Still, it is remarkable how well the Dunce's theory fits the record of scientific discovery as it has now come to be understood (Miller, 1996). Countless examples culled from scientists' journals and notes soundly refute the notion that induction plays a key role in the discovery of order or regularity in nature—this, despite the fact that great scientists often pretended that they followed the path of "Baconian induction." So ingrained was the commitment to this aspect of nominalist philosophy that even Darwin adhered to the methodological convention, as Ghiselin points out: "Darwin, like other scientists of his day, gave much lip service to 'induction,' and such hypocrisy has long obscured the real nature of scientific discovery" (1969, p. 35). While induction has been exposed in science as the emperor with no clothes, the process continues to be held in high esteem amongst progressive educators. Before exploring the educational implications of Scotus's alternative to Ockham's nominalism, more needs to be said about why Ockham won the great debate seven hundred years ago.

Peirce is clear in his mind about the process that dubbed Ockham the clear winner. The latter was a better politician, he writes, pure and simple (*CP* 6: 361). Scotus's belief in order or regularity was perceived to be a conservative doctrine; the regularity he touted, his opponents suggested, is best located through the good offices of the Catholic Church. The humanists, who were intent on countering what they viewed as the excessive power of the church, were inclined on this basis alone to reject Scotism. More than this perception was at issue, however. The battleground that the humanists had staked out was control of the universities. Boler (1963) describes what happened this way, "In the struggle to control the universities, the humanists sided with the followers of Ockham in an attempt to overthrow the Dunces, who were then in power. As a political favor, but with little concern for or understanding of the real issues involved, the humanists championed nominalism" (p. 20). The humanists, who were to lay the ground work for early modern science (cf., Shapin, 1996, p. 76), may have outsmarted themselves. This, at least, was Peirce's conclusion: Nominalism was to prove "anti-science in essence," he argues (*CP* 2: 166). The important point to keep in mind, Peirce emphasizes, is that the dominance of nominalism is an historic accident.

Philosophers agree that nominalism did not prevail over realism because of the strength of its philosophical argument. Freddoso, for one, maintains that Ockham's arguments against Scotus's position are uneven at best; the former often simply asserts that the Dunce's positions are unjustified (1999, p. 342). Be that as it may, intellectual historians agree that Ockham's main objection to Scotus's theory was that it did not provide for a powerful enough God. The world that Scotus thought God created, as argued above, met man half-way when it came to knowledgeability. God imbued things with an order or regularity that man could tease out if he put his mind to it. Not so in what Farrell calls Ockham's "thinned out" world (1994). God is not about to tie his hands even to the order he creates: He cannot be held to the laws he has laid down; in fact, he can decide at a moment's notion to throw them out and start all over again (Langer, 1990, p. 8). Man is thus left entirely to his own devices in nominalist theory, as we have seen. Blumenberg (1993, p. 171) picks up on this idea well when he writes, "The [nominalist] formula that the Creator has done His work for no other purpose than to demonstrate His power omitted man entirely from the determination of the world's meaning." Little is to be gained by belaboring the point; the important thing to keep in mind is that Ockham, like all scholastics, was as much influenced by theology in his argument as by philosophy.

THE EDUCATIONAL IMPLICATIONS OF "REALIST CONSTRUCTIVISM"

I begin this last section with a question that, hopefully, will not sound as strange now as it might have at the beginning of the chapter: What if the Dunce was right, after all? What if his views, instead of Ockham's, had prevailed, especially in the field of education? The primary way that nominalism surfaces in education today is in what Duns Scotus, were he to be suddenly resurrected as a latter day pundit, might characterize as an excessive, even compulsive concern on the part of educators for the students' own experience. Nominalists view the child's experience as the starting point for all progressive education. It is almost heretical to suggest otherwise. Education is about making sense of one's experience, the motivation for which must come from within, as the early (nominalist) Dewey emphasized: "To appreciate a problem as such," he wrote in 1896 while still under James's nominalist influence, "the child must feel it as his own difficulty, which has arisen within and out of his own experience" (*EW* 5: 145). The teacher's role, given this assumption, is that of a provocateur—an individual who plays an indirect role in getting the student to recast prior experience and deal in more appropriate ways (i.e., more disciplinarily sound ways) with new experience. The expression that is often used to describe this role is that of the "guide on the side;" this, in marked

Table 4.1

Epistemology	What	How	Where	When	Why
Nominalism ("progressive" approach only)	Concepts, language & logic	Induction	In the head	Input enters system	Need to make sense of personal experience
Realist Constructivism	Ideas	"Abduction" (semiotic process)	Between mind & world	Sense of deeper meaning arises	Need to create harmony in a disharmonious situation

Teacher Role	Goal	Motivation	Strategy	Initial Test
"Guide on the side"	To get students to recast personal experience	Blockage of need or goal	Involvement in "hands on" activity	Checking propositions against the "logic" of experience
"Sage on the side"	To open up the child's world, to see it with "new eyes"	To be more completely "in" the situation	Working the metaphor	The ability to tease the general out of the particular

contrast to the didactic approach, also inspired by nominalism, which is said to view the teacher as the "sage on the stage."

Table 4.1 contrasts nominalism with realism on a number of dimensions such as the one just presented. Phillips (1997), in an analysis of constructivism, suggests that philosophers and educators make use of the first five headings in the table: *What* is constructed, *how* does the construction occur, *why, when, and where* does this process take place? All these seem like sensible questions to ask. As Table 4.1 reveals, nominalists and realists—or, as I prefer to label them, "realist constructivists"—are likely to respond to the questions Phillips raises in dramatically different ways. While I have speculated about their probable response, the answers attributed to advocates for the two approaches should make sense in light of what has already been said.

The differences between nominalist and realist thinking on a second set of issues, those pertaining directly to education, are also explored in Table 4.1. The teacher's role, to return to the issue just mentioned, is described as being that of the "sage on the side" for those who oppose nominalism. This variant on the now familiar contrast between the expert being at the head of the class or working behind the scenes to guide the student, both of which fit the nominalist approach to a tee, is meant to connote the fact that, in the realist alternative to traditional (or progressive) education, the teacher does not relinquish the role of expert in the classroom. This expertise, however, is expressed in a novel way, which is not unlike the way tour guides express their knowledge when they stand alongside their charges in front of an important site that must be jointly explored. The teacher, as a kind of intellectual "tour guide," works with students in a collective effort to tease out what the teacher knows to be an interesting regularity lurking just beneath the surface of the phenomenon in science, in social studies, or in other disciplines. It might be helpful at this point to contrast the realist constructivist approach with an interesting and popular variant on the nominalist approach, widely known as "conceptual change" teaching.

Arguably, conceptual change teaching is the best developed of the current experiential approaches inspired by nominalist thought. It is a misnomer, however, to categorize this approach as being primarily about "induction." Teachers play a frontal role in conceptual change, at least in the beginning, inasmuch as it is their responsibility to make sure that students bump up against the limits of their current knowledge. A better description for this approach, therefore, might be that of "guide on the stage." Regardless of how one views the guiding role in conceptual change, it is the teacher in this approach who bears responsibility for presenting an interesting kind of event—one that appears, at first blush, to be a common or everyday occurrence but that turns out to be much more provocative then anyone had initially imagined. The inability of the students to adequately (i.e., scientifically) explain what has occurred supposedly sets in motion the search for alternative, more "workable" ways of construing these experiences (Posner, Strike, Hewson, & Gertzog, 1982). The hoped for result is the same as that which would be obtained in hands on, problem oriented learning: The "teachable moment," where students are suddenly receptive to new ways of construing the situation.

I recently observed an example of this approach in a ninth grade science classroom. Students were asked to comment on a reasonably common event, the sudden extinguishing of flame from a lighted candle, which had been placed in an open container. The event was unusual in that the cause of the flame going out was not immediately evident. In actuality, the casual agent responsible for putting out the flame was carbon dioxide emanating from a mixture of vinegar and baking soda at the bottom of the container. The carbon dioxide reduced the oxygen supply to the candle, which extinguished the flame. The problem was that the students seemed only moderately interested in this "provocative" event. The teacher, despite the fact that he presented this anomalous occurrence with great energy and dispatch, was able to elicit only a few timid explanations for the phenomenon that had been observed. One student suggested that the bubbles (produced from the mixture of chemicals) had "blown the candle out." Several others nodded in agreement. This explanation apparently fit with students' current ways of construing flame-related experiences: Namely, that a flame expires when something or someone suddenly cools the source of the fuel feeding the flame, in this case the wick. The thought that the bubbles, which were in plain view at the bottom of the container, might play a role akin to that of a person blowing out a birthday candle, was thus not an unreasonable one given the students' past experience.

Following the "bubble solution" suggestion, which the teacher tactfully described as not being the one a scientist would prefer, it was obvious to the observer that the rest of the class had lost interest in the "game." The teacher later puzzled over the fact that an inability to account for the event did *not* appear to be provoking students in the manner prescribed by conceptual change theory. He speculated about why that was the case: First, the group, being teenagers, quickly caught on to the fact that they lacked adequate knowledge to account for the event in a scientifically acceptable way; the situation could easily have been viewed by them as yet another instance of not being able to respond correctly to a teacher's question.

However, even if he had been able to overcome this egocentric response, the teacher went on, another difficulty might arise. This difficulty, perversely, relates to what conceptual change theorists see as a real strength in their approach: Namely, that the teacher is presenting a phenomenon that students are eager to talk about. This assumption appeared not to apply to the present situation, presumably because the students had already "solved" the problem that the teacher was trying to get them to rethink, at least to their own satisfaction. The conceptual change approach might work, the science teacher lamented, if in fact the phenomenon was one that students found worthy of further pursuit. This teacher, however, found himself in the unenviable position of saying to students, in effect: "Look. Here's a problem of minor interest to you personally. I realize that you have already worked out a solution to this problem that 'works' for you; thus, there is little to be gained by opening it up again. Still, I want you to do just that and to risk being considered wrongheaded at the same time!"

At the heart of the problem, I submit, is the traditional focus on student experience and the resulting effort to change how students interpret that experience. The teachers' role in this process is to assist students in their cognitive restructuring efforts. The teacher relies on carefully crafted language to achieve this goal (Shapiro, 1994). Children are encouraged to use this language to go back over and "rename" or, more appropriately, to reclassify and rename their own experience in the approach that throughout this paper has been referred to as nominalism.

What does the realist theory gain for the teacher in the candle example that is lacking in the nominalist, conceptual change alternative just described? It gains the same thing for the teacher that it gains for the scientist. It assumes that the possibility for understanding is there for the taking—present in any qualitatively rich situation present to the learner or to the inquirer. All that is necessary to bring this possibility to fruition is a well-conceived metaphor or analogy. As indicated earlier, ideas are generated through a metaphoric process, one that Scotus, Peirce, and Dewey all thought lies outside language (Prawat, 1999). These metaphor-ideas, as we have seen, offer sudden new insights about phenomena. They open up an aspect of the world to the student (or the scientist) that otherwise would remain closed off, perhaps forever.

Our teacher, had he opted for Scotus's "realist constructivist" approach, would have gotten to the point in a much less circuitous way. In effect, he would say to students, "Here is a familiar, even everyday phenomenon (i.e., a flame). You can continue to view it in the same old way— as something that just is, something that can move from place to place, that people can "start" in various ways, but that, in the end, is not much more than this. That's all right. That's how most people down through history would have viewed this phenomenon. However, there was this interesting person who suggested that we think about fire in a different way, as a strange kind of 'living/non-living' thing." The teacher would then develop with students the implications of this new metaphor. "In what ways might fire be a 'living/non-living' thing?" Together, the community could elaborate the expectations associated with the new idea: "Fire is living in the sense that it feeds off oxygen and a food supply just like other living things. There is a metabolic process in fire just as there is in the human body; that is, there are differences in the rate at which fire consumes 'food;' those differences are a function of the nature of the 'food' and the size or intensity of the fire.... Fire is non-living in the sense that it is inanimate and man- (or nature-) made..." The teacher, using this approach, would have gotten the students to perceive a familiar phenomenon in an entirely new and different manner in the most direct way possible.

In the realist constructivist approach, interesting objects or events in the environment are singled out and students are encouraged to view these phenomena with new eyes, as it were. The strength of this approach is that the ability to see new and wondrous things is *inherently* motivational for the child. A glance at Table 4.1 illustrates this; the goal, "opening up the world for the child" maps onto, in a seamless way, the motivation that prompts the movement toward this goal. This is not the case in the "frustration-recasting of experience" operation favored by the nominalists. The motivation in this approach, frustration resulting from the blockage of need, "kick starts" the meaning making process but is not an integral part of it.

Dewey explained the advantages of the realist approach best when he introduced a notion that he said is too little appreciated in education— the notion, to use his language, that ideas are "self-propelling," that they have the ability to carry the alert mind along with it into new territory (*LW* 8: 334). There is not much preparation time associated with this approach, Dewey adds. The value of an idea is determined on the spot by individuals who agree to test it out. "The individual qua individual is the organ or instrument of truth," Dewey wrote, even when that person has not authored the idea him or herself (in Diggins, 1994, p. 140). The validity of an idea like photosynthesis, to cite one example, lies in its ability to uncover a fascinating new regularity in the world, a regularity that connects green leafy things to other regularities having to do with food production and consumption that affects all other living things.

As Table 4.1 indicates, the shift in focus from a nominalist to a realist approach is subtle but terribly important. If possibility can be directly sensed and immediately given ideational form, there is less reason to focus on the child's existing experience and the role of language in getting the child to rework or reorganize that experience. The need to "rename" experience, however, is axiomatic in progressive education as Freire makes clear (1982, p. 76). The realist position developed seven hundred years ago by the Dunce questions this hallowed assumption. If adopted, even at this late date, it might fulfill the ambitious goal Dewey set for it in the nineteen thirties and forties—that of helping to eliminate what he anticipated would be a series of back and forth swings of the pendulum from didactic to experiential teaching. This, of course, is exactly what has happened, starting with the progressive movement that Dewey had a hand in initiating, occurring in the United States again in the 1960s and, most recently, in the 1990s. The choice between language and definition, which is primarily deductive, and the so-called hands on or activity based approach, which is inductive, is a false choice according to Dewey. Had the Dunce prevailed, these two nominalist options would likely not have served as focal points in education and philosophy from the middle ages on. The strong possibility that realist constructivism, if widely embraced by educators, might eliminate or at least ameliorate the insidious distinction between didactic and progressive education is reason enough to regard it as more than a viable alternative to nominalism; it is, I believe, a significantly better belief for teachers to hold when they ponder important philosophical questions like what is knowledge and where does it come from.

NOTES

1. References to Dewey's writings are from the collected works published by Southern Illinois University Press under the editorship of J. A. Boydston. The standard way of citing pieces in this collection lists initials for each of the three series first (i.e., *The Early Works* [*EW*], 1882-1898, 5 vols., *The Middle Works* [*MW*], 1899-1924, 15 vols., *The Later Works* [*LW*], 1925-1953, 15 vols.), followed by the volume and page numbers.

2. References to Peirce's writings are from the *Collected Papers of Charles Sanders Peirce* edited by C. Hartshorne, P. Weiss, and A. Burks (1931-1935). The volume and paragraph numbers follow the *CP* designation.

3. I beg the reader's indulgence for use of the term "man" here and in the remainder of the paper. Throughout the middle ages and modern era, as the reader must appreciate, writers used the term with its primary meaning in mind—that of "human being;" I follow this convention.

REFERENCES

Almeder, R. (1980). *The philosophy of Charles S. Peirce: A crical introduction*. Oxford, UK: Basil Blackwell.

Ashman, K. M., & Baringer, P. S. (Eds.). (2001). *After the science wars*. London: Routledge.

Blumenberg, H. (1983). *The legitimacy of the modern age.* Cambridge, MA: MIT Press.

Boler, J. (1963). *Charles Peirce and scholastic realism: A study of Peirce's relationship to John Duns Scotus.* Seattle, WA: University of Washington Press.

Brehier, E. (1965). *The middle ages and the renaissance.* Chicago: University of Chicago Press.

Cantor, N. F. (1993). *The civilization of the middle ages.* New York. HarperCollins.

Carre, M. H. (1950). *Realists and nominalists.* Oxford, UK: Oxford University Press.

Cobb, P. (1994). Where is the mind? Constructivist and sociocultural perspectives on mathematical development. *Educational Researcher, 23*(7), 13-20.

Dewey, J. (1940). *Education today.* New York: Greenwood Press.

Diggins, J. P. (1994). *The promise of pragmatism.* Chicago: University of Chicago Press.

Durant, W. (1953). *The story of philosophy.* New York: Simon & Schuster.

Farrell, F. B. (1994). *Subjectivity, realism, and postmodernism—the recovery of the world.* Cambridge: University of Cambridge.

Freire, P. (1982). *Pedagogy of the oppressed.* New York: Continuum.

Flavell, J. (1963). *The developmental psychology of Jean Piaget.* New York: D. Van Nostrand.

Freddoso, A. J. (1999). Ockham on faith and reason. In P. V. Spade (Ed.), *The Cambridge companion to Ockham* (pp. 326-349). Cambridge: Cambridge University Press.

Furth, H. G. (1981). *Piaget and knowledge.* Chicago: University of Chicago Press.

Ghiselin, M. T. (1969). *The triumph of the Darwinian method.* Berkeley: University of California Press.

Ghiselin, M. T. (1969). *The triumph of the Darwinian method.* Berkeley: University of California Press.

Gilson, E. (1937). *The unity of philosophical experience.* New York: Charles Scribner.

Grant, E. (1986). Science and technology is the middle ages. In D. C. Lindberg & R. L. Numbers (Eds.), *God and nature* (pp. 49-75). Berkeley, CA: University of California Press.

Haack, S. (1998). *Manifesto of a passionate moderate.* Chicago: University of Chicago Press.

Hale, J. (1993). *The civilization of Europe in the renaissance.* New York: Macmillan.

Hausman, C. R. (1993). *Charles S. Peirce's evolutionary philosophy.* Cambridge: Cambridge University Press.

Hemisoeth, H. (1994). *The six great themes of western metaphysics and the end of the middle ages.* Detroit, MI: Wayne State University Press.

Howe, K. R., & Berv, J. (2000). Constructing constructivism, epistemological and pedagogical. In D. C. Phillips (Ed.), *Constructivism in education. Ninety-ninth yearbook of the national society for the study of education* (pp. 19-40). Chicago: University of Chicago Press.

James, W. F. (1950). *The principles of psychology: Vol. 1.* New York: Dover Publications. (Original work published 1890)

James, W. F. (1956). Stanford's ideal destiny. In W. James (Ed.), *The will to believe and other essays in popular philosophy.* New York: Dover Publications. (Original work published 1906)

Jensen, A. (1969). How much can we boost IQ and scholastic achievement? *Harvard Educational Review, 39*(1), 1-123.

Ketner, K. L., & Kloesel, C. J. W. (Eds.). (1986). *Peirce, semeiotic, and pragmatism. Essays by Max H. Fisch*. Bloomington: Indiana University Press.

Kliebard, H. M. (1987). *The struggle for the American curriculum 1893-1958*. New York: Routledge & Kegan Paul.

Knowles, D. (1988). *The evolution of medieval thought*. Longman: London.

Kretzmann, N., Kenny, A., & Pinborg, J. (Eds.). (1982). *The Cambridge history of later medieval philosophy*. Cambridge, UK: Cambridge University Press.

Langer, U. (1990). *Divine and poetic freedom in the renaissance*. Princeton, NJ: Princeton University Press.

Lindberg, D. C. (1992). *The beginnings of western science*. Chicago: University of Chicago Press.

Miller, A. I. (1996). *Insights of genius. Imagery and creativity in science and art*. Cambridge, MA: MIT Press.

Montgomery, S. L. (1996). *The scientific voice*. New York: Guilford Press.

Neisser, U. (1976). *Cognition and reality*. San Francisco: W. H. Freeman.

Nelson, J. S., Megill, A., & McCloskey, D. N. (1987). Rhetoric of inquiry. In J. S. Nelson, A. Megill, & D. N. McCloskey (Eds.), *The rhetoric of the human sciences* (pp. 3-18). Madison, WI: University of Wisconsin Press.

Owens, J. (1994). Thomas Aquinas. In J. J. E. Gracia (Ed.), *Individuation in scholasticism* (pp. 173-194). Albany: State University of New York Press.

Panaccio, C. (1999). Semantics and mental language. In P. V. Spade (Ed.), *The Cambridge companion to Ockham* (pp. 53-75). Cambridge: Cambridge University Press.

Pepper, S. G. (1942). *World hypotheses*. Berkeley: University of California Press.

Phillips, D. C. (1997). How, why, what, when, and where: Perspectives on constructivism in psychology and education. *Issues in Education, 3*(2), 151-194.

Porter, R. (2000). *Enlightenment. Britain and the creation of the modern world*. London: Penguin Books.

Posner, G. T., Strike, K. A., Hewson, P. W., & Gertzog, W. A. (1982). Accommodation of a scientific conception: Towards a theory of conceptual change. *Science Education, 66*, 211-227.

Prawat, R. S. (1995). Misreading Dewey: Reform, projects, and the language game. *Educational Researcher, 24*(7), 13-22

Prawat, R. S. (1999). Dewey, Peirce, and the learning paradox. *American Educational Research Journal, 36*(1), 47-76.

Prawat, R. S. (2000). The two faces of Deweyan pragmatism: Inductionism versus social constructivism. *Teachers College Record, 102*(4), 805-840.

Prawat, R. S. (2001). Dewey and Peirce, the philosopher's philosopher. *Teachers College Record, 103* (4), 667-721.

Rochberg-Halton, E. (1986). *Meaning and modernity*. Chicago: University of Chicago Press.

Rorty, R. (1979). *Philosophy and the mirror of nature*. Princeton, NJ: Princeton University Press.

Rorty, R. (1989). *Contingency, irony, and solidarity*. Cambridge, UK: Cambridge University Press

Rosenthal, S. B. (1994). *Charles Peirce's pragmatic pluralism*. Albany: State University of New York Press.

Shapin, S. (1996). *The scientific revolution*. Chicago: University of Chicago Press.

Shapiro, B. (1994). *What children bring to light: A constructivist perspective on children's learning in science*. New York: Teachers College

Skorupski, J. (1998). Mill on language and logic. In J. Skorupski (Ed.), *The Cambridge companion to Mill* (pp. 35-56). Cambridge: Cambridge University Press.

Sobel, D. (1999). *Galileo's daughter.* New York: Walker & Company.

Tachau, K. H. (1988). *Vision and certitude in the age of Ockham*. Leiden, the Netherlands: E. J. Brill.

Uljens, M. (1997). *School didactics and learning*. East Suusex, UK: Taylor & Francis.

Weinberg, S. (1996, August). Sokal's hoax. *New York Review of Books*, 11-15

Wolter, A. B., O.F.M. (1990). *The philosophical theology of John Duns Scotus*. Ithaca, NY: Cornell University Press.

CHAPTER 5

AT THE HEART OF TEACHING

The Role of Emotion in Changing Teachers' Beliefs[1]

Patricia Ashton
University of Florida
and
Michele Gregoire-Gill
University of Central Florida

"Emotions are ways with which we know the world around us.... Emotions inform you whether something needs to change" (Zembylas, 2002, pp. 92, 94). These quotes from Catherine, an elementary-school teacher who was the subject of a 3-year ethnographic study of the impact of emotions on teaching, reveal an important insight that has eluded educational researchers seeking to explain why it is so difficult to change teachers' beliefs and teaching practices. That is, emotions play a crucial role in motivating change in beliefs. Using Foucault's genealogical method, Zembylas showed how Catherine's emotions, particularly her feelings of excitement, influenced her professional and personal identity, her relationships with students and colleagues, her curriculum decisions, her instruction, and her views and reactions to her school culture. On the basis of Catherine's reactions, Zembylas concluded that discourse about teachers' emotional reactions can be used to understand and transform their teaching.

Advances in Teacher Education 99–121

In keeping with Zembylas's (2002) conclusion, our purpose in this chapter is to offer a model of belief change for guiding researchers and practitioners in enhancing preservice and inservice teachers' ability to foster the development of their students. Our model reflects Catherine's crucial insight about the role of emotions in influencing teachers' beliefs and actions. For our purposes here, we adopt Koestler's definition of emotion (as cited in Hargreaves, 1998): "Emotions are mental states accompanied by intense feeling and (which involve) bodily changes of a widespread character" (p. 835).

Numerous widely held beliefs about the nature of teaching and the role of the teacher and the learner limit teachers' effectiveness in increasing their students' learning (Kagan, 1992; Pajares, 1992). Despite recent advances in understanding the nature of motivation and learning, researchers continue to document difficulties in changing these beliefs. For example, considerable research on reforming mathematics instruction has offered compelling evidence of the difficulty of changing teachers' core beliefs about the nature of teaching and learning (e.g., Ball, 1990).

In light of this research, it is evident that teacher educators need more informative conceptual frameworks to guide their efforts to effect change in teachers' beliefs. Understanding the process of change is important for two reasons: It is essential for understanding (a) how to effect change in teachers' thinking and (b) how to enable teachers to effect change in their students' thinking. Research on conceptual change[2] offers a useful foundation for understanding the process of change in teacher beliefs (Winitzky & Kauchak, 1997); however, researchers' failure to incorporate the role of emotion in models of conceptual change has limited our understanding of the process by which changes in belief occur.

In this chapter we examine the theory of conceptual change to identify strengths and limitations of this perspective for providing insights into the psychological processes that promote significant and enduring change in teachers' beliefs. Then we propose a model that integrates the research on conceptual change with research on motivation and emotional and social psychological processes. (For an alternative model, see Gregoire, 2003.)

THE EMOTIONAL BASIS OF BELIEF CHANGE

Conceptual change theory emerged from the efforts of Posner and his colleagues (Posner, Strike, Hewson, & Gertzog, 1982) to describe the kinds of evidence involved in changing the core concepts in people's belief systems. Posner et al. drew parallels between Kuhn's (1970) description of scientists' use of evidence in the creation of revolutions in scientific thought and the process of conceptual change in students as they discard intuitive conceptions in favor of more scientific understandings of the physical world.

The central assumption of the theory of conceptual change is that "learning is a rational activity" (Posner et al., 1982, p. 212). This assumption was not meant to imply that "motivation or affective variables are unimportant to the learning process. [Rather] the claim that learning is a rational activity [is] meant to focus on what learning is, not what learning depends on" (p. 212). Despite the researchers' claim that they were not denying the role of motivation or affect in learning, we believe that their failure to include emotion as an intrinsic component of the process of learning limits their conception of learning and ultimately their understanding of the process of conceptual change.

Interestingly, Piaget and Vygotsky, two of our foremost developmental theorists, recognized the intrinsic relationship between affect and reason, but their critical insight has not influenced research in either development or education. Piaget (1981) rejected the typical conception of intelligence and affect as a dichotomy composed of two "distinct but analogous mental faculties acting on each other" (p. 74). Instead he argued that intelligence and affect are inseparable. To Piaget, affect is always involved in intellectual activity, and intelligence is always involved in affective experiences: "Without affect there would be no interest, no need, no motivation; and consequently ... there would be no intelligence" (as cited in Bearison & Zimiles, 1986, p. 3); correspondingly, he asserted that "affectivity is nothing without intelligence. Intelligence furnishes affectivity with its means and clarifies its ends" (Piaget, 1967, p. 69).

In sum, Piaget (1981) conceived of affect, including interests, drives, and feelings, as the energizer of intellectual activity, like "gasoline, which activates the motor of an automobile but does not modify its structure" (p. 5). For Piaget, the incentive for action is always affect, because it determines the value of activities and allocates energy to them. Intelligence, on the other hand, he suggested, is like the engine that gives the automobile structure.

Vygotsky shared Piaget's belief in the inseparable nature of emotion and cognition:

> The separation of the intellectual side of our consciousness from its affective, volitional side is one of the fundamental flaws of all of traditional psychology. Because of it, thinking is inevitably transformed into an autonomous flow of thoughts thinking themselves. It is separated from all the fullness of real life, from the living motives, interests, and attractions of the thinking human. (as cited in Goldstein, 1999, p. 648)

The failure to incorporate an understanding of the intrinsic relationship between emotion and cognition in educational and psychological research has severely limited the development of our understanding of teachers' thinking and action. Further Vygotsky (1986) agreed with Piaget on the role of affect in motivating thought: "Thought is not begotten by thought; it is engendered by motivation, i.e., by our desires and needs, our interests and emotions" (p. 252).

Although Posner et al. (1982) separated reason and affect in their conception of the processes of learning, the first condition of conceptual change that they proposed as necessary for change is emotional—a feeling of dissatisfaction. They proposed that conceptual change involves a shift in perspective that occurs when an individual becomes dissatisfied with a current conception and finds an alternative conception intelligible, plausible, and fruitful. Despite having grounded the process of conceptual change in the emotional reaction of dissatisfaction, Posner et al. conceived of conceptual change theory as a cognitive theory, thus ignoring the affective nature of the state of discomfort that initiates the process of cognitive change and without which no change will ensue.

THE DIFFICULTY OF INDUCING BELIEF CHANGE

Similar to the conception of conceptual change that Posner et al. (1982) posited, Piaget (1974) based his view of instruction on the role of cognitive conflict as a motivator of cognitive development:

> [The teacher] is needed to provide *counter-examples* that compel reflection and reconsideration of over-hasty solutions. What is desired is that the teacher cease being a lecturer, satisfied with transmitting ready-made solutions; [the teacher's] role should rather be that of a mentor stimulating initiative and research. (emphasis added, p. 16)

Applying Piaget's cognitive conflict (i.e., equilibration) theory or the conceptual change theory of Posner et al., teacher educators have begun to design instructional interventions that induce cognitive conflict in students' existing beliefs about teaching in the hope of creating dissatisfaction with these beliefs and thus motivating them to adopt innovative conceptions of teaching (Borko & Putnam, 1996). Recently, however, researchers have pointed out that counter-evidence does not necessarily change students' views (Duit, 1999). In the case of deeply held beliefs, such as many of the entering beliefs of preservice teachers, the original belief is not replaced but rather continues to influence their thoughts and behavior. Chinn and Brewer (1993) reviewed the role of conflicting or anomalous data in knowledge acquisition and identified six ways students resist significant conceptual change: ignoring, rejecting, excluding, reinterpreting, holding anomalous information in abeyance, or making merely peripheral changes in their beliefs. Duit concluded that in most studies of conceptual change in science instruction students achieve only peripheral change at best.

At the end of their review, Chinn and Brewer (1993) pointed out that preservice and inservice teachers also resist conceptual change in entrenched beliefs such as racist stereotypes, beliefs about intelligence as a fixed entity, and their beliefs about instruction and learning. The research on belief change in teacher education provides strong support for their claim. Changes in teachers' beliefs are difficult to create and tend to be peripheral rather than central (Wideen, Mayer-Smith, & Moon, 1998). These studies indicate that inducing enduring cognitive change is an intractable and complex process. To further our understanding of the process of change, Chinn and Brewer identified four types of prior beliefs that influence whether students resist or engage in belief change: entrenched prior beliefs, ontological beliefs, epistemological commitments, and background knowledge. We consider each of these beliefs in the following sections.

Entrenched Prior Beliefs

Chinn and Brewer (1993) defined an entrenched belief as "a belief that is deeply embedded in a network of other beliefs.... A deeply entrenched belief ... (a) has a great deal of evidentiary support and (b) participates in a broad range of explanations in various domains" (p. 15). Most important for the purposes of this chapter, they added that "a belief may be entrenched because it satisfies strong personal or social goals" (p. 15). They pointed out that the more entrenched the belief, the more difficult it is to change. In fact, social-psychological research suggests that the beliefs that educators are likely to have the most difficulty in influencing or those that are ingrained by strong affective needs.

Vosniadou's (1994) notion of children's framework theories offers a useful way of conceiving of preservice teachers' entrenched views of teaching. She proposed that children develop misconceptions that are resistant to change because their early conceptions of the physical world originate from their personal experiences and are organized in a framework theory that acts as the basis for acquiring further knowledge. Children's framework theories are unconscious and may hinder learning, because the concepts children have constructed from their everyday experience differ in important ways from currently accepted explanations of scientific phenomena. Similarly, preservice teachers have constructed idiosyncratic framework theories of teaching that include entrenched beliefs about the role of teachers and the nature of effective instruction from spending thousands of hours as students observing their teachers. For example, in three case studies of preservice teachers, Anderson and Bird (as cited in Anderson, 2001) found that the prospective teachers held surprisingly diverse beliefs that did not reflect the traditional model of "teaching as telling and learning as passive reception based on educational experiences in fairly traditional and teacher-centered classrooms," (p. 210), or the constructivist model of their teacher education instructors. Similar to other researchers (e.g., Weinstein, 1989), Anderson and Bird found that the three preservice teachers were confident about the effectiveness of their views of the role of the teacher and they resisted making changes in those views throughout the course:

> It was as if [the three students] approached the study of the cases as an opportunity to fill in the missing details in their existing schemas of teaching, to learn how to do whatever they already imagined they should learn to do. . . . [When the students responded to the cases,] they did not do so by expanding their belief systems for what it is possible to notice, consider, and value in teaching. Rather, they interpreted each case through the lens of their initial images of teaching. (p. 197)

From an analysis of six additional case studies, Anderson (2001) concluded that when teacher educators understood and built upon the preservice teachers' initial conceptions, they enabled the preservice teachers to expand their conceptions into "more powerful frames for thinking about instruction" (p. 211).

Vosniadou (1999) offered an alternative hypothesis about how to overcome the resistance to conceptual change that results from the highly entrenched beliefs in framework theories. She pointed out that novice learners lack metaconceptual awareness. That is, they are unaware of the hypothetical nature of their beliefs and presuppositions, which they treat as facts rather than as hypotheses that are falsifiable. Vosniadou proposed that development of metacognitive awareness fosters conceptual change, as understanding that others hold different perspectives from one's own motivates individuals to submit their perspectives to empirical test and may enable them to adopt new perspectives. Vosniadou recommended research to determine if the development of metacognitive awareness is a necessary step in conceptual change.

Thus, Anderson (2001) and Vosniadou (1999) have proposed two methods of fostering belief change in entrenched beliefs that differ from the approach that Posner et al. (1982) initially advocated. Research that compares the approach of gradually suggesting refinements in preservice teachers' beliefs (Anderson, 2001), with the approach of direct challenges of their prior beliefs (Posner et al., 1982), and the approach of promoting the development of metacognitive awareness of the hypothetical nature of beliefs (Vosniadou, 1999) is needed to determine the relative effectiveness of these three different approaches to changing entrenched beliefs. This research might also provide insight into how to change the second category of beliefs that Chinn and Brewer described as highly resistant to change. These beliefs, which they referred to as ontological beliefs, are discussed next.

Ontological Beliefs

Chinn and Brewer (1993) used this category to refer to entrenched beliefs about the fundamental properties of the world. These beliefs are particularly resistant to change, because they are so entrenched that students find alternative views difficult if not impossible to understand. Ontological beliefs of preservice and inservice teachers include deeply held beliefs about human nature that influence their expectations of students and their motivation to persist in helping students who are experiencing learning difficulties. In drawing conclusions from her nine case studies, Anderson (2001) pointed out that such ontological beliefs emerged as significant dimensions in preservice teachers' entering conceptions, and she called for research to clarify how ontological beliefs interact with the ideas that teacher educators present in their programs.

Epistemological Commitments

In addition to entrenched and ontological beliefs, preservice teachers' beliefs about the type of evidence that is necessary to warrant belief change may also contribute to their resistance to efforts to influence change in their beliefs. Chinn and Brewer (1993) referred to this category of beliefs that deals with people's criteria for evaluating the evidence for belief change as epistemological commitments. Citing research by Samarapungavan, Chinn and Brewer pointed out that in evaluating whether evidence is sufficiently convincing to warrant a change in beliefs even young children use a "commonsense" epistemology that includes internal consistency, consistency with empirical observations, and consistency with a wide range of evidence. They noted, however, that children lack awareness of the value of experimental testing of hypotheses and the need for rigorous controls. Like Vosniadou (1999), Chinn and Brewer recommended developing students' metaconceptual awareness of how beliefs relate to evidence to promote a more rational approach to the evaluation of beliefs. Of greatest relevance to this chapter, recent theorists interested in the role of epistemological beliefs in affecting belief change have pointed out that emotion may influence the impact that epistemological beliefs have on conceptual change. For example, Hofer and Pintrich (as cited in Bendixen, 2002) noted that individuals may retreat to "safer, more established positions when in new environments and that there may be affective issues involved, such as the effects of anxiety and negative feelings associated with challenges to strongly held ideas" (p. 193). Bendixen explored the experience of epistemic doubt in interviews with 12 undergraduates and concluded that emotions associated with their experience of doubt facilitated as well as interfered with epistemic change. Thus, it is likely that understanding the role of epistemological beliefs in belief change requires an understanding of how emotions are involved in the maintenance and development of epistemological beliefs.

Along with prior beliefs, ontological beliefs, and epistemological commitments, other beliefs not directly salient but connected to the conception at hand within individuals' framework of beliefs influence their openness to considering alternative perspectives. These beliefs, referred to as background knowledge, are considered next.

Background Knowledge

According to Chinn and Brewer (1993), background knowledge consists of beliefs that people assume to be true that are not part of the belief under consideration. Because background knowledge acts as a filter separating salient from irrelevant information, it can have a profound effect on whether individuals attend to and ultimately accept an alternative core belief. For example, consider Jessica, one of the prospective teachers in Anderson's (2001) study. When analyzing a case illustrating an open classroom, Jessica "noticed those features of the case that she already believed, and she ignored other features that represented new or alternative interpretations" (p. 197). Emotion is particularly important in determining whether background beliefs support acceptance of or resistance to a new belief. Anderson illustrated this point in her case study of Greg, who despite being in an exemplary teacher education program, failed to modify his entering conceptions because "his affective reactions to the program were so negative" (p. 209). The need to develop a model that incorporates the critical role of emotion in belief change is discussed in the remainder of the chapter.

THE NEED FOR A
HOTTER MODEL OF CONCEPTUAL CHANGE

Chinn and Brewer's (1993) description of the four types of beliefs that influence belief change and the instructional strategies that they recommend to overcome resistance to change may be helpful to teacher educators in understanding the process of change, but by failing to include the emotions that energize belief change in their discussion Chinn and

Brewer omitted the most important component of belief change. Without an understanding of the critical role of emotion in motivating belief change, efforts to foster change in teachers' beliefs are likely to remain ineffectual.

In their 1992 revision of conceptual change theory, Strike and Posner admitted that their initial formulation of the theory was overly rational, and they recommended that motives, goals, epistemological views of the subject matter, and their institutional and social origins need to be included in their theory of conceptual change. This recommendation was a response to their recognition that not all students engage in a rational assessment of competing concepts. Some may be engaged in behaviors motivated by affective concerns, such as protecting their self-esteem.

Reacting to similar concerns, Pintrich, Marx, and Boyle (1993) criticized the overly rational model of conceptual change of Posner et al. (1982) and emphasized the importance of a supportive motivational context that includes task, authority, and evaluation structures that promote the adoption of learning goals. In elaborating further on a "hot" model of conceptual change, Pintrich (1999) identified five motivational factors that should be included in a comprehensive model of conceptual change: (a) a mastery goal orientation, (b) constructivist epistemological beliefs, (c) high levels of personal interest in and valuing of the topic as personally relevant, (d) a strong sense of efficacy or confidence in one's ability to use thinking and learning strategies to change one's ideas and synthesize new ideas, and (e) a belief in personal control over one's learning.

Although Pintrich and his colleagues added crucial components to our understanding of why students resist changing their beliefs by pointing out the need to incorporate motivational and contextual factors into a "hot" model of conceptual change, their model is still overly rational and, thus, not hot enough. To advance our understanding of effective conceptual change, researchers need to recognize the critical role that emotion plays in the development and maintenance of conceptual beliefs.

Cognitive theories dominate our views of motivation and instruction in part due to the influence of Weiner's (1986) attribution theory, which focuses on the explanations (i.e., attributions) that individuals adopt to account for their experiences. In an article that received little attention, Weiner (1980) presented evidence demonstrating that *emotions*, not thought, motivate action, including the actions required for academic achievement. For example, in most instances when a student attributes her failure to lack of effort, feelings of guilt ensue; in contrast, when she attributes her success to ability, she feels pride and a sense of competence. These emotions, Weiner showed in his research, not the thoughts that preceded them, motivate achievement behavior. In the case of the attributions mentioned above, for example, the emotions of guilt and pride that the attributions elicited motivate students to engage in the behavior of studying for future tests. Weiner qualified his argument by explaining that guilt and pride do not always influence students' academic behaviors because other factors such as the general affective climate of the classroom may counteract their effect, creating other emotions, perhaps fear or helplessness, that elicit behaviors such as withdrawal.

In later more extensive treatments of the role of emotion in motivation in which he integrated insights from theories of emotion, Weiner (1985, 1986) contended that in the temporal sequence between the outcome of an event such as success or failure and the attribution the individual adopts to explain the outcome, a general positive or negative feeling is experienced—happiness in response to success for example and sadness in response to failure. He labeled these emotions *outcome dependent-attribution independent*, because they are evoked by success or failure in achieving a goal, not by the individuals' attribution for the success or failure. Following this initial emotional experience, the individual searches for an explanation for the outcome. The attribution, in turn, evokes a more complex emotion; for example, when failure is attributed to lack of effort, the individual experiences guilt, and when success is attributed to ability pride ensues. Weiner referred to these more complex emotions as *attribution dependent*.

In sum, Weiner (1980, 1985, 1986) concluded that the central role that emotion plays in motivation needs to be integrated into cognitive theories of motivation. Unfortunately researchers' failure to recognize the importance of this insight and to incorporate it into theories of motivation has limited our understanding of conceptual change and learning in general and our effectiveness in promoting students' academic achievement.

THE INTELLIGENCE OF EMOTION

The thesis of this chapter is that emotion plays a role in motivating belief change that is similar to the role Weiner (1980) posited for emotion in academic motivation. That is, emotions motivate the thoughts and behavior that lead individuals to reject or accept a new belief. Traditional conceptions of emotion as inhibiting thought, however, have impeded researchers' recognition of the positive role that emotion plays in fostering conceptual change. The predominance of the cognitive paradigm in psychology and education has supported and strengthened the widely held cultural view of emotion as a detour or obstacle to rational thinking (Bearison & Zimiles, 1986). Recent developments in our understanding of the role of emotion in human psychology, however, provide support for Weiner's view of emotion as the motivator of thought and action. No

longer considered an inevitable threat to rationality, emotions are conceived as internal guides to action that are "an integral component of the
machinery of reason" (Damasio, 1994, p. xii). Drawing on these new
developments in psychological research, Nussbaum (2001) made a powerful argument for a Neo-Stoic view of emotions as "highly discriminating
responses to what is of value and importance," "suffused with intelligence," that "shape the landscape of our mental and social lives" (p. 1).
As an extension, we argue that emotions shape the landscape of teachers'
professional lives. Nussbaum's conception of emotion as intrinsic to our
reasoning is reflected in the decision making of the teacher whose words
began this chapter. Nussbaum's conception of emotion as "upheavals of
thought" deepens our understanding of the process of belief change in
teachers. Nussbaum wrongly dismissed the essential role of feeling—the
physiological basis of emotion—in her Neo-Stoic analysis of emotion, but
her effort to dispel the cultural belief that emotions are "blind forces that
have no selectivity or intelligence about them," forces that are antithetical
to rationality (p. 11) helps elucidate the intelligence that emotion may
offer in the process of belief change.

Oatley and Jenkins (as cited in Hargreaves, 1998) effectively described
the intelligence of emotions:

> In real life, a purely logical search through all possibilities is not possible
> (because of limitations of resources, multiple goals and problems of coordi-
> nation with others). Nevertheless, we must act ... despite our limitations we
> must take responsibility for our actions and suffer their effects. This is why
> emotions, or something like them are necessary to bridge across the unex-
> pected and the unknown, to guide reason, and to give priorities among
> multiple goals. (p. 841)

In their quote, Oatley and Jenkins aptly described why recognition of the
role of emotion in teaching is so important. With the continual press of
decision making and the multiple and often contradictory goals of teaching (Lampert, 1985), teachers, as seen in the case of Catherine described
at the beginning of this chapter, use emotions consciously and uncon-
sciously as a basis for their instructional decisions.

Lewis (1990) proposed that one of the six bases for people's beliefs is
the emotion or feeling that something is true or right. Any teacher educator who has studied the rationales that preservice and inservice teachers
give for their instructional goals and practices recognizes that, of the six
bases of beliefs that Lewis identified (i.e., authority, deductive logic, emotion, the experience of the senses, rational intuition, and personal use of
the scientific method), emotion is one of the most prevalent bases for
their beliefs. However, the argument we make for emotion here is stronger than that posed by Lewis or by Hargreaves (1998) who made a com-

pelling case for the importance of emotion in teaching. Like Piaget (1981) and Vygotsky (1986), we are arguing that emotion and cognition are inextricably linked. Every cognition is suffused with feeling, and those feelings motivate teachers' belief changes and their subsequent actions. Neuroscientific data are providing support for this claim. As Damasio (1999) explained, when cognitions are induced, magnetic resonance images (MRIs) show that emotions are also elicited. These data support Nespor's (1987) description of the role of emotion in enhancing the storage and recall of beliefs in long-term memory.

The Motivation of Deep Processing in Belief Change

Chinn and Brewer (1993) proposed that deep processing of contrasting beliefs is the basis for achieving belief change. However, the impetus for engaging in the hard work required in deep processing is unclear in cognitive models of belief change, such as those of Posner et al. (1982) and Chinn and Brewer. With the integrated model of emotion and cognition described here that posits emotion as the motivator of thought and behavior, we have a basis for understanding where the motivation for deep processing originates. In the next section we distinguish between types of processing and the implications these types of processing have for belief change.

SYSTEMATIC AND HEURISTIC PROCESSING

Chinn and Brewer (1993) described deep processing as including the following cognitive processes: attending carefully to the information contradictory to the current belief, attempting to understand the competing belief, elaborating the relationships between the evidence and the alternative belief, and evaluating the full range of available evidence. They pointed out that people are more likely to change and maintain their beliefs when they process information on the competing belief deeply, but they noted that people have a natural conservative tendency and are, consequently, more likely to attend to evidence supporting their beliefs than to evidence that contradicts those beliefs. To overcome this tendency, Chinn and Brewer recommended two strategies: (a) expose people to personally relevant information that contradicts their belief and (b) require them to justify their belief to others. Chinn and Brewer presented research showing the effectiveness of those two strategies in increasing students' deep processing of information. We propose that the reason these two strategies are effective is that they arouse emotions that motivate and sustain the effort required to engage in deep processing. Next, we describe recent social-psychological research that supports this hypothesis.

In the development of a social-psychological model of attitude[3] change called the *heuristic-systematic model* (HSM), Chaiken (1987) identified two types of information processing—systematic and heuristic processing—that provide insight into the nature of deep processing and the factors necessary to motivate people to engage in deep processing. Chaiken, Liberman, and Eagly (1989) defined systematic processing as "a comprehensive analytic orientation in which perceivers access and scrutinize all informational input for its relevance and importance to their judgment task" and by thinking about the information in relation to other knowledge they may possess, they "integrate all useful information in forming their judgments;" Chaiken et al. defined heuristic processing as "a more limited processing mode that demands much less cognitive effort and capacity than systematic processing. [In heuristic processing] people focus on that subset of available information that enables them to use simple inferential rules, schemata, or cognitive heuristics to formulate their judgments and decisions" (pp. 212-213). Numerous research studies (Chaiken et al., 1989) indicate that, in comparison to heuristic processing, systematic processing yields greater maintenance of belief change and greater consistency between beliefs and behavior—two important goals of belief change in preservice and inservice teachers (Chaiken et al., 1989).

Heuristic processing is often automatic and unconscious. Perceivers use minimal information and simple decision rules, such as "Experts' statements can be trusted," or "Consensus implies correctness," to judge the validity of information. Thus individuals may be relatively unaware of the extent to which simple rules influence their judgments and behavior. Because heuristic processing is based on such superficial cues as the expertise and likeability of the messenger, message length, and group consensus, perceivers may accept information without having fully analyzed or absorbed its meaning. Heuristic cues vary in their availability and perceived reliability. For example, Chaiken et al. reported that college students generally consider the expertise heuristic to be more reliable than the likeability heuristic.

Systematic processing, in contrast, tends to be controlled and intentional. Because systematic processing requires greater effort and cognitive capacity than heuristic processing, it is more directly affected by constraining factors, including (a) motivational factors, such as processing goals; (b) situational factors, such as time limits, and (c) individual differences, such as lack of domain-specific expertise. Consequently, as Chinn and Brewer (1993) suggested in their recommendations for increasing deep processing, when people see information as more personally relevant and having important consequences, they are more likely to engage in systematic processing. Chaiken et al. argued that when people are highly motivated and capable of systematic processing, their beliefs are less likely to be influenced by heuristic cues. Thus, perceived self-efficacy is an important prerequisite for systematic processing. That is, people must believe that they can increase their confidence in the accuracy of the belief by engaging in systematic processing of information about the belief.

Chaiken et al. (1989) emphasized that, although systematic and heuristic processing may seem like two ends of a continuum, they are not. They may occur simultaneously; when conditions are conducive, the two types of processing may have additive or interactive effects on people's beliefs, and when motivation and ability for systematic processing is high, systematic processing can override the effect of heuristic processing. In instances in which people lack confidence in their ability for systematic processing, however, heuristic processing may predominate or may bias systematic processing. For example, if a belief is attributed to experts, preservice students who consider themselves to be novices may accept the belief in deference to the expert without engaging in systematic processing. This tendency is likely to be exacerbated when preservice teachers feel they do not have time to engage in systematic processing. Chaiken et al. identified important sources of bias in systematic processing that we review in the next section.

Sources of Bias in Systematic Processing

Motivational Biases

Chaiken et al. (1989) reviewed research indicating that vested interests, commitments to particular values, ideologies, or reference groups, and preferences for particular conclusions may bias systematic processing, and they attributed this bias to one overarching motive—the desire to protect ego-involved beliefs. In teacher education, for example, preservice teachers' unrealistic optimism about their ability to assume the responsibilities of teaching (Weinstein, 1989) may limit their motivation to think systematically about the evidence for a belief. Secure in their belief that they already possess the skills necessary to teach effectively, preservice teachers may not feel a need to comply when teacher educators encourage them to think deeply about the dilemmas of teaching.

Cognitive Biases

Strong prior beliefs may also bias systematic processing. For example, if prior beliefs seem consistent with information about a new belief, perceivers may not feel a need to process the information systematically. Conversely, if information about a new belief contradicts a current belief, especially a personally relevant belief, perceivers may quickly dismiss the new information without examining it carefully. These cognitive biases appear to be prevalent in teacher education students' reactions to instruction. Consider Holt-Reynolds's (1992) conclusions after interviewing preservice teachers about what they understood in their teacher education classes:

> When preservice teachers believe that teaching well depends rather exclusively on making school work interesting, they reject as irrelevant parts of the course that focus on teaching students to use metacognitive strategies for reading to learn.... When they believe that students' effort is the salient factor contributing to success as a learner, they reject as irrelevant learning how to foster comprehension skills.... When they believe all students will be like themselves—able learners a bit bored by school—they find little reason to learn how to analyze the demands inherent to subject matter texts.... When they believe that teacher telling—lecturing—is a primary vehicle for communicating teacher's enthusiasm for subject matter, they react negatively to ideas for cooperative learning. (p. 63)

Emotional Biases

In addition to the motivational and cognitive biases Chaiken et al. (1989) described, we believe that emotional biases play an important role in influencing whether people engage in systematic processing. Chaiken et al. offered evidence of such emotional biases when they noted that people probably use heuristic cues frequently in situations where they continually confront the need to process information, which no doubt applies to preservice and inservice teachers, whose lives are fraught with stressful demands for information processing. For example, the role of emotional biases has implications for the trend toward the development of brief alternative certification programs. Such programs are likely to increase prospective teachers' dependence on heuristic cues because of the time pressures such programs impose, particularly those programs in which students are immersed in full- or half-time teaching assignments.

In the next section we integrate the research on motivation and systematic processing in a model of belief change that emphasizes the role of emotion in motivating systematic processing and ultimately changes in beliefs and practices. Then we present recommendations for research to determine the adequacy of the model for representing the process of belief change.

A MODEL OF THE ALTERNATIVE EFFECTS OF
EMOTIONS ON BELIEF CHANGE

Based on Weiner's (1980, 1985) view of emotion as a motivator of thought and action, Figure 5.1 illustrates our model of the role emotion plays in belief change. In the model, whether individuals change core beliefs depends, first, on whether individuals feel dissatisfaction with their current belief, and, ultimately, on whether cognitive and motivational factors elicited by the feeling of dissatisfaction with the current belief trigger positive or negative emotions that motivate the information processing that, in turn, induces the emotions that motivate belief change. Whether belief change results in changes in teaching practice is further determined by the emotions evoked in the process of changing beliefs. Although emotion and cognition are separated in the model for the purposes of illustration, we assume, consistent with Piaget's (1981) and Vygotsky's (1986) developmental theories and Damasio's (1999) neurological research, that cognition and emotion are inseparable processes in normal human consciousness.

To illustrate how emotion motivates belief change, we offer an example of how the process might evolve in three preservice teachers who hold the belief Holt-Reynolds (1992) found prevalent in her interviews with beginning preservice teachers that "teaching well depends rather exclusively on making school interesting" (p. 63). In our fictional scenario, the students have strong positive feelings about this belief, because they believe that it has been validated by their own educational experiences. To challenge this belief, their instructor presents a case of an experienced teacher who shares their belief and works diligently and creatively to find exciting activities for her students. Her students loved being in her class and found the class activities exciting, but their scores on the end-of-the-year achievement test were markedly lower than the scores of students at the same grade and of similar ability whose teachers were less concerned about making class activities fun and more concerned about developing students' metacognitive skills.

This case distresses the first preservice teacher, as she reflects on the possibility that if her belief is inaccurate she might someday confront a similar problem. Thus she experiences the dissatisfaction that Posner et al. (1982) posited as essential to conceptual change. Let us assume also that she has the cognitive and motivational characteristics that elicit the positive emotion of excitement at the possibility of learning new skills to help students learn or alternatively she experiences the negative emotion of fear that if she does not develop new skills to help her students learn she faces the fate of the teacher in this case. Whether her emotion is negative or positive, it motivates her to systematically process the information

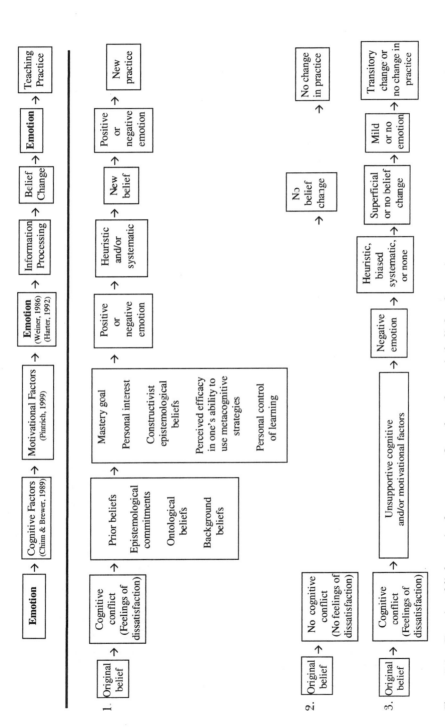

Figure 5.1. Emotional linkages in the process of teacher change in belief and practice

her instructor offers to support the belief that metacognitive strategies can increase students' understanding and achievement, and she develops positive feelings about the importance of helping students develop these strategies. The outcome will be her revised belief—making school work interesting is not sufficient to teach well, teachers must also foster the development of students' metacognitive skills.

The second preservice student, in contrast, dismisses the outcome of the case on the basis of a background belief that tests do not measure important outcomes of teaching. Consequently, this student does not experience the feeling of dissatisfaction and cognitive conflict that might initiate the process of belief change. Like the first, the third student experiences dissatisfaction with her belief, but she lacks either the cognitive or motivational factors or both that elicit the emotion that would motivate her to engage in systematic processing. Instead she may experience anxiety, which serves as a heuristic cue that motivates her to change her belief superficially, perhaps on the basis of her instructor's expertise, but her belief is weak and vulnerable to change. If no heuristic comes to mind to support belief change, she is likely to resist change.

IMPLICATIONS FOR RESEARCH

Three research thrusts are needed to determine whether the integrated model of belief change presented in Figure 5.1 helps teacher educators to foster changes in beliefs and teaching practices that enable prospective and experienced teachers to enhance their students' learning. We hope that researchers will investigate the usefulness of the model in (a) designing effective approaches to belief change in teacher education, (b) enabling teachers to regulate their own teaching and learning more effectively, and (c) developing more effective instruction for fostering belief change in content knowledge.

The Integrated Model of Belief Change as a Guide to Effective Approaches to Belief Change in Teacher Education

The importance of relating new information to existing knowledge is one of the most widely accepted tenets of teacher education. However, the nature of the beliefs that preservice teachers bring to teacher education and the processes by which to access them are not well understood. Teacher educators have designed numerous approaches for fostering belief change in prospective and experienced teachers (Borko & Putnam,

1996). The results, however, have been relatively unimpressive (Wideen et al., 1998).

Vosniadou (1999) proposed that resistance to belief change occurs because the individual's initial beliefs are supported by a "relatively coherent and systematic explanatory system, which works relatively well in the everyday world," and, as a consequence, is rather difficult to change" (p. 8). Although Vosniadou's description of initial beliefs may fit some of the beliefs held by prospective teachers, Winitzky and Kauchak (1997) in their studies of beginning preservice teachers' concept maps of teaching found that their students' "anemic" maps suggest that many of the students' beliefs about teaching are vague and fragmented. Consequently, Winitzky and Kauchak recommended that when students' beliefs are sturdy and well organized, they may need an instructional approach that involves directly challenging their beliefs with counter-examples and discussions; whereas, when their beliefs were vague and fragmented, an instructional approach that involves the construction of a coherent belief system is more appropriate. This recommendation suggests that Anderson (2001) and Duit (1999) who challenged the view of Posner et al. (1982) that it is necessary to create dissatisfaction with current beliefs in order to induce conceptual change may have been working with students who had vague and fragmented beliefs. Increasing our understanding of the kinds of approaches needed to foster belief change requires systematic investigation of prospective and experienced teachers' beliefs to determine which are well organized and resistant to change and require emotional arousal to initiate change and which are less entrenched and require less emotional stimulation and support. In addition, students' emotional reactions to current approaches to belief change in teacher education, including analyses of personal metaphors of teaching, the construction of concept maps, the writing of personal philosophies and journals, and analyses of personal beliefs and cases (Woolfolk & Murphy, 2001) need to be explored to determine the impact of each on students' emotions and to assess their relative effectiveness in motivating sustained belief change and ultimately improvements in classroom practice.

The Integrated Model of Belief Change as a Guide to Self-Regulation in Teaching

In the case study of Catherine, whose comments introduced this chapter, Zembylas (2002) presented a vivid illustration of how Catherine's reflections on her emotional reactions provided her with a powerful tool for enriching her knowledge about herself, her students, and her pedagogy. Catherine was chosen for the study because of her interest in the role of emotions in teaching. Consequently, it is unclear whether other teachers view their teaching in terms of their emotional reactions as Catherine did, whether other teachers would find reflections on their emotional reactions as informative about their professional identities, and ultimately whether emotions have the power to transform beliefs to the extent that they did for Catherine. Zembylas has provided a provocative basis for the design of further research on the role of emotion in changing beliefs and teaching practices.

The Integrated Model of Belief Change as a Guide to Effective Approaches to Belief Change in the Instruction of Content Knowledge

Researchers of conceptual change from early childhood through the college years have been frustrated by the difficulty of inducing conceptual change. Clearly, the cognitive approaches that have characterized the approaches to stimulating conceptual change in students have for the most part failed to produce significant and enduring change. Research is needed to determine if interventions that focus on the emotional basis of conceptual change increase the likelihood of sustaining changes in students' core beliefs.

CONCLUSION

In her review of the implications of research on teacher belief, Kagan (1992) concluded that teacher belief "lies at the very heart of teaching" (p. 85). Interestingly, her use of the metaphor of the heart did not include common associations of the heart with emotion. Instead she emphasized the cognitive components of belief in her paper. Our goal in this chapter is to highlight the integral role of emotion in changing and maintaining beliefs. We believe that exploring this perspective in research on belief change holds promise for helping teacher educators and teachers better understand the processes of teaching and learning and, consequently, more effectively foster human development.

NOTES

1. Knowledge and belief are used synonymously in this chapter in keeping with Chinn and Brewer's (1993) perspective that the term *belief* emphasizes the fallibility of knowledge and Kagan's (1992) assumption that "most of a

teacher's professional knowledge can be regarded more accurately as belief" rather than knowledge (p. 65). Nespor (1987) and Pajares (1992) discussed important distinctions between the two terms, but we decided that for the issues we raise here the distinctions can be ignored, though they are not forgotten.

2. The use of the term *conceptual change* seems to be sufficiently similar to the conception of belief change that we explore in this paper that we will use the terms conceptual change and belief change interchangeably. Again, we recognize that important distinctions can be made between these two terms, but we believe that the distinctions can be ignored here.

3. Chaiken et al. (1989) proposed that their model of attitude change applies to belief change as well.

REFERENCES

Anderson, L. (2001). Nine prospective teachers and their experiences in teacher education: The role of entering conceptions of teaching and learning. In B. Torff & R. J. Sternberg (Eds.), *Understanding and teaching the intuitive mind: Student and teacher learning* (pp. 145-185). Mahwah, NJ: Erlbaum.

Ball, D. (1990). Reflections and deflections of policy: The case of Carol Turner. *Educational Evaluation and Policy Analysis, 12*, 247-259.

Bearison, D., & Zimiles, H. (1986). Developmental perspectives on thought and emotion: An introduction. In D. J. Bearison & H. Zimiles (Eds.), *Thought and emotion: Developmental perspectives* (pp. 1-10). Hillsdale, NJ: Erlbaum.

Bendixen, L. (2002). A process model of epistemic belief change. In B. K. Hofer & P. R. Pintrich (Eds.), *Personal epistemology: The psychology of knowledge and knowing* (pp. 191-207). Mahwah, NJ: Erlbaum.

Borko, H., & Putnam, R. (1996). Learning to teach. In D. C. Berliner & R. C. Calfee (Eds.), *Handbook of educational psychology* (pp. 673-708). New York: Macmillan.

Chaiken, S. (1987). The heuristic model of persuasion. In M. P. Zanno, J. M. Oldson, & C. P. Herman (Eds.), *Social influence. The Ontario Symposium* (Vol. 5, pp. 3-39). Hillsdale, NJ: Erlbaum

Chaiken, S., Liberman, A., & Eagly, A. H. (1989). Heuristic and systematic information within and beyond the persuasion context. In J. S. Uleman & J. A. Bargh (Eds.), *Unintended thought* (pp. 212-252). New York: Guilford Press.

Chinn, C. A., & Brewer, W. F. (1993). The role of anomalous data in knowledge acquisition: A theoretical framework and implications for science instruction. *Review of Educational Research, 63*, 1-49.

Damasio, A. (1994). *Descartes' error: Emotion, reason, and the human brain*. New York: Avon Books.

Damasio, A. (1999). *The feeling of what happens. Body and emotion in the making of consciousness*. New York: Harcourt.

Duit, R. (1999). Conceptual change approaches in science education. In W. Schnotz, S. Vosniadou, & M. Carretero (Eds.), *New perspectives on conceptual change* (pp. 263-282). Oxford, UK: Elsevier Science.

Goldstein, L. (1999). The relational zone: The role of caring relationships in the co-construction of mind. *American Educational Research Journal, 36*, 617-673.

Gregoire-Gill, M. (2003). Is it a challenge or a threat? A dual-process model of teacher's cognition and appraisal processes during conceptual change. *Educational Psychology Review, 15*, 147-179.

Hargreaves, A. (1998). The emotional practice of teaching. *Teaching and Teacher Education, 14*, 835-854.

Holt-Reynolds, D. (1992). Personal history based beliefs as relevant knowledge in course work. *American Educational Research Journal, 29*, 325-349

Kagan, D. (1992). Implications of research on teacher belief. *Educational Psychologist, 27*, 65-90.

Kuhn, T. S. (1970). *The structure of scientific revolutions* (2nd ed.) Chicago: University of Chicago Press.

Lampert, M. (1985). How do teachers manage to teach? Perspectives on problems in practice. *Harvard Educational Review, 55*, 178-194.

Lewis, H. (1990). *A question of values*. San Francisco: Harper & Row.

Nespor, J. (1987). The role of beliefs in the practice of teaching. *Journal of Curriculum Studies, 19*, 317-328.

Nussbaum, M. (2001). *Upheavals of thought. The intelligence of emotions*. New York: Cambridge University Press.

Pajares, M. F. (1992). Teachers' beliefs and educational research: Cleaning up a messy construct. *Review of Educational Research, 62*, 307-332.

Piaget, J. (1967). *Six psychological studies*. New York: Random House.

Piaget, J. (1981). *Intelligence and affectivity. Their relationship during childhood*. Palo Alto, CA: Annual Reviews.

Pintrich, P. (1999). Motivational beliefs as resources for and constraints on conceptual change. In W. Schnotz, S. Vosniadou, & M. Carretero (Eds.), *New perspectives on conceptual change* (pp. 33-50). Oxford, UK: Elsevier Science.

Pintrich, P. R., Marx, R. W., & Boyle, R. A. (1993). Beyond cold conceptual change: The role of motivational beliefs and classroom contextual factors in the process of conceptual change. *Review of Educational Research, 63*, 167-199.

Posner, G. J., Strike, K. A., Hewson, P. W., & Gertzog, W. (1982). Accommodation of a scientific conception: Toward a theory of conceptual change. *Science Education, 66*, 211-227.

Strike, K. A., & Posner, G. J. (1992). A revisionist theory of conceptual change. In R. A. Duschl & R. J. Hamilton (Eds.), *Philosophy of science, cognitive psychology, and educational theory and practice* (pp. 147-176). Albany, NY: SUNY Press.

Vosniadou, S. (1994). Capturing and modeling the process of conceptual change. *Learning & Instruction, 4*, 45-69.

Vosniadou, S. (1999). Conceptual change research: State of the art and future directions. In W. Schnotz, S. Vosniadou, & M. Carretero (Eds.), *New perspectives on conceptual change* (pp. 3-13). Kidlington, Oxford, UK: Elsevier Science.

Vygotsky, L. S. (1986). *Thought and language*. Cambridge, MA: MIT Press.

Weiner, B. (1980). The role of affect in rational (attributional) approaches to human motivation. *Educational Researcher*, 4-11.

Weiner, B. (1985). An attributional theory of achievement motivation and emotion. *Psychological Review, 92*, 548-573.

Weiner, B. (1986). *An attributional theory of motivation and emotion*. New York: Springer-Verlag.

Weinstein, C. S. (1989). Teacher education students' preconceptions of teaching. *Journal of Teacher Education, 40*, 53-60.

Wideen, M., Mayer-Smith, J., & Moon, B. (1998). A critical analysis of the research on learning to teach: Making the case for an ecological perspective on inquiry. *Review of Educational Research, 68*, 130-178.

Winitzky, N., & Kauchak, D. (1997). Constructivism in teacher education: Applying cognitive theory to teacher learning. In V. Richardson (Ed.), *Constructivist teacher education: Building a world of new understandings* (pp. 59-83). Washington, DC: Falmer Press.

Woolfolk, A., & Murphy, P. K. (2001). Teaching educational psychology to the implicit mind. In B. Torff & R. J. Sternberg (Eds.), *Understanding and teaching the intuitive mind: Student and teacher learning* (pp. 145-185). Mahwah, NJ: Erlbaum.

Zembylas, M. (2002). Constructing genealogies of teachers' emotions in science teaching. *Journal of Research in Science Teaching, 39*, 79-103.

CHAPTER 6

TEACHER EDUCATION AND TEACHERS' BELIEFS

Theoretical and Measurement Concerns

Maria Teresa Tatto and Daniel Bryan Coupland
Michigan State University

INTRODUCTION

It can be said that one of the most prolific areas of research in teacher education is that having to do with attitudes, dispositions or beliefs. In this chapter we will use the term "belief" to encompass commonly used terms such as teachers' beliefs, dispositions, and attitudes (see Pajares, 1992 for an excellent discussion of the meaning of the terms attitudes, beliefs and dispositions, especially pp. 313-316). We use the term "belief" in association with teacher-oriented interventions (such as preservice teacher preparation) over the other terms based on the notion that *beliefs* are convictions of the truth largely reliant on examination of evidence by individuals or by a social group (as opposed to personal preferences or opinions) for their validation.

Indeed, after a series of calls in the literature for more research on teacher beliefs as a way to inform educational practice, educators have

Advances in Teacher Education 123–182
Copyright © 2003 by Information Age Publishing

been busy defining beliefs, drawing profiles of beliefs deemed important for good teachers to have, designing programs to teach and mold these beliefs, and measuring belief change (Fenstermacher, 1994; Nespor, 1987; Pajares, 1992; Richardson, 1994). As per this body of literature, one of the most important outcomes of teacher preparation would seem to be belief change among prospective and current teachers. This is in congruence with the education literature describing teaching as being concerned with the modification and formation of belief systems (Green, 1971).

It is intriguing that such intangible constructs as attitudes, dispositions and beliefs have commanded so much interest and effort among teacher educators. The term *attitude* has been defined as a mental position, a feeling or emotion with regard to a fact or state; an organismic state of readiness to respond in a characteristic way to a stimulus (as an object, concept, or situation). The term attitude is said to be equivalent to point of view, bias, predilection, prejudice, or prepossession. The terms *dispositions* and *beliefs* appear in the teacher education literature as equivalent to attitudes and have also been an object of study and desired transformation. *Dispositions* are defined as the tendency to act in a certain manner under given circumstances, or as the dominant quality or qualities distinguishing a person or group, and it implies customary moods and attitudes toward the life around one (e.g., a cheerful disposition). *Belief*, another term used as equivalent to attitudes, is defined as a tenet or body of tenets held by a group, and as a conviction of the truth of some statement or the reality of some being or phenomenon, especially when based on examination of evidence (Merriam-Webster, 2001).

As these definitions demonstrate, and in spite of Pajares' (1992) early attempt at "cleaning and defining a messy construct," what teacher educators have been attempting to understand and mold does not only continue to have a wide range of definitions, but it is also deeply personal and rooted in the culture and norms held by individuals and society. This chapter attempts to examine three issues that are relevant to a critical examination of how beliefs are taught and measured in teacher education: (a) the theoretical basis for the kind of belief change that is currently seen as important in reformed teacher education; (b) the current approaches used to measure belief change in teachers as a result of a given intervention; (c) the degree to which current measurements indeed capture the kinds of belief change advocated by teacher education reform. This chapter first presents a summary of major tendencies in the teaching and measurement of beliefs in the field of preservice teacher education based on a review of studies from the last five years. We looked for peer-reviewed research articles from the last five years (1996-2001) in the ERIC and EdAbstracts databases. We used the key words "preservice teacher," "attitudes," "beliefs," "dispositions," and "measurement" to identify articles that would relate to our focus. From the more than one hundred pieces, we chose 26 articles representing major trends in the literature from a variety of contexts, publications, and subject areas in education that represent this field of study. All of these articles demonstrate researchers' efforts to measure change in the beliefs/attitudes/dispositions of preservice teachers as a result of some kind of intervention. We assumed that in this time-period research on belief change would reflect not only accountability influences but also effects of teacher education interventions. Next, we present the particular case of a teacher preparation program's self-study of beliefs and conclude that examining teacher candidates' beliefs as outcomes provides only partial evidence of program influence. We conclude with recommendations for future work in this area.

THE ROLE OF TEACHER BELIEFS IN EDUCATIONAL REFORM

Although traditional definitions of good teaching have included references to belief change, reformed ideas about what it means to know and what it means to teach seem to have placed belief change at the core of these reforms. The idea that teacher education programs socialize their students to acquire a set of beliefs accepted by the profession has not been as controversial as could be expected. A more in-depth exploration of the kinds of beliefs advocated by different approaches to teacher preparation, however, indicates that the field lacks general agreement as to what are acceptable beliefs (see Tatto, 1996, 1998, 1999). Whether or not it is ethical and even effective to target beliefs as a major outcome of successful teacher preparation, current reforms implicitly support belief change as central to improving quality and equality in teaching and learning (see, e.g., Darling-Hammond, 1998). In her vice-presidential address presented at the 2000 Annual Meeting of the American Educational Research Association, Cochran-Smith discusses the "professional image" of the teacher with important implications for the role of teacher education in "shaping" this image: "[I]t is important to ask, ... whether this emerging professional image also includes images of the teacher as activist, as agent for social change, as ally in anti-racist initiatives. As we construct the outcomes question in teacher education, we need to clarify and interrogate what it means to teach "all students" well and what it means to adjust teaching practices according to the needs and interests of "all children" (Cochran-Smith, 2000a). In a 1999 chapter on preparing teachers for diversity, Ladson-Billings (1999) suggests that "the changing demographics of the nation's schoolchildren have caught schools, colleges, and departments of teacher education by surprise. Students are still being prepared to teach in idealized schools that serve white, monolingual, middle class children from homes with two parents" (pp. 86-87). In an article that same year on culturally relevant approaches to teacher assessment, Ladson-Billings (2000) further asserts that these are "dangerous times" for teachers of students of color; she suggests that some aspects of the new presumably more authentic evaluations of teacher competency "may actually serve to [reinstate] a narrow set of teaching practices that fail to serve all children well—particularly children of color and children living in poverty" (p. 255). Similarly Jackie Jordan Irvine has suggested that some aspects of assessments such as those of NBPTS are not in keeping with what we know about the strategies, relationships, and beliefs of teachers who teach children of color most effectively (Irvine, 2000; Irvine & Fraser, 1998)."

An important influence in the reform agenda is the notion that knowledge is constructed and that as such, beliefs toward teaching and learning are crucial to this enterprise (Richardson, 1994). Although there is not a unified conception of how knowledge becomes constructed in teacher education, educators—from developmental to cognitive to critical theorists—agree that teacher change requires learning opportunities that support in-depth examination of theories and practices in light of teachers' *beliefs* and *experiences* if they are to help pupils develop conceptual understandings of subject matters and a critical view of education (Ashton, 1992, p. 322). Reformed views of teaching and learning generally argue that teachers need to know that knowledge is constructed by individuals and their society; they need to be able to construct knowledge themselves in order to demonstrate such an assertion, and they need to make sense of their learning within a sociohistorical context in order to help their pupils find meaning in what they learn (see, e.g., Duckworth, 1996; Prawat, 1992).

According to these arguments, two necessary points of departure for developing a reformed approach to teacher education are: (a) the development of a theoretically grounded *view* of learning that shifts traditional conceptions of knowledge as being "out there" to knowledge developed by those who are involved in the teaching and learning process, including deeper understandings of subject matters, a discipline-based curriculum, teaching to accommodate different learning needs and styles, and the arrangement of learning opportunities so that all participants in the teaching-learning process are contributors in mastering knowledge and constructing understandings, and (b) the development of learning communities able to create opportunities for teachers and students to encourage reflection, dialogue, critical thinking, knowledge ownership, and understanding in context, including the *development of norms* to guide the program's progress and insure coherence and continuity (Ashton, 1992;

Black & Ammon, 1992; Cochran, DeRuiter, & King, 1993; Condon, Clyde, Kyle, & Hovda, 1993; O'Loughlin, 1992; Schon, 1987; Tatto, 1997; Zeichner & Gore, 1990). In the United States, these learning communities are principally located in teacher education programs and in schools, and their norms are not necessarily consistent. For instance while teacher educators may want their students to spend more time in the program analyzing teaching and learning practices, teachers in schools may feel that the best place to learn is in schools, and the best way to learn to teach is by actually teaching.

Reformed tendencies toward teaching and teacher education require dramatic changes in views and behaviors. The most important challenge in teaching and teacher education is in shifting views from traditional to reformed teaching and in the creation of communities of learning requiring the development of norms to guide program's progress and consistency. The creation of norms in teacher preparation imply working toward program consistency.

Although these conditions seem to make good common sense when thinking about teacher education programs, these assertions are still in need of empirical test. Is it possible for teacher education programs to develop consistent communities able to socialize teachers as professionals and, more importantly, to translate these beliefs into good practices?

Indeed, this is a question that is not easily resolved in the field. Many educators argue that teaching is a deeply personal act (Carter, 1998). But to the extent that beliefs influence behavior, then beliefs held by teachers as professionals must not be dictated by personal preferences or long held opinions (e.g., girls are not good at math), but must be regulated by norms according to a larger professional community. And teacher educators—as important representatives of the professional community—must endeavor to encourage their students to examine these beliefs in light of empirical evidence, and to question views based on prejudice. Other educators argue that in spite of established norms, teachers still make decisions based on their personal preferences and beliefs (Buchmann & Schwille, 1993; Raths, 2001; Richardson, 1996). Nevertheless, teacher education programs for the most part strive to mold beliefs in teachers with the assumption that a set of beliefs is preferred over others. Teachers are expected to share professional beliefs toward teaching and learning, teaching diverse learners, purposes of education, roles and practice, and instructional choice among others according to generally understood professional norms. The locus of these norms are to be found more within programs (e.g., program faculty) as the lack of consistency in the field in these areas is remarkable (see Tatto 1996, 1998, 1999).

Important questions regarding belief change for teacher educators are: what kinds of beliefs do teacher education programs look to address, and how? What does the belief research help us understand about theories of belief change and methods to measure belief change? We turn now to the literature to look for answers.

What Kinds of Beliefs do Teacher Education Programs Seek to Address, and How?

While numerous studies have examined teachers' beliefs and thinking, studies examining beliefs within the teacher education context are less numerous. Important research reviews such as those by Nespor (1987) and Pajares (1992) have begun to bring more awareness of the need to understand and address belief change while learning to teach. These reviews indicate that teachers' beliefs may be important in understanding classroom practices. In our review, we found four dominant strands of beliefs meriting attention by teacher educators as they indicate important theoretical tendencies in the field (see Table 6.1).

These tendencies can be conceptualized as notions about what makes a good teacher and the way that beliefs influence these factors, such as the ability to use technology in one's classroom, the ability to conceptualize and learn rigorous subject matter to be able to teach it in depth and for understanding, the ability to teach diverse students, and how beliefs influence teachers' thinking about their practice. We proceed to describe the studies we found below. The studies' findings are summarized in Table 6.1.

Beliefs toward Technology

Teaching via CAI (computer assisted instruction) seems to be increasing in popularity, and, as such, we found studies that both attempted to measure the impact of content taught via this medium, as well as beliefs toward the medium itself. In our small sample, we found five studies that used technology to replace actual courses in a teacher education program in areas such as reading/language arts methods (Abbott & Faris, 2000), field experience in an elementary mathematics methods course (Atkins, 1998), curriculum based-measurement (Foegen, Espsin, & Allinder, 2001), gender equity (Levin & Matthews, 1997), and a literacy course (Yildirim, 2000). In all these studies, the object was not only to teach content but also to explore the impact of technological instruction on preservice teachers' beliefs toward computers. Other studies explored teachers' beliefs toward the use of computers. One study explored the impact of a course that was directed at training preservice teachers to use computers (Robin, Tellez, & Miller, 1998); another reports the role of personal characteristics facilitating computer use (Ropp, 1999), and yet another reports perceptions of computers as related to level of skills (Sherry, 2000). In all

Table 6.1. Literature Review of Teaching Beliefs in Preservice Teacher Education

Article, journal, design, and purpose of study	Study design	How beliefs are taught	Indicators	How beliefs are measured	Findings
Abbott & Faris (2000) *Journal of Research on Computing in Education* Explores the impact of focused technology instruction on preservice teachers' attitudes towards computers.	Longitudinal (one college semester) and self-report	Seven technology modules presented in an integrated reading/language arts methods course.	Attitudes towards computers as measured by the Computer Attitude Questionnaire (CAQ), Computer Attitude Scale for Secondary Students (CASS), and E-mail Attitude Survey (EMAS).	Three instruments were administered to 63 preservice teachers on the first and last days of an integrated reading and language arts methods course.	The increase in positive attitudes towards computers resulted from modular technology instruction and the integration of the technology skills and strategies into the existing assignments required for an integrated reading/language arts methods course.
Atkins (1998) *The Journal of Computers in Mathematics and Science Teaching* Examines whether the effective use of technology could serve as a viable alternative for a field experience component in shaping the vision of effective teaching practices.	Longitudinal (one college semester) and self-report	Increased use of technology in place of field experience in an elementary mathematics methods course.	Preservice teachers' perception of mathematics teaching as measured by a Perception of Mathematics Teaching questionnaire.	Questionnaires at the beginning and end of the course completed by 38 (of 45) students enrolled in an elementary mathematics methods course. The exit questionnaire had an additional question about the course activities.	The use of videotape cases did contribute to the preservice teachers' conceptualization of mathematics teaching. The preservice teachers viewed the elimination of a field experience as the elimination of an opportunity.

Continued on next page

Table 6.1. Continued

Article, journal, design, and purpose of study	Study design	How beliefs are taught	Indicators	How beliefs are measured	Findings
Carter (1998) *Action in Teacher Education* Investigates the impact of weekly journal writing on preservice teachers' attitude toward teaching.	One-shot and self-report/researcher observation	Basic educational psychology class in which students were required to write a total of eleven journal entries (approximately 2 or 3 pages).	Preservice teachers' attitude toward teaching as measured by student interviews, student surveys, and informal conversations.	72 students completed a survey designed by the researcher. 6 students were chosen at random for interviews. Personal observations (informal conversations) with students.	Writing journals helped the majority of the students to reflect on their previous beliefs and to consider other beliefs.
Cooney et al. (1998) *Journal of Research in Mathematics Education* Examines the belief structure and change in preservice teachers.	Longitudinal (one year) and self-report	A yearlong sequence of 4 courses in the secondary mathematics education program.	Preservice teachers' belief structure and change in beliefs as measured by interviews.	4 preservice secondary math teachers (selected from a pool of 15) were interviewed at five different times during the year.	Preservice teachers' conception of knowledge moves from something emanating from external beings toward something emanating from interrelationships between self and others.
Crawford (1998) *Reading Improvement* Examines the impact of systematic desensitization on reducing reading anxiety in preservice teachers.	Longitudinal (eight weeks) and self-report	An 8-week, voluntary, three-step desensitization program (that includes deep muscle relaxation).	Reading anxiety as measured by a self-rating of high, moderate, low, and none.	23 preservice teachers ranked their reading anxiety before, during (at the 2-week and 4-week mark), and after the program.	The use of systematic desensitization proved to be an effective means for reducing anxiety in these preservice teachers.

| Foegen et al. (2001) *The Journal of Special Education* Studies preservice teachers beliefs regarding curriculum-based measurement (CBM) and the effects of presentation format on beliefs. | One-shot and self-report | Two different video presentations (one statistical and the other anecdotal) on CBM. | Preservice teachers' beliefs about the validity and utility of one particular CBM reading measure as measured by a 15-item Teacher Belief Survey (TBS) developed by the researcher. | 45 preservice teachers (randomly assigned to either the statistical or anecdotal version of the video) completed the survey following the showing of the video. | Preservice teachers generally held positive beliefs about CBM (more positive about utility and less positive about validity). Beliefs were not affected by the format of the presentation. |
| Groulx (2001) *Urban Education* Examines change in preservice teachers' attitudes toward working in urban schools. | Longitudinal (one college semester) and self-report | Teacher preparation program. | Preservice teachers' interest and comfort levels toward working in urban schools as measured by a survey designed by the researcher. | 112 preservice teachers enrolled in several sections of an educational psychology class completed an initial survey. 29 (of the initial 112) preservice teachers who completed student teaching responded to the survey a second time. | Preservice teachers were not ready or willing to face the challenges of urban schools. Shifts occurred more for students in elementary certification programs and particularly for those whose field experiences involved substantial contact with teachers and children at the urban sites. |

Continued on next page

Table 6.1. Continued

Article, journal, design, and purpose of study	Study design	How beliefs are taught	Indicators	How beliefs are measured	Findings
Harlin (1999) *Reading Research and Instruction* Describes changes in preservice teachers' images and perceptions of teaching and literacy.	Longitudinal (one college semester) and self-report	Six-credit reading and language arts class (8 hours per week) and included a six-week practicum.	Preservice teachers' images and perceptions of teaching and literacy as measured by semantic maps and accompanying narratives.	Preservice teachers' semantic maps and accompanying narratives of 18 urban preservice teachers enrolled in a reading and language arts course. Collected at the beginning, middle, and end of the course.	The first set of maps indicated that the preservice teachers had traditional images of themselves as teachers. The second set of maps showed influence of the course content. The third set of maps demonstrated the influence of the field experience.
Harper et al. (1998) *Action in Teacher Education* (a) Explores what factors originally contributed to math anxiety of elementary preservice teachers. (b) Examines the effects of a mathematics methods course on the math anxiety of preservice teachers.	Longitudinal (one college semester) and self-report	Undergraduate elementary mathematics methods course.	Math anxiety as measured by the Mathematics Anxiety Rating Scale (MARS), Factors Influencing Mathematics Anxiety (FIMA), and Methods Course Reflection (MCR).	Three instruments (one pretest, one posttest, and one pretest and posttest) were administered to 53 elementary preservice teachers enrolled in a mathematics methods course. Follow-up interview with 11 students from the original sample who had exhibited the greatest differences between their MARS pretest and posttest scores.	By the end of the mathematics course, the level of math anxiety of the preservice elementary teachers had lowered significantly from the level of math anxiety at the beginning of the course.

Hart & Rowley (1996) *Reading Research and Instruction* Explores the professional decision making of preservice elementary teachers in selecting specific types of children's literature for classroom use and how participation in a children's literature course that included multicultural perspectives influenced decision-making.	One-shot and self-report	Children's literature course (a 3-semester-hour course). There were 4 types of instructional activity: (1) Lecture and materials on multicultural education; (2) Introduction of different literature (3) Oral student reports on books written about various cultures (4) Cooperative learning activity based on a chapter entitled "Teaching Multicultural Literature."	Choice and written explanation of the choice of selections from a "Page Packet" including "one page" selections from each of 13 children's literature books for use in grades 1 to 6.	40 undergraduate students enrolled in a children's Literature course were shown a booklet with one page each of specific types of children's literature for classroom use. They were asked to select among the different texts. Researchers analyzed students' written explanations to understand how they made their selections.	The reasons for choices were: Instructional Personal Production quality Many subjects in the study showed a notable shift in their willingness to select other than mainstream literature.
Hodge (1998) *The Physical Educator* Studies the attitudes of prospective General Physical Education (GPE) teachers towards teaching students with disabilities.	Longitudinal (ten weeks) and self-report	Introductory Adapted Physical Education (APE) courses, with and without practica experiences.	Attitudes towards teaching students with disabilities as measured by the Physical Educators' Attitude towards Teaching Individuals with Disabilities – III (PEATID – III).	195 students completed pretest-posttest surveys (from 7 colleges and universities across 5 states) in the first and last week of class.	GPE teachers' attitudes towards teaching students with disabilities improved significantly following 10 weeks of instruction in the APE courses, with and without practica experiences.

Continued on next page

Table 6.1. Continued

Article, journal, design, and purpose of study	Study design	How beliefs are taught	Indicators	How beliefs are measured	Findings
Johnson & Landers-Macrine (1998) *The Teacher Educator* Examines the effects of student teaching on the thinking of student teachers at the elementary level and elicits their explanation for changes or lack of changes in that thinking.	Longitudinal (one college semester) and self-report	Semester-long student teaching experience.	Preservice teachers' perceptions of classroom teaching as measured by a Managing Students Scale, Teacher Efficacy Scale, concept maps, and interviews.	55 student teachers completed surveys and concept maps at the beginning and end of the student teaching experience. 6 students were chosen for interviews based on their answers from the surveys.	Most of the student teachers' posttest exhibited a richer increased awareness of classroom life. However, there was also a small group who exhibited very little change.
Levin & Matthews (1997) *Journal of Research on Computing Education* Studies learning of preservice teachers (college juniors and seniors) from interacting with a hypermedia stack about gender equity.	Longitudinal (one week) and self-report	A hypermedia presentation was developed around five content themes (classroom interactions, language, role models, gender expectations, and curriculum) and five interaction categories (initial responses, background information, responses, strategies and scenarios),	Change in levels of awareness, attitudes toward and knowledge of gender equity in the classroom as measured by the pre and post Gender Equity Questionnaire and card-sorting activities.	51 preservice students in elementary education from a teacher education program completed a 50-item pre-test and post test questionnaire and a card sorting activity, individual completion of hyperstudio stack (40-90 min.), and questions about how thinking about gender equity changed, and what material from the hypermedia stack they would use in their classroom.	The hyperstudio stack can significantly influence the thinking of preservice teachers, in addition to providing with background information and strategies about gender equity issues needed by the teacher education curriculum.

Study	Design	Variables	Method	Findings
Linek et al. (1999) *Reading Research and Instruction* Investigates the changes in preservice teachers' beliefs about literacy instruction.	Longitudinal (one college semester) and self-report	Three literacy methods courses (at 2 different universities): a university-based course with no field experience, a university-based course with unsupervised field experience, and a field-based course.	Preservice teachers' beliefs, change in beliefs, and factors contributing to the changes as measured by the Philosophical Orientation to Literacy Learning (POLL), interviews, and collected artifacts.	Pretest and posttest of 40 preservice teachers. Interviews with 9 preservice teachers (3 from each course) at the beginning, middle, and end of the semester.	Preservice teachers gained conceptual knowledge about learning and teaching literacy, the process of reading and writing, and instructional strategies.
Mason (1997) *Multicultural Education* Explores the impact of urban-based field experiences on the attitudes of preservice teachers.	Longitudinal (eight weeks) and self-report	An eight-week, field-based practicum.	Interest in pursuing teaching in the inner city and beliefs about a series of educational issues that posed difficulties for teachers in inner-city schools as measured by a two-part questionnaire designed by the researcher.	A questionnaire given at the beginning and end of the practicum to 176 preservice teachers enrolled in a number of instructional methods courses within an elementary certification program.	The effect of field experience on interest in urban teaching was positive overall for all participants regardless of field placement (urban vs. suburban). All participants perceived urban schools as generally more "problematic" than suburban schools.

Continued on next page

Table 6.1. Continued

Article, journal, design, and purpose of study	Study design	How beliefs are taught	Indicators	How beliefs are measured	Findings
Maxson & Sindelar (1998) *Teacher Education Quarterly* (a) Identifies the images, ideas, and knowledge that entry-level students bring into an elementary teacher education program. (b) Explores how and if those images changed as a result of coursework designed to challenge and clarify those images.	Longitudinal (one college semester) and self-report	A "Research in Elementary Education" course.	Preservice teachers' perspectives and implicit beliefs about teaching as measured by an analysis of two writing exercises (papers).	Two writing exercises (one at the beginning and one at the end of the course) from 12 students (6 from each of two concurrent sections)	Students entered the course with a wide variety of images. Some students evidenced very thoughtful and reasoned analysis of their images. Others took the coursework and readings in but appeared to use them only superficially or to misuse them.
Peterson et al. (2000) *Action in Teacher Education* Examines the impact of a focus on diversity on preservice teachers in a foundations class.	One-shot and self-report	A foundations of education course.	Change in preservice teachers' views regarding intolerance and multicultural issues.	3-question posttest completed by 26 students in the foundation class.	Most students claimed that the course changed their views regarding intolerance and multicultural issues.

Pigge & Marso (1997) *Teaching and Teacher Education* Looks longitudinally (seven years) at the factors that affect teaching concerns development through teacher preparation and early years of teaching.	Longitudinal (seven years) and self-report	Teacher preparation program	Change in concerns as mediated by personal characteristics, basic skills, concerns, locus of control, and academic achievement	Data from teachers (personal characteristics, basic skills, concerns, locus of control, and academic achievement) was collected via questionnaires from the beginning of preservice preparation through the fifth teaching year.	Results found developmental changes in concerns about teaching over time, indicating relationships between changes in teaching concerns and teachers' capabilities and feelings.
Quinn (1997) *Journal of Educational Research* Studies the effects of elementary and secondary mathematics methods courses based on NCTM standards on meaningful mathematical coherent knowledge and attitudes toward mathematics.	Longitudinal (one college semester) and self-report	Elementary and secondary mathematics methods courses based on NCTM standards (emphasizing the use of manipulatives, technology, and cooperative learning across a variety of topics).	1. Attitudes defined as the level of like or dislike felt by an individual toward mathematics. 2. Meaningful knowledge of mathematical content refers to a conceptual and intuitive understanding of mathematics.	1. Attitudes were measured (pre- and post-) by the score attained on the Aiken's Revised Mathematics Attitude Scale (Aiken, 1963). 2. Meaningful knowledge of mathematical content was measured (pre- and post-) by the score obtained on the revised version of the Essential Elements of Elementary School Mathematics Test (White 1986) on 19 preservice secondary teachers and 28 preservice elementary teachers	Elementary preservice teachers improved their attitudes and knowledge of mathematics. Problem areas in mathematics for these teachers were fractions, long division, geometry, statistics and probability. Secondary preservice teachers showed no change in attitudes and in their knowledge. Problem areas in mathematics for these teachers were fractions, geometry, statistics and probability.

Continued on next page

Table 6.1. Continued

Article, journal, design, and purpose of study	Study design	How beliefs are taught	Indicators	How beliefs are measured	Findings
Robin et al. (1998) *Journal of Technology and Teacher Education* Investigates differential use and preferences of preservice teachers for Graphic-User-Interfaces (GUI) versus Command Line Interface (CLI) for a variety of personal computer software applications.	Longitudinal (one college semester) and self-report	Students were divided into two groups and assigned to one of two elementary schools where they served as teaching interns. One group received GUI training and the other CLI training.	Self-efficacy in personal computer use and time spent on computer activities as measured by a researcher-modified survey.	21 preservice teachers completed surveys at the beginning and end of the semester.	The group of preservice teachers using the GUI resources was more comfortable using the computer and they used electronic mail more than the comparison group of preservice teachers that used a CLI system.

Ropp (1999) *Journal of Research on Computing in Education* Explores the change in preservice teachers' characteristics associated with learning to use computers	Longitudinal (one college semester) and self-report	Identification of individual characteristics associated with learning to use computers and two hands-on technology sessions for a total of three hours.	Change in preservice teachers' a) attitudes toward computers and technology as measured by the Attitude Toward Technology scale and the Computer Attitude Scale, b) computer anxiety as measured by the Computer Anxiety Scale, c) computer self-efficacy as measured by the Computer Self-Efficacy Scale, d) self-report of technology proficiency as Measured by the Technology Proficiency Self-Assessment (TPSA), and e) computer coping strategies as measured by Computer Coping Strategies.	46 preservice teachers completed the surveys at the beginning and end of a teacher preparation course. They also completed a "fast write" response at the end of the hands-on technology sessions.	Teacher candidates who are confident in their ability to perform computer tasks are also less anxious about using computers, hold more positive attitudes toward technology and computers and more confident in their ability to perform tasks related to teaching with technology, and they use more computer coping strategies. At the end of the semester, students felt more confident performing computer tasks and they reported using more computer coping strategies.

Continued on next page

Table 6.1. Continued

Article, journal, design, and purpose of study	Study design	How beliefs are taught	Indicators	How beliefs are measured	Findings
Sherry (2000) *Journal of Technology and Teacher Education* Takes a broad view of school-based preservice teachers' developing attitudes towards computers and computer skills	Longitudinal (two years) and self-report	College-sponsored computer instruction activities over two years in a school-based teacher education program.	Preservice teachers' perceptions of computers as measured by a Computer Attitude Survey (CAS), verbal, and freehand drawing formats. Preservice computer skills as measured by a Computer Skill Questionnaire (CSQ)	30 preservice teachers completed 1) the CAS and CSQ at the beginning and end of the two-year program and 2) exit interviews and free hand draw at the end of the course.	There was a significant increase in the preservice teachers' computer skills and overall perception of the positive impact of computers.
Tatto (1996) *Educational Evaluation and Policy Analysis* Studies longitudinally nine teacher education programs to understand the influence of different modalities of teacher preparation on beliefs and knowledge about teaching subject matter (mathematics and literacy) to diverse learners. This study was part of the National Center for Research on Teacher Learning at Michigan State University.	Longitudinal and self-report	Different approaches to teacher preparation (preservice, inservice, alternative routes).	Beliefs and knowledge about teaching subject matter to diverse students.	Questionnaires were gathered from 113 faculty members, 552 student teachers at the moment of entering their program, and 265 student teachers at the moment of exiting their programs. This sample included data from nine different teacher education programs located in various regions of the United States.	Evidence gathered from a study of nine teacher education programs shows that lay culture norms among education students are strongly ingrained. Teacher education as it is currently structured is a weak intervention to alter views regarding the teaching and management of diverse learners.

Teicher (1997) *Journal of Research in Music Education* Explores the influence of multicultural music lesson planning and classroom implementation on preservice elementary teachers' attitudes regarding future multicultural music teaching.	Longitudinal (six weeks) and self-report	Two music methods courses that required students to develop a lesson plan and implement a lesson plan that used "European/American" music; two methods courses that required students to use non-European/American music.	1) Willingness to teach multicultural music activities, 2) preparedness to teach multicultural music activities, and 3) willingness to teach in a culturally diverse setting as measured by an "opinionnaire" developed by the researcher.	Pretest and posttest "opinionnaires" given to 60 preservice elementary teachers in 4 music method classes. 29 students had the "multicultural" music assignment and 31 students had the "mainstream" assignment.	The "multicultural" group showed an increase in attitude scores compared to a decrease for the "mainstream" group. There was no significant difference between the groups in attitude of preparedness in multicultural music or in willingness to work in a culturally diverse setting.

Continued on next page

Table 6.1. Continued

Article, journal, design, and purpose of study	Study design	How beliefs are taught	Indicators	How beliefs are measured	Findings
Vacc & Bright (1999) *Journal of Research on Mathematics Education* Examines the effect of introducing preservice elementary school teachers to cognitively guided instruction (CGI). This approach is designed to help teachers use knowledge from cognitive science to make their own instructional decisions.	Longitudinal (two years) and self-report/ researcher observation	3-semester-hour mathematics methods course (process learning, national curriculum reform, problem solving, communicating mathematically, reasoning and mathematical connections). CGI was introduced through a 5-session module (problem types for the basic operations and children's solution strategies and knowledge of children's geometrical thinking).	Change on beliefs (as measured by the CGI beliefs scale) in four areas: Role of the learner Relationships between skills and understanding Sequencing of topics Role of the teachers	34 members of an undergraduate cohort of preservice teachers took part in the study. They were commencing their 2-year sequence of professional course work. They were observed 8 times onsite. 2 teachers were selected as cases for in depth study. They had reflective journals and 4 videotapes mathematics lessons during the student teaching semester and 3 openended interviews. Change in beliefs was measured by the CGI Belief Scale at 4 points: beginning of program, beginning of math methods course, beginning of student teaching and end of student teaching.	Teachers' beliefs about teaching and learning mathematics significantly affect the form and type of instruction they deliver. The beliefs of preservice teachers changed to a more constructivist orientation as a result of their preservice preparation program. The module was effective though should last longer. Results also indicate that extensive field experiences, linkages between theory and practice, are essential elements for changing beliefs. The on-site teacher educators' support proved important.

| Yildirim (2000) *Journal of Research on Computing in Education* Examines the impact of a computer literacy course on preservice and inservice teachers' attitudes towards and use of computers. | Longitudinal (one college semester) and self-report | State of California mandated educational computing course. | Computer anxiety, confidence, and liking as measured by a computer competency survey developed by the researcher. | Pretest and posttest of 114 students attending an educational computing course using a computer competency survey. Follow-up questionnaire and interview with 21 volunteers from the original sample. | Teachers with the least amount of computer knowledge and experience gained the most from the course in regard to increasing confidence, reducing anxiety, and improving positive attitudes towards computers. |

these cases, the studies report increased positive attitudes, and in cases where content was taught, studies report positive results as well.

Beliefs toward Subject Matter Content and Pedagogy

A significant number of studies show that teacher educators' are concerned about understanding, jointly examined ideas, and learned responses to teaching and learning. For instance, Carter (1998) explored the impact of weekly journal writing on preservice teachers' attitude toward teaching. Cooney, Shealy, and Arvold (1998) examined the impact of a yearlong sequence of four math courses on the belief structure about conceptions of knowledge (externally versus internally situated) in four preservice secondary math teachers. Harlin (1999) describes changes in preservice teachers' images and perceptions of teaching and literacy as a result of a six-credit reading and language arts class (8 hours per week) which included a six-week practicum. Hart and Rowley (1996) explored how decision-making of preservice elementary teachers in selecting specific types of children's literature for classroom use was influenced by their participation in a children's literature course (a 3-semester-hour course) that included multicultural perspectives. Peterson, Cross, and Johnson (2000) studied the impact of a foundations of education course on preservice teachers' ideas about diversity. Teicher's (1997) study sought to determine the effects of multicultural music lesson planning and classroom implementation on preservice elementary teachers' beliefs regarding future multicultural music teaching. Two studies attempted to research the effects of reformed teacher education on standards. Quinn (1997) studied the effects of elementary and secondary mathematics methods courses based on NCTM standards (emphasizing the use of manipulatives, technology, and cooperative learning across a variety of topics) on meaningful mathematical content knowledge and attitudes toward mathematics. Vacc and Bright (1999) attempted to document the effect of introducing preservice elementary school teachers to cognitively guided instruction (CGI) as a result of a 3-semester-hour mathematics methods course (process learning, national curriculum reform, problem solving, communicating mathematically, reasoning and mathematical connections). Linek, Nelson, & Sampson (1999) investigated the changes in preservice teachers' beliefs about literacy instruction as a result of three literacy methods courses (at two different universities): a university-based course with no field experience, a university-based course with unsupervised field experience, and a field-based course.

Beliefs toward Diverse Students

We found proportionally fewer studies that examined the influence of teacher education on teachers' beliefs about teaching and learning diverse students. Mason (1997) explored the impact of an eight-week, urban-based field practicum on the beliefs of preservice teachers. Groulx (2001) examined change in preservice teachers' attitudes toward working in urban schools as a result of participation in a teacher preparation program. Hodge (1998) examined the attitudes of prospective general physical education (GPE) teachers toward teaching students with disabilities as a result of introductory adapted physical education (APE) courses, with and without practica experiences. Tatto (1996) explored longitudinal findings of research in nine teacher education programs (preservice, inservice, alternative routes) to understand the influence of different modalities of teacher preparation on beliefs and knowledge about teaching subject matter (mathematics and literacy) to diverse learners.

Beliefs Influencing Teachers' Thinking

In the literature we found that certain beliefs seem to have a strong influence on the way teachers think about their practice. For instance teachers who believe that they are not good at math, tend to avoid teaching the subject, consequently we found two studies that focused on strategies to reduce anxiety toward subject matter in preservice teachers. Crawford (1998) examined the impact of an eight-week systematic desensitization program on reducing reading anxiety in preservice teachers. Harper and Daane (1998) explored attempts to determine what factors originally contributed to math anxiety of elementary preservice teachers, and the effects of a mathematics methods course on the math anxiety of preservice teachers. In addition, we found three studies that attempted to explore the influence of teacher preparation on teachers' beliefs and their thinking. Johnson and Landers-Macrine (1998) examined the effects of a semester-long student teaching experience designed to change beliefs about teaching practice, and thus the thinking of student teachers at the elementary level about what it means to be a teacher. Maxson and Sindelar (1998) sought to identify the images, ideas, and knowledge that entry-level students bring into an elementary teacher education program, and how and if those images changed as a result of a "Research in Elementary Education" course designed to challenge and clarify those images. Pigge and Marso (1997) studied longitudinally for seven years the factors (such as personal characteristics, basic skills, concerns, locus of control, and academic achievement) that seem to affect the development of teacher concerns through preservice teacher preparation and early years of teaching.

Understanding those strategies that have been used by teacher educators to influence such views is helpful to the field. We describe those below.

Interventions Designed to Influence Beliefs

Little is known about the effectiveness of mechanisms though which programs attempt to affect teacher candidates' beliefs and the outcomes of these efforts (e.g., how belief change affects teaching practice and children's learning). Across the literature reviewed for this chapter, we found that preservice programs have engaged in a limited range of activities to affect beliefs (see Table 6.1).

Individualized Strategies

One study reports attempts at affecting beliefs through discrete interventions such as specific reflective strategies. Carter (1998) explored the impact of weekly journal writing on preservice teachers' attitude toward teaching.

Discrete Courses

This seems to be the predominant style preferred mechanism by which teacher educators attempt to alter the belief systems among future teachers. An alternative explanation can be that classroom-based studies are the most likely to be reported. We found that discrete courses are used to help teachers to feel more comfortable with computers both to learn through this medium and to use it to help pupils learn (Abbott & Faris, 2000; Atkins, 1998; Levin & Matthews, 1997; Robin et al., 1998; Ropp, 1999; Sherry, 2000; Yildirim, 2000). Similarly, the use of discrete courses is reported in attempts at affecting teachers beliefs ("desensitizing") toward mathematics and reading anxiety (Crawford, 1998; Harper & Dane, 1998); toward affecting images and perceptions when teachers enter a teacher education program (Maxson & Sindelar, 1998) and when teaching different subject matters (Harlin, 1999; Teicher, 1997; Quinn, 1997; Vacc & Bright, 1999) in the manner teachers make decisions affecting multicultural populations (Hart & Rowley, 1996) and when the attempt was directed at helping teachers to understand themselves when teaching in unfamiliar contexts and/or diverse populations (Mason, 1997; Peterson et al., 2000).

Programmatic Efforts

Fewer studies document more holistic attempts, such as teacher preparation programs, on belief change on specific areas. Among the articles we reviewed, these efforts included change on belief structure regarding conceptions of knowledge in math, literacy, toward working in urban schools, and with diverse populations (Cooney et al., 1998; Groulx, 2001; Hodge, 1998; Linek et al., 1999; Tatto, 1996). Programmatic efforts were also designed to affect prospective elementary teachers' thinking and concerns development (Johnson and Landers-Macrine, 1998; Pigge and Marso, 1997).

Discussion

The results of these interventions are reported to be positive and the results on teachers seem to be as expected. Exceptions are studies that seemed to be designed expecting more complexity. These studies include Groulx (2001), reporting that preservice teachers were not ready or willing to face the challenges of urban schools; Quinn (1997), reporting that secondary preservice teachers showed no change in beliefs and in their knowledge; Tatto (1996), who reports that lay culture norms among education students are strongly ingrained and that teacher education as it is currently structured is a weak intervention to alter views regarding the teaching and management of diverse learners; and Vacc and Bright (1999), who report that the beliefs of preservice teachers changed to a more constructivist orientation as a result of their preservice preparation program, and that extensive field experiences, linkages between theory and practice, are essential elements for changing beliefs. Indeed, looking at these studies, there seems to be a sense that belief change among teacher candidates is a self-justifiable activity. And that belief change will, by implication, result in better practice and benefit pupil's learning. Although this may be true to a degree, most of the studies reviewed above, spent little time justifying why working in beliefs is an important activity in teacher education and if justifications are given (e.g., expected improved practice, etc.) they are rarely proved. Most of the studies reviewed above, report positive results, but only three studies are longitudinal, looking at the effect of these strategies in teachers' classrooms. Similarly, few studies attempted to make connections between the intervention itself and evidence of belief change other than by participants' self-report. This indeed may be a reason that results are so positive. Only few (six) studies correlated belief change with other important program outcomes such as knowledge acquisition (Pigge & Marso, 1997; Quinn, 1997), decision making regarding classroom materials (Hart & Rowley, 1996), conceptualization of subject matter teaching and learning (Atkins, 1998; Linek et al., 1999), strategies to increase gender equity (Levin & Matthews, 1997), and the form and type of instruction teachers deliver (Vacc & Bright, 1999). Only one study attempted to document the effects of belief change on actual teaching practice (Vacc & Bright, 1999), and no studies documented the effects of belief change on pupils learning. Also, no studies researched the beliefs and disposition of teacher educators. It is conceivable that the scarcity of empirical research connecting belief change with changes in practices and pupil learning leaves the field lacking on a solid theoretical basis to justify and to organize these efforts.

Belief Research: Theory and Methods

Up to now, we have been mostly describing our findings from the selected studies included in this chapter. We take now a more analytical stance and examine questions that are fundamental to the development of sound research on the influence of teacher education. We look at the theories of change put forward in the research reported, discuss the importance of reporting validity and reliability on the instruments used calling attention to the absence of social science research protocol among the majority of the studies reviewed, and analyze the appropriateness of the kinds of measurements used to determine whether teacher preparation is an effective intervention on prospective teachers' belief change.

Theories of Belief Change

A central question to ask of the selected studies we analyzed had to do with the theories of belief change used by researchers to explain the credibility of their results. These theories are expected to be reflected on the instruments used to confirm such theories. The rigor used in developing these instruments and the manner in which they were administered are indicators of the level of validity and reliability of the results reported in these studies. Table 6.2 shows the espoused theory of change, the instruments used and whether indices of reliability and validity were reported in the methodology section of the article.

We found four theoretical strands regarding belief change. Beliefs are expected to change (according to the studies here reviewed) if educational interventions provide more and better: (a) field and classroom experiences for prospective teachers (Atkins, 1998; Groulx, 2001; Hart & Rowley, 1996; Hodge, 1998; Linek et al., 1999; Mason, 1997; Pigge & Marso, 1997; Quinn, 1997; Teicher, 1997); (b) opportunities for reflection either individual or with peers (Carter, 1998; Cooney et al., 1998; Harlin, 1999; Levin & Matthews, 1997; Maxson & Sindelar, 1998; Peterson et al., 2000); (c) opportunities for understanding one-self vis-à-vis challenging and novel situations in a secure environment (Crawford, 1998; Harper et al., 1998; Johnson & Landers-Macrine, 1998; Robin et al., 1998; Ropp, 1999; Sherry, 2000; Yildirim, 2000); and (d) theoretical and applied knowledge about subject matter, pedagogy, curriculum, teaching, learning, diverse

Table 6.2. Teaching Beliefs in Preservice Teacher Education: Theory of Change and Methodology

Article, journal, and purpose of study	Theory of Change	Instruments	Reported in the article (yes/no)?	
			Reliability	Validity
Abbott & Faris (2000) *Journal of Research on Computing in Education* Explores the impact of focused technology instruction on preservice teachers' attitudes towards computers.	Bridging the gap between the education theory and instructional approaches of the university faculty and the situated practices of the public school teachers will affect preservice teacher attitudes.	Computer Attitude Questionnaire (CAQ)	Y	N
		Computer Attitude Scale for Secondary Students (CASS)	Y	Y
		E-Mail Attitude Survey (EMAS)	N	N
Atkins (1998) *The Journal of Computers in Mathematics and Science Teaching* Examines whether the effective use of technology could serve as a viable alternative for a field experience component in shaping the vision of effective teaching practices.	The effective use of technology can serve as a viable alternative for a field experience in shaping preservice teachers' visions of effective practices.	Perceptions of Mathematics Teaching questionnaire	N	N
Carter (1998) *Action in Teacher Education* Investigates the impact of weekly journal writing on preservice teachers' attitude toward teaching.	Preservice teachers need to understand how their previous experience impact their beliefs about teaching.	Survey designed by researcher	N	N
		Personal observation by researcher	N	N
		Interviews	N	N
Cooney et al. (1998) *Journal of Research in Mathematics Education* Examines the belief structure and change in preservice teachers.	Preservice teachers' beliefs can be changed by creating opportunities for them to reflect on their own belief structures.	Interviews	N	N

Continued on next page

Table 6.2. Continued

Article, journal, and purpose of study	Theory of Change	Instruments	Reported in the article (yes/no)?	
			Reliability	*Validity*
Crawford (1998) *Reading Improvement* Examines the impact of systematic desensitization on reducing reading anxiety in preservice teachers.	Systematic desensitization techniques can help teachers remove barriers of fear and anxiety that can create obstacles to learning.	Self-report rankings	N	N
Foegen et al. (2001) *The Journal of Special Education* Studies preservice teachers beliefs regarding curriculum-based measurement (CBM) and the effects of presentation format on beliefs.	Presentation format has an impact on preservice teachers' beliefs.	Teacher Belief Survey (TBS)	N	N
Groulx (2001) *Urban Education* Examines change in preservice teachers' attitudes toward working in urban schools.	Direct experience and sustained human contact are key elements for facilitating multicultural understanding.	Survey designed by researcher	N	N
Harlin (1999) *Reading Research and Instruction* Describes changes in preservice teachers' images and perceptions of teaching and literacy.	When preservice teachers organize, examine, and share their beliefs with peers, they are able to bridge the gap between pre-existing beliefs and new knowledge.	Semantic maps and accompanying narratives	N	N
Harper et al. (1998) *Action in Teacher Education* a) Explores what factors originally contributed to math anxiety of elementary preservice teachers. b) Examines the effects of a mathematics methods course on the math anxiety of preservice teachers.	Creating a supportive environment will help preservice teachers to build confidence, alleviate math anxiety, and promote effective teaching and learning.	Math Anxiety Rating Scale (MARS) Factors Influencing Mathematics Anxiety (FIMA) Methods Course Reflection (MCR) Interviews	N N N N	N N N N

Study	Description	Measure		
Hart & Rowley (1996) *Reading Research and Instruction* Explores the professional decision making of pre-service elementary teachers in selecting specific types of children's literature for classroom use and how participation in a children's literature course that included multicultural perspectives influences decision-making.	Preservice teachers need the opportunity to explore and clarify their own cultural identities and develop more positive attitudes toward other racial, ethnic, and culture groups. This can be achieved by experiencing multi-ethnic children's literature in the context of a children's literature course.	Choice of text Written reasons for choice	N N	N N
Hodge (1998) *The Physical Educator* Studies the attitudes of prospective General Physical Education (GPE) teachers towards teaching students with disabilities.	Preservice teachers with past experience, knowledge, and newly acquired knowledge of teaching students of disabilities will have a more favorable attitude towards teaching students with disabilities.	Physical Educator's Attitude Toward Teaching Individuals with Disabilities-III (PEATD-III)	Y	Y
Johnson & Landers-Macrine (1998) *The Teacher Educator* Examines the effects of student teaching on the thinking of student teachers at the elementary level and elicits their explanation for changes or lack of changes in that thinking.	Preservice teachers' thinking can change when they are able to try out theories from their course work, get a feel for the tempo of the classroom, and develop a sense of their own efficacy as professionals.	Managing Students Scale Teacher Efficacy Scale Concept maps Interviews	N N N N	N N N N
Levin & Matthews (1997) *Journal of Research on Computing Education* Studies learning of preservice teachers (college juniors and seniors) from interacting with a hypermedia stack about gender equity.	Reading or hearing about gender equity issues in single, simple, or abstract presentations is not as effective at changing preservice teachers' beliefs as seeing, thinking about and reflecting in writing on multiple, specific, and complex examples.	Gender Equity Questionnaire Card-sorting activity	N N	N N

Continued on next page

Table 6.2.   Continued

Article, journal, and purpose of study	Theory of Change	Instruments	Reported in the article (yes/no)?	
			Reliability	Validity
Linek et al. (1999) *Reading Research and Instruction* Investigates the changes in preservice teachers' beliefs about literacy instruction.	The student teaching experience might facilitate the gestalt shift that can lead to changes in the beliefs of preservice teachers.	Philosophical Orientation to Literacy Learning (POLL)	N	N
		Interviews	Y	Y
		Collected artifacts	Y	Y
Mason (1997) *Multicultural Education* Explores the impact of urban-based field experiences on the attitudes of preservice teachers.	Urban-based field experiences can impact preservice teachers' attitudes toward teaching in urban, low SES settings.	Questionnaire designed by researcher	N	N
Maxson & Sindelar (1998) *Teacher Education Quarterly* a) Identifies the images, ideas, and knowledge that entry-level students bring into an elementary teacher education program. b) Explores how and if those images changed as a result of coursework designed to challenge and clarify those images.	Preservice teachers need to surface and begin to confront their implicit beliefs about teaching early and continuously.	Writing exercises (papers)	N	N
Peterson et al. (2000) *Action in Teacher Education* Examines the impact of a focus on diversity on preservice teachers in a foundations class.	Preservice teachers must understand the stereotypes that they have learned and how these attitudes can influence their interactions with students.	Questionnaire designed by researcher	N	N

Reference	Description	Instrument		
Pigge & Marso (1997) *Teaching and Teacher Education* Looks longitudinally (seven years) the factors that affect teaching concerns development through teacher preparation and early years of teaching.	Appropriate preservice and inservice experiences are essential to the passage of teachers through Fuller's (1969) three concern phases (self, task, and impact).	Teacher Concern Questionnaire (TCQ)	Y	Y
Quinn (1997) *Journal of Educational Research* Studies the effects of elementary and secondary mathematics methods courses based on NCTM standards on meaningful mathematical coherent knowledge and attitudes toward mathematics.	Preservice teachers' knowledge, assumptions, feelings, and beliefs about their role as teachers in the classroom can be changed as a result of a mathematics methods course.	Essential Elements of Elementary School Mathematics Test	Y	N
Robir et al. (1998) *Journal of Technology and Teacher Education* Investigates differential use and preferences of preservice teachers for Graphic-User-Interfaces (GUI) versus Command Line Interface (CLI) for a variety of personal computer software applications.	Preservice teachers will have a more positive attitude towards computers if their experience with computers is not too difficult, too technical, and too unfamiliar.	Researcher modified survey from University of Virginia	Y	N
Ropp (1999) *Journal of Research on Computing in Education* Explores the change in preservice teachers' characteristics associated with learning to use computers	Preservice teachers can use their individual strengths as pedagogical tools for learning to use computers.	Attitudes Towards Technology scale	Y	Y
		Computer Anxiety scale	Y	Y
		Computer Self-Efficacy scale	Y	Y
		Computer Attitude scale	Y	Y
		Technology Proficiency Self-Assessment (TPSA)	Y	Y
		Computer Coping Strategies scale	Y	Y
		A fast write	N	N

Continued on next page

Table 6.2.   Continued

Article, journal, and purpose of study	Theory of Change	Instruments	Reported in the article (yes/no)? Reliability	Validity
Sherry (2000) *Journal of Technology and Teacher Education* Takes a broad view of school-based preservice teachers' developing attitudes towards computers and computer skills.	Prior computer experience, access to computers, and involvement with computer instruction while in college may lessen computer anxiety and increase perception of usefulness.	Computer Attitude Survey (CAS)	Y	N
		Computer Skill Questionnaire (CSQ)	Y	N
		Interview	N	N
		Free-hand draw	Y	Y
Tatto (1996) *Educational Evaluation and Policy Analysis* Studies longitudinally nine teacher education programs to understand the influence of different modalities of teacher preparation on beliefs and knowledge about teaching subject matter (mathematics and literacy) to diverse learners. This study was part of the National Center for Research on Teacher Learning at Michigan State University.	Preservice teachers may be better socialized regarding student diversity by teacher education experiences resembling more closely social constructivist views of teaching and learning rather than experiences that follow a more conventional (or transmission) approach.	TELT (Teaching and Learning to Teach) Questionnaire	N	Y
Teicher (1997) *Journal of Research in Music Education* Explores the influence of multicultural music lesson planning and classroom implementation on preservice elementary teachers' attitudes regarding future multicultural music teaching.	Training can make positive changes in preservice teachers' attitudes, especially if it is (1) of an experiential nature, (2) includes peer observation, and (3) includes relevant resource materials.	"Opinionnaire" designed by the researcher	Y	N

Citation / Description	Instrument		
Vacc & Bright (1999)			
Journal of Research on Mathematics Education			
Examines the effect of introducing preservice elementary school teachers to cognitively guided instruction (CGI). This approach is designed to help teachers use knowledge from cognitive science to make their own instructional decisions.	CGI Belief Scale	Y	N
	Observation	N	N
	Reflective journals	N	N
	Video-taped lessons	N	N
In order to change beliefs, preservice teachers need (1) extensive field experience, and (2) linkages between theory and practice.	Interviews	N	N
Yildirim (2000)			
Journal of Research on Computing in Education			
Studies the impact of a computer literacy course on preservice and inservice teachers' attitudes towards and use of computers.	Computer competency survey developed by researcher	Y	N
	Follow-up questionnaire	N	N
Participating in a computer literacy course helps develop positive attitudes towards computers and increases computer use in the classroom.	Interviews	N	N

students, and technology (Abbott & Faris, 2000; Foegen at al., 2001; Tatto, 1996; Vacc & Bright, 1999).

Reporting Validity and Reliability

Reporting validity and reliability of the measures and procedures used to determine whether a teacher education intervention has had the desired outcome—in this case belief change—seemed to be the exception rather than the rule. Of the 26 studies here reviewed half reported some indicator of reliability (e.g., whether the instruments *consistently* measure a given outcome), but only seven studies reported attempts at determining validity (e.g., whether the instruments *actually measure the construct they are expected to measure*—in this case belief change) according to the theory put forth by the teacher educators (see Table 6.2). Simply put, in more than two-thirds of the studies reviewed it is impossible to ascertain, according to the rules of social science research, whether a given intervention may be having the expected /hypothesized effect. Reports of reliability without validity simply tell us that researchers have been measuring the same thing consistently. Reporting reliability is not a substitute for reporting validity. Use of qualitative methods would seem to have weakened across the field the need to develop rigorous research. It should be stated clearly here that both qualitative and quantitative methodologies have developed strategies to determine validity and reliability of measurements. We are thus puzzled by the lack of these indicators of research quality in the studies here reviewed. We encourage researchers to work hard at following social research protocols and ask journals to develop more rigorous criteria when making decisions about publishable scholarship on the influence of teacher education.

Measuring Beliefs

A useful way of looking at the way beliefs are measured is by analyzing the hypothesized indicators of belief change (or outcomes); the "closer" the measurement, the safer would be our assumption that we are capturing the outcomes of our intervention. Figure 6.1 shows different methods to measuring indicators. Sound research approaches usually include more than one measurement over time and across nested contexts allowing for triangulation, validity and reliability of the results obtained. In belief research, it is conceivable to expect data from the first three points of measurement (such as observations, teachers' daily logs, and interviews and/or questionnaires). We would also expect to see these kinds of measurements taken across nested contexts or different groups (e.g., program level, classroom level, and pupil level). This multiple strategies would better measure the expected influence of belief change on teacher candidates as a result of their preparation. In addition, and congruent with the type of change expected, longitudinal methodologies, rather than one-shot studies, would be more appropriate to document belief change.

The studies reviewed here used for the most part measurements in the point 3 of the continuum (e.g., questionnaires, interviews, and/or surveys) and the measurement is located in the first context, at the program level (e.g., preservice teachers answers to questionnaires). Most studies (15) used only one measurement (e.g., questionnaire, survey or interview). Ten studies included more than one type of measurement such as surveys, interviews and observations (Carter, 1998); semantic maps and accompanying narratives or surveys and interviews (Harlin, 1999; Johnson & Landers-Macrine, 1998); a Math Anxiety Rating Scale, factors influencing mathematics anxiety, and a survey on a methods course (Harper et al., 1998); pretest and posttest questionnaires, a card sorting activity, and individual completion of a hyperstudio stack (Levin and Matthews, 1997); an Aiken's Revised Mathematics Attitude Scale and the Essential Elements of Elementary School Mathematics Test (Quinn, 1997); an Attitude Toward Technology scale, a Computer Attitude Scale, a Computer Anxiety Scale, a Computer Self-Efficacy Scale, a self-report of technology proficiency measured by the Technology Proficiency Self-Assessment (TPSA), and the Computer Coping Strategies scale (Ropp, 1999); a Computer Attitude Survey (CAS), verbal, and freehand drawing formats, and a Computer Skill Questionnaire (CSQ) (Sherry, 2000); survey, interviews and observations (Tatto, 1996); observations on-site, reflective journals, videotapes, open-ended interviews, and the Change on Beliefs Scale (or CGI) (Vacc and Bright, 1999); a Computer Competency Survey, follow-up questionnaires, and interviews (Yildirim, 2000). In what it is a basically longitudinal process (belief change and its effect on classroom practice and pupil learning), only three studies used comparative and /or longitudinal approaches to research teacher education influence on beliefs (Linek et al., 1999; Pigge & Marso, 1997; Tatto, 1996).

As the idea was to measure change, most of these studies are a "before-and-after" design consisting in the administration of a questionnaire or an interview at the beginning and at the end of the intervention expected to affect such change. The sample size varies but is, for the most part, purposeful (versus random), in a contained course, and thus subject to validity and reliability concerns.

Contexts/ Measurements	Point 1	Point 2	Point 3	Point 4	Point 5
	Closeness to outcomes ← →		← Remoteness to outcomes →		
Program Classroom Pupil	• Observation • Video/audio • Performance assessments • Portfolio-Based Assessments • Tests of Knowledge	• Situated descriptions of teaching • Responses to hypothetical situations • T's daily logs • Vignettes • Semantic maps	• Interviews • Questionnaire • Surveys	Reports of how: • Innovations affect teaching and learning. • Beliefs affect teaching and learning.	Document analysis of: • Curricular materials • Assessments • Lesson plans • Internal vs. external standards

←————— Longitudinal Methodology —————→

Figure 6.1. Measuring the Influence of Teacher Education

Discussion

Most of the studies reviewed here seek to serve the primary purpose of informing educators of the outcomes of particular interventions. Although beneficial for program faculty, the studies are problematic in that they have not attempted to discriminate between the *net effects* of particular interventions from other confounding factors and design effects. In other words, these studies contribute little to developing a theory of how beliefs are effectively taught and learned in teacher preparation. The most important conclusion from what we have learned here is the need to develop more rigorous and programmatic studies of belief change in teacher preparation programs. A programmatic research agenda would view beliefs as part of program inputs, process and outcomes. Most of the research here discussed is *not* programmatic, nor is it designed to respond to external accountability concerns. In the next section we present a design for programmatic research and use the Teacher Preparation Program at MSU as a case study of exploration of program impact on graduates' beliefs.

Understanding the Influence of Teacher Preparation on Beliefs through Programmatic Research

In this section, we present an attempt to begin building a programmatic research agenda for the Teacher Preparation Program at MSU. Figure 6.2 represents the programmatic agenda for research in our teacher education program. The shadowed squares represent the research we present below. The first stage in our programmatic agenda included measuring beliefs as a program outcome. In this instance, the question was whether interns' views grouped themselves around the program's major themes. A second step was to examine faculty's views about teaching and learning and contrasting these with the views of interns (at the end of the program). For the program to have an effect, the views of the interns should be very close to those of teacher educators (representing the norms of the teaching profession according to program faculty). In addition, we began to explore the influence of collaborating teachers during the internship year on interns' views about teaching and learning subject matter. The framework for this research and some preliminary results were presented in the AACTE meeting in 2001 and at AERA 2001. See Tatto, 2001; Tatto & Papanastasiou, 2001).

We are not presenting this research as an example of what the field should do; rather we believe that developing programmatic research on teacher education effects is a complex and difficult journey, and that these

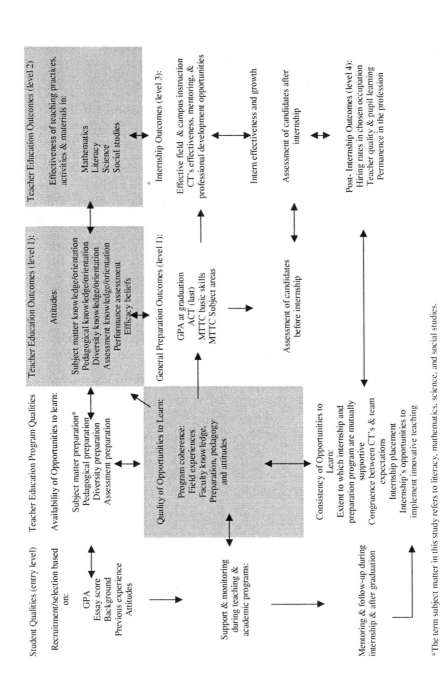

Figure 6.2. Teacher Education Quality and Impact

*The term subject matter in this study refers to literacy, mathematics, science, and social studies.

efforts should be shared with the larger teacher education professional community for consideration and feedback. Our intent with this research is to find empirical evidence for program assertions that holding a specific set of beliefs is essential to good teaching.

Teacher Education Program at Michigan State University

The MSU Teacher Preparation Program is a three-year teacher certification program in which students enter as juniors, take two years of courses and field work, and then do a one year internship in schools. The internship, or "guided practice," is a yearlong developmental apprenticeship with veteran teachers and MSU faculty which mixes practice and reflection. According to the Team leaders, the aim of the program is to create "a brand of teacher education grounded in sound theory, the good example and wisdom of veteran teachers, and thoughtful reflection on experiences in the field" (Team 1 Student Handbook, 1999, Foreword).

Currently, the MSU teacher certification program is divided into four teams of university and school faculty, each with a diverse cohort of prospective teachers. Three teams work with elementary and one with secondary candidates. Each team is developing long-term connections with a small cluster of school districts. Each team also places seniors and juniors in schools for particular kinds of field experiences. Within the framework of a common program, each team is developing a unique identity and geographical base.

The MSU teacher preparation program has several general goals, a number of which imply that some beliefs are preferable to others:

1. New teachers prepared at MSU should achieve a deep understanding of subject matters and of methods for *"teaching for understanding."*
2. They should form a *democratic commitment* to the education of all children and to classrooms and schools that *embrace diversity.*
3. They should learn how to establish learning communities in classrooms and schools.
4. They should learn how to participate in the improvement of teaching, of schools, and of the teaching profession to help make a better world.
5. They should learn how to integrate theory with practice and teaching experience with reflection on that experience (Student Handbook Team 2, 1998-99, italics are ours).

The teams have organized the program so that each year has a general theme. In the junior year, students begin learning to "think and feel like a teacher" through course experiences in which, among other things, they do a careful study of classroom management, student motivation, and lesson planning. In the senior year, students begin learning to "know like a teacher," integrating subject matter knowledge, curriculum and pedagogy. In the intern year, students begin learning to "act like a teacher," putting it all together in supervised practice. The program relies on a strong disciplinary knowledge base and a mentoring relationship between teacher learners and experienced teachers as a model for knowledge, skill and beliefs development. The idea that candidates *should think* in particular ways to become teachers as stated in the program documents is somewhat vague and raises important empirical and ethical questions. Faculty would argue that these statements should not be taken in isolation and need to be used along with program *assumptions* and *standards*. Still, to date, we (at MSU or in any other teacher preparation in the United States) do not have strong empirical evidence that teachers who believe in say, democratic ideals, make better teachers. In addition, the statement that teachers should think in certain ways brings about the question of indoctrination (e.g., to imbue with a usually partisan or sectarian opinion, point of view or principle). Although in the dictionaries indoctrination is also identified with the action "to teach" (e.g., to cause to know something) the MSU Teacher Preparation Program intent identifies more with the term *educate* which implies development of the mind and attempts to encourage reflection and critical thinking. Still the issue of values prevails as a developed mind can lean either toward good or evil. Through our work we hope to begin to explore these and other important empirical questions.

The program's pedagogy seeks to reinforce these themes and it is based on a number of assumptions. (1) "Because teachers should grow steadily over a lifetime of practice, during their teacher preparation they should learn the intellectual habits conducive to steady growth." The program tries to give students tools to reflect on their own practice as it affects student's learning through the professional life span (e.g. study of one child, writing journals, writing one's evolving teaching philosophy). (2) "People learn not from activity alone, but from activity combined with reflection on that activity." The program aims to provide students with a one-year internship combined with courses on reflection and inquiry in teaching and teachers' professional role. These courses are expected to give students the opportunity to connect study with practice (e.g., connect their studies on the teaching of subject matter with their actions as teachers) so that they can continue to draw on those studies over a period of years in teaching. These courses are also expected to give students opportunities to clarify issues in teaching such as decisions about how to teach the curriculum, make or choose instructional materials or assessments, relationships with parents and so on. (3) "Good teachers work at learning about their students." The program provides opportunities throughout for students to understand how children learn. This is the specific aim of the early stages of the program in the courses TE150, TE250 (through a Service Learning Project where teacher learners tutor individual children for a semester or more), and TE301. (4) "Good teachers work at learning from their colleagues." Students are placed in cohorts throughout their course experience. This aspect of the preparation program is underlined during the internship year when students have the opportunity to work with a "collaborating teacher" or mentor and field instructors throughout an entire school year. (5) "Learning communities are as important to teachers as to students." Students are expected to understand, first through their course work (starting in TE 401) and then during the internship year, how to develop learning communities in their classroom. (6) "Effective teaching combines the sort of wisdom that comes from direct experience and practice, and from systematic study and inquiry." Students are asked to participate in the internship year which is designed to bring together learning to teach effectively through direct experience and practice under a mentor in a guided practice format. At the same time, students take courses that are designed to help them understand and reflect in these experiences. During the internship year, students carry out inquiry projects in their coursework and in their schools.

Throughout the teacher preparation program, teacher learners are assessed by their individual instructors according to program standards. In the case of the major and minor areas, they are assessed by their particular departments. The program standards developed by the faculty and collaborating teachers represent understandings, skills, commitments and dispositions that are needed to be an effective teacher. There are four major general standards:

- Knowing subject matters and how to teach them: (a) the intern understands the subject matter(s) as needed to teach it (them); (b) the intern thoughtfully links subject matter and students, creating a responsive curriculum; (c) the intern plans and implements a curriculum of understanding; (d) the intern is thoughtful about assessment and its relationship to planning and teaching.
- Working with students: (a) the intern respects and cares for all students in his/her charge; (b) the intern promotes active learning and thoughtfulness; (c) the intern build on students' interests, strengths, and cultural backgrounds; (d) the intern treats all students as capable of learning.

- Creating and managing a classroom learning community: (a) the intern creates a safe, caring, productive environment in the classroom; (b) the intern makes the classroom an inclusive community; (c) the intern helps students develop personal and social responsibility.
- Working and learning in a school and profession: (a) the intern works well as a teacher in a school community; (b) the intern works productively with his/her MSU liaison, collaborating teacher, field instructor, and seminar instructors in ways that support his/her learning to teach; (c) the intern reflects on his or her experience and seeks opportunities for continued learning and improvement; d) the intern is open to alternatives and constructive feedback.

During the fall semester, program instructors seek evidence that interns are making satisfactory progress in meeting each of the Program Standards. A recommendation for continuing the internship will be based on the professional judgement of the field instructor, the collaborating teacher, and others who are familiar with the intern's teaching practice. During the spring semester, program instructors and /or cluster coordinators seek evidence that the interns have met the Program Standards and are ready to assume responsibilities of beginning teaching.

In addition to fulfilling these standards, during the internship year, students are required to prepare and eventually present a professional portfolio. In order to be recommended for teacher certification by the end of the internship year, an intern will need to show that she or he is capable of responsible, autonomous teaching based on the Program Standards and the other program requirements.

In short, the program heavily depends on the judgement of teacher education instructors to implement the program and to educate, assess and certify future teachers. An area of special concern is the degree of coherence with which the program is implemented as it is assumed that coherent views will have an important influence on those of the graduates. Similarly, because the internship is the section in the program that represents the intersection between teacher educators, collaborating teachers, field instructors and the interns, coherence is very relevant. As with teacher education programs across the nation, belief change is extremely important given the program philosophy in which educators aim to effect profound changes in the manner the intern conceives of the nature of the subject matter, the nature of knowledge acquisition, the nature of teaching and learning, and perspectives about pupils.

Given these programmatic priorities, we begin by examining interns' beliefs regarding the teaching and learning of literacy and mathematics. We then move to examining the degree of consistency that exists between faculty and interns across the program in matters considered essential in learning to teach these two subjects. Consistency in attitude between faculty and interns is considered both a program outcome and a mediating condition to program influence. The degree of consistency among faculty around specific goals and assumptions reflects program views about the beliefs they expect interns to hold.

Beliefs about Teaching and Learning Literacy and Mathematics

We collected general background information, and views on opportunities to learn, perceptions on acquired knowledge, knowledge orientation and ability to teach from interns in their last semester in the program, and from their faculty. We used a questionnaire based on a form used by the National Partnership for Excellence and Accountability in Teaching (NPEAT) project but adapted to fit the MSU program theory and strategies. In May of 2000, the questionnaire composed of mostly Likert-based-scale items was administered to the interns of the TPP elementary (teams 1, 2 and 3), and secondary team in the second semester of their internship (their fifth year). In November of 2000, questionnaires containing questions similar to those answered by the interns were sent to instructors in the internship component of the program.

Table 6.3 shows the results of the factor analysis we performed to understand the particular beliefs that seem to contribute to larger views interns have about the teaching of literacy and mathematics. Table 6.3 shows the mean responses of the interns for the particular items we offered them, and the weight of each item as contributor to explaining the total variance to overall views on teaching subject matter. For instance, interns' overall "Orientation toward Literacy" is influenced by their beliefs toward reform and traditional oriented literacy teaching, as well as by the knowledge they have of these particular approaches (reform or traditional oriented). Indeed we see by the pattern of their responses that interns' literacy beliefs tend to favor reform oriented views, and that these beliefs help explain almost 30% of the variance in this area (see "Variance %" column). Regarding understanding of the knowledge that conforms reformed and traditional literacy tendencies, interns' responses help explain close to 35% each of their overall orientation to literacy. The interpretation of these results tells us that even if interns have more positive beliefs toward reformed literacy teaching, they also believe it is important to understand the content and teaching approaches used in both, reformed and traditional literacy teaching. Table 6.4 shows interns' mean responses to the same items but now in comparison across the elementary teams and with the responses given by their faculty, and Figures 6.3 and 6.4 show, in a diagrammatic form, the pattern of these responses. The similarity and proximity of the figures indicate that the literacy and mathematics views of faculty and interns in the teacher preparation program at MSU are highly consistent with each other (or possibly what could be called a program effect, but we refrain from asserting this here as we do not have data of the views of interns at the point of entry to the program. We expect to collect these views in the Fall of 2002).

Similarly in mathematics, interns have strong beliefs toward reform oriented mathematics teaching and quite negative views about traditional oriented mathematics teaching. Indeed these views contribute about 25% of the variance of interns' overall "Orientation toward Mathematics Teaching." We see in Table 6.3 under *Mathematics breath vs depth*" that interns' beliefs have a tendency toward in-depth study of selected topics in mathematics rather than toward comprehensive superficial coverage. As with literacy, the similarity in views across teams and with faculty seems very consistent. We now proceed to explain in detail our findings.

Literacy

Table 6.3 shows the pattern of responses our interns gave toward questions reflecting their particular beliefs (or beliefs and understanding) in literacy. Our factor analysis shows that interns' views grouped around reformed and traditional views.

Literacy Reform Oriented

The views of elementary interns grouped around two areas (in six questions which contributed 27.2% of this factor total variance). Consistent with program's philosophy, interns tended to agree that a primary goal of schooling is to develop readers and writers who are critical and thoughtful in using reading and writing to improve the world in which they live, and that schools must develop readers who are independent and motivated to choose, appreciate, and enjoy literature. Conversely, and also in accordance with the program's orientation, interns were less uniform in their views regarding the idea that the skills and processes involved in teaching students to read and write are best thought of as repeated, with increasingly sophisticated texts and activities, across grade levels, and that a primary goal of schooling is to develop readers who are skillful and strategic in word identification, fluency, and reading comprehension.

Literacy Traditional

Interns' patterns of response regarding traditional beliefs in literacy teaching (in four questions contributing 16.8% of this factor's total variance) tended to disagree with ideas such as mastery of the mechanics of

Table 6.3. Factor Analysis of Program Effectiveness Indicators

	Mean*	Loadings	Variance %
Orientation Toward Literacy (beliefs and understanding). *N*=218 (elementary interns)			
Literacy Reform Oriented Beliefs (1 = strongly disagree; 5 = strongly agree)			27.2
65) A primary goal of schooling is to develop readers and writers who are critical and thoughtful in using reading and writing to improve the world.	4.5	.781	
62) Schools must develop readers who are independent and motivated to choose, appreciate, and enjoy literature.	4.6	.732	
61) Mastery of mechanics can be best developed by engaging students in authentic writing activities.	4.4	.692	
63) Schools must develop readers who can read and evaluate the quality and accuracy of information in prose.	4.2	.678	
67) The skills and processes involved in teaching students to read and write are best thought of as repeated, with increasingly sophisticated texts/activities	4	.523	
64) A primary goal of schooling is to develop readers who are skillful and strategic in word identification, fluency, and reading comprehension.	4.3	.469	
LITERACY TRADITIONAL BELIEFS			16.8
60) Mastery of the mechanics of writing precedes progress in other writing features, such as style, organization, and voice.	2.8	.776	
66) The skills and processes involved in teaching students to read and write are best thought of as being carefully sequenced within and across grades	3.7	.720	
58) It is necessary for students to develop decoding and word recognition processes in order to facilitate comprehension and response to literature.	4	.499	
59) If students are taught to emphasize comprehension and response to literature, decoding and word recognition skills will often develop in the process.	3.8	.318	
KNOWLEDGE OF TRADITIONAL LITERACY (1=poor; 5=excellent)			36.3
69) Phonics and phonemic awareness	3.3	.886	
70) Children's word recognition strategies	3.4	.832	
68) Language and literacy development	3.7	.805	
71) Syntax and semantics	3.2	.754	
72) Reading comprehension strategies	3.8	.599	

Continued on next page

Table 6.3. Continued

	Mean*	Loadings	Variance %
KNOWLEDGE OF REFORM ORIENTED LITERACY			35.0
76) Narrative writing processes and conventions	3.5	.904	
77) Expository writing processes and conventions	3.4	.885	
75) Literary genres, conventions, and criticism	3.5	.773	
73) Reading strategies in the content area	3.7	.642	
74) Children's literature (narrative and information books)	4	.592	
Orientation Toward Mathematics (beliefs and understanding). $N = 218$ (elementary interns)			
MATHEMATICS: TRADITIONAL (1=strongly disagree; 5=strongly agree)			24.4
82) The skills and processes involved in understanding Math require the teaching of basic facts and computation skills before discussing underlying principles of mathematics.	2.5	.770	
78) A primary goal of schooling is to help students learn mathematical terms and master computational skills.	3.4	.764	
84) The main job of a teacher is to transmit the knowledge and content of mathematics.	2.6	.715	
MATHEMATICS: REFORM ORIENTED			23.4
85) The main job of a teacher is to encourage students to think and question mathematically.	4.5	.794	
79) A primary goal of schooling is to help students achieve a deeper conceptual understanding of mathematics.	4.6	.766	
83) The skills and processes involved in understanding Mathematics require teaching basic facts after (or at the same time as) the underlying principles of mathematics.	3.9	.709	
MATHEMATICS BREATH vs DEPTH			14.3
80) Schools must aim for in-depth study of selected topics in Math lessons, even if it means sacrificing comprehensive coverage.	3.5	.760	
81) Schools must aim for comprehensive coverage in Math lessons, even if it means sacrificing in-depth study.	2.6	-.693	

writing precedes progress in other writing features (e.g., style, organization, and voice). They were more in agreement with the notion that the skills and processes involved in teaching students to read and write are best thought of as being carefully sequenced within and across grade levels. Less common were assertions that it is necessary for students to develop decoding and word recognition processes in order to facilitate comprehension and response to literature, and that teaching students to emphasize comprehension and response to literature, decoding and word recognition skills will often develop in the process.

Knowledge of Traditional Literature

In rating their knowledge of a number of traditional literary forms (in five questions contributed 36.3% of this factor's total variance) most interns saw their knowledge as adequate regarding phonics and phonemic awareness and children's word recognition strategies, but rated as good their knowledge of language and literacy development. Reading comprehension strategies seem to be less important components in this factor.

Knowledge of Reform Oriented Literature

Interns' pattern of responses grouped around five questions (which contributed 35% of this factor's total variance) to form the factor we termed knowledge of the reform-oriented literature. For instance, most interns believe they have adequate to good knowledge of narrative writing processes and conventions, making this a powerful driving force in their belief system. Similarly they rated as adequate their knowledge of expository writing processes and conventions. Less emphasis was given to their knowledge of reading strategies in the content area, and to children's literature (narrative and information books) though for those who aligned with this "knowledge type" they believe their knowledge to be good.

Mathematics

Table 6.3 shows the pattern of responses our interns gave to questions reflecting their particular beliefs (or beliefs and understanding) in mathematics. Our factor analysis shows that our interns' views favored reformed mathematics. Regarding knowledge their views reflected a tension between breath and depth in mathematics teaching.

Mathematics Reform Oriented

Interns' patterns of responses grouped around three questions characteristic of reform-oriented mathematics (accounting for 23.4% of this factor's total variance). Interns expressed a tendency to agree with reform oriented ideas of mathematics that see the main job of a teacher as encouraging students to think and question mathematically, and the primary goal of schooling as helping students achieve a deeper conceptual understanding of mathematics. Interns were ambivalent to the idea that the skills and processes involved in understanding mathematics mostly require teaching basic facts.

Mathematics Traditional

Interns' patterns of responses grouped around three questions characteristic of traditional mathematics teaching (these questions account for 24.4% of this factor's total variance). Congruent with program tendencies, interns expressed their inclination to disagree with ideas reflecting traditional math such as the idea that skills and processes involved in understanding mathematics require the teaching of basic facts and computation skills before discussing underlying principles of mathematics, the idea that the main job of a teacher is to transmit the knowledge and content of mathematics, and that a primary goal of schooling is to help students learn mathematical terms and master computational skills.

Mathematics Knowledge: Breath vs. Depth

Two questions characterize the interns' views regarding mathematics knowledge (and account for 14.3% of this factor's total variance). On the one hand, interns tended to agree with the idea that schools must aim for in-depth study of selected topics in math lessons, even if it means sacrificing comprehensive coverage. On the other hand, and according to program's philosophy, interns tended to reject the idea that schools must aim for comprehensive coverage in math lessons, even if it means sacrificing in-depth study.

In sum, interns views about teaching and learning mathematics and literacy are indicative of program's influence. These views are also informed by ideas about what it means to know mathematics and literacy that are consistent with the program's philosophy. An additional question, however, is how consistent are the faculty and the interns regarding these views?

Coherence in Views among Program Participants

Coherence in Views between Faculty and Interns

If we conceive of the program as socialization into the teaching profession, for the program to be successful the views of the interns at the end of the program should be very similar to those of their faculty. Although we would need measures of interns' views before they enter the program to have more certainty on the assumption that the faculty (for purposes of this comparison conceptualized as espousing the program's views) has had an influence, observing great disparity in views would be a worrisome sign indicating that the program does not seem to be having the desired effect (see Tatto, 1996, 1998, 1999). We found that the patterns of views among faculty and interns were very consistent (see Table 4 and Figure 3). Faculty views were internally consistent as well. In all cases the standard deviation for all items was less than 2, this indicates no significant differences among faculty regarding these views.

Literacy

Table 6.4 presents the list of items we gave interns and faculty for their consideration and Figure 6.3 shows the pattern of responses for literacy. The programs' literacy approach is integrated, that is, it incorporates the newer tendencies that see as complementary whole language and other more traditional approaches such as the use of phonics. Still the emphasis in the program is toward conceptual thinking and understanding. An illustration of these views can be found in the answer of interns and faculty to the proposition, "the mastery of the mechanics of writing precedes progress in other writing features, such as style, organization, and voice," to which respondents tended to disagree (with the mean for the elementary teams of 2.86 and the faculty of 2.9). Conversely, interns and faculty uniformly tended to strongly agree toward the idea that "schools must develop readers who are independent and motivated to choose, appreciate, and enjoy literature" (with an overall mean for the elementary interns of 4.7 and the faculty of 4.71). Agreement was observed towards the idea that "a primary goal of schooling is to develop readers and writers who are critical and thoughtful in using reading and writing to improve the world in which they live" (with an overall mean for the elementary interns of 4.47 and the faculty of 4.52). Faculty and interns also tended to agree with the idea that "the skills and processes involved in teaching students to read and write are best thought of as repeated, with increasingly sophisticated texts and activities, across grade levels (with an overall mean for the elementary interns of 4 and the faculty of 4).

Mathematics

Table 6.4 presents the list of mathematics items we gave interns and faculty for their consideration and Figure 6.4 shows the pattern of responses for this subject.

The Mathematics approach in the program is distinctly constructivist and is aligned with NCTM standards. These views are strongly reflected among interns and faculty. An illustration of this is the responses to an item representing a traditional view of mathematics teaching, "schools

Table 6.4. Beliefs About Literacy and Mathematics for Interns and Faculty

	Team 1	Team 2	Team 3	Faculty
Literacy (1 = strongly disagree; 5 = strongly agree)				
It is necessary for students to develop decoding and word recognition processes in order to facilitate comprehension and response to literature	3.93	4.22	3.65	4.04
If students are taught to emphasize comprehension and response to literature, decoding and word recognition skills will often develop in the process	3.75	3.98	3.71	3.85
Mastery of the mechanics of writing precedes progress in other writing features, such as style, organization, and voice	2.61	3.16	2.81	2.9
Mastery of mechanics can be best developed by engaging students in authentic writing activities	4.52	4.5	4.37	4.5
Schools must develop readers who are independent and motivated to choose, appreciate, and enjoy literature	4.7	4.72	4.69	4.71
Schools must develop readers who can read and evaluate the quality and accuracy of information in prose	4.33	4.3	3.63	4.26
A primary goal of schooling is to develop readers who are skillful and strategic in word identification, fluency, and reading comprehension	4.36	4.44	4.19	4.38
A primary goal of schooling is to develop readers and writers who are critical and thoughtful in using reading and writing to improve the world in which they live	4.6	4.51	4.31	4.52
The skills and processes involved in teaching students to read and write are best thought of as being carefully sequenced within and across grade levels	3.57	3.96	3.94	3.79
The skills and processes involved in teaching students to read and write are best thought of as repeated, with increasingly sophisticated texts and activities, across grade levels	4.1	3.97	3.94	4.02
I rate my understanding of language and literacy development as (1=poor; 5=excellent):	3.78	3.72	3.53	3.73
I rate my understanding of phonics and phonemic awareness as:	3.18	3.26	3.24	3.23
I rate my understanding of children's word recognition strategies as:	3.41	3.48	2.94	3.41
I rate my understanding of syntax and semantics as:	3.19	3.26	3.19	3.23
I rate my understanding of reading and comprehension strategies as:	3.82	3.83	3.47	3.8

I rate my understanding of reading strategies in the content area as:	3.69	3.77	3.24	3.69
I rate my understanding of children's literature (narrative and information books) as:	3.86	4.13	3.94	3.99
I rate my understanding of literary genres, conventions, and criticism as:	3.56	3.54	2.76	3.49
I rate my understanding of narrative writing processes and conventions as:	3.55	3.39	3.24	3.45
Mathematics (1=strongly disagree; 5=strongly agree)				
A primary goal of schooling is to help students learn mathematical terms and master computational skills	3.41	3.65	3.38	3.52
A primary goal of schooling is to help students achieve a deeper conceptual understanding of mathematics	4.73	4.68	4.56	4.69
Schools must aim for in-depth study of selected topics in Math lessons, even if it means sacrificing comprehensive coverage	3.51	3.59	3.13	3.52
Schools must aim for comprehensive coverage in Math lessons, even if it means sacrificing in-depth study	2.33	2.81	3.13	2.64
The skills and processes involved in understanding math require the teaching of basic facts and computation skills before discussing underlying principles of mathematics	2.41	2.59	2.88	2.55
The skills and processes involved in understanding Mathematics require teaching basic facts after (or at the same time as) the underlying principles of mathematics	4.01	3.96	3.69	3.96
The main job of a teacher is to transmit the knowledge and content of mathematics	2.62	2.75	2.44	2.68
The main job of a teacher is to encourage students to think and question mathematically	4.65	4.53	4.63	4.59

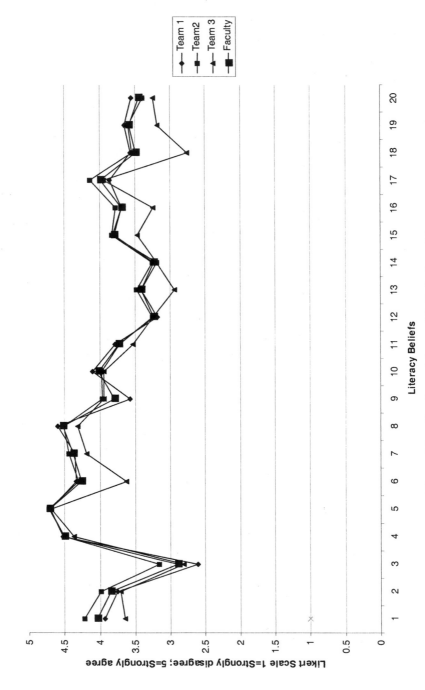

Figure 6.3. Faculty and Interns' Beliefs about Literacy

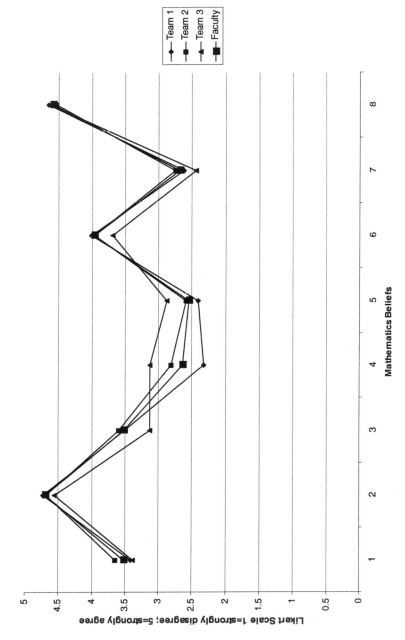

Figure 6.4. Faculty and Interns' Beliefs about Mathematics

must aim for comprehensive coverage in Math lessons, even if it means sacrificing in-depth study." In accordance with program philosophy, faculty and interns disagreed (with an overall mean of 2.7 for interns and of 2.64 for faculty). Similar levels of disagreement were observed toward the following items, "the skills and processes involved in understanding math require the teaching of basic facts and computation skills before discussing underlying principles of mathematics (with an overall mean of 2.6 for interns and of 2.55 for faculty); and "the main job of a teacher is to transmit the knowledge and content of mathematics (with an overall mean of 2.6 for interns and of 2.68 for faculty). A view that represents more closely the programs' philosophy was seen approvingly by interns and their faculty, "the main job of a teacher is to encourage students to think and question mathematically (with an overall mean of 4.6 for interns and of 4.59 for faculty).

In sum, the elementary interns show significant agreement with their faculty regarding the teaching and learning of subject matter. This finding is remarkable given the disparate views the larger society and even the educational community hold in these areas (see Tatto, 1996, 1998; 2000).

We recognize that we are just beginning to build our programmatic research in this area. This year, we will initiate a longitudinal study to measure conceptions of teaching and learning at three points in time (entry, exit and follow-up). We have begun an intensive study of the internship for elementary teachers in order to understand the influence of the different learning opportunities on their practice.

Research on belief change as an indicator of the effectiveness of teacher preparation design is an emerging line of scholarship for teacher educators. In this chapter, our purpose was to begin to provide examples of what has been done in the field.

CONCLUSION

This chapter attempted to examine a number of issues that were seen as relevant to a critical examination of how beliefs are taught and measured in teacher education, we will briefly discuss these in light of our findings.

- *The theoretical basis for the kind of belief change that is currently seen as important in reformed teacher education, is somewhat thin.* The kinds of changes seen as theoretically relevant in teacher education can be conceptualized as originated in notions about what makes a good teacher and the way that beliefs seem to influence these factors. In most cases, the empirical basis for upholding such theories is yet to be realized. Although our collection of studies show that important emphasis is placed on equipping future teachers with beliefs that will prepare for the classroom (e.g., to know how to use technology, to conceptualize and learn rigorous subject matter to teach it in depth and for understanding, to teach diverse students, and to think in powerful ways about their practice) studies to empirically test these theories (e.g., whether these teachers are better because they hold certain beliefs) are lacking in the literature.

- *The theory of belief change is in need of empirical confirmation.* According to the studies here reviewed, beliefs are expected to change if educational interventions provide more and better field and classroom experiences for prospective teachers; opportunities for reflection either individual or with peers; opportunities for understanding one-self vis-à-vis challenging and novel situations in a secure environment; theoretical and applied knowledge about subject matter, pedagogy, curriculum, teaching, learning, diverse students, and technology. As the arrangement of these opportunities to change beliefs require a great deal of effort, understanding their relative effectiveness may help design more powerful teacher education.

- *The current approaches used to measure belief change in teachers as a result of a given intervention in teacher preparation lack programmatic focus.* Few studies here reviewed document programmatic efforts, while most report the use of discrete courses as the principal context for belief change. Indeed, this seems to be the preferred vehicle by which teacher educators attempt to alter the belief systems among future teachers. If we are going to call teacher preparation interventions *programs*, then more holistic and consistent efforts to increase program influence need to be explored and studied.

- *Given the lack of triangulation procedures and of reported validity and reliability in the studies here reviewed it is difficult to ascertain the degree to which current measurements capture the kinds of belief change advocated by teacher education reform.* Qualitative and quantitative studies of teacher preparation influence on belief change need to report validity and reliability of measurements. Regarding methodology, the studies reviewed here used for the most part purposeful samples and measurements that were quite removed from the actual knowledge and practice of teachers. Most studies lacked the use of triangulation. In what it is a basically longitudinal and comparative process, only three studies used comparative and /or longitudinal approaches to research teacher education influence on beliefs. We encourage researchers to follow social research conventions and ask journals to develop more rigorous criteria when making decisions about publishable scholarship on teacher education influence.

- *The ethics of belief change in teacher preparation needs careful thought and review.* In no study we reviewed was there serious questioning of the ethics of belief change. Although the field of ethics and educational change has explored this issue (see for instance Imel, 2000; Tisdell, Hanley, & Taylor 2000), we need to revisit this question in light of new theories about teaching and learning, about teacher preparation effects, and about whether these outcomes guarantee the efforts and resources placed in this area.

Research on belief change as a result of teacher preparation design is an emerging line of scholarship for teacher educators. In this chapter, our purpose was to begin to provide examples of what has been done in the field. Given what we have learned, we urge teacher educators interested in belief change as an avenue to forming caring and excellent teachers, to undertake the development of programmatic research agendas. This research should use multiple designs and multiple measures that are capable of capturing the opportunities to learn different beliefs among teachers. We urge researchers to consider belief change strategies in light of program purposes and impact in classroom contexts.

NOTE

1. See Kennedy (1999) for a similar framework on measurements for complex student learning.

REFERENCES

Abbott, J. A., & Faris, S. E. (2000). Integrating technology into preservice literacy instruction: A survey of elementary education students' attitudes towards computers. *Journal of Research on Computing in Education, 33*(2), 149-161.

Ashton, P. T. (1992). Editorial. *Journal of Teacher Education, 43*(5), 322.

Atkins, S. L. (1998). Windows of opportunity: Preservice teachers' perceptions of technology-based alternatives to field experiences. *The Journal of Computers in Mathematics and Science Teaching, 17*(1), 95-105.

Black, A., & Ammon, P. (1992). A developmental constructivist approach to teacher education. *Journal of Teacher Education, 43*(5), 323-335.

Buchmann, M., & Schwille, J.R. (1993). Education, experience, and the paradox of finitude. In M. Buchmann, & R. E. Floden (Eds.), *Detachment and concern* (pp. 19-33). London. Cassell

Carter, C. W. (1998). The use of journals to promote reflection. *Action in Teacher Education, 19*(4), 39-42.

Cochran, K. F., DeRuiter, J. A., & King, R. A. (1993). Pedagogical content knowing: An integrative model for teacher preparation. *Journal of Teacher Education, 44*, 263-272.

Cochran-Smith, M. (2000a). Blind vision: Unlearning racism in teacher education. *Harvard Educational Review, 70*(2), 157-190.

Cochran-Smith, M. (2000b). *The outcomes question in teacher education.* Vice-presidential address presented at the 2000 Annual Meeting of the American Educational Research Association, New Orleans, LA. Available: http://www2.bc.edu/~cochrans/mcsvpaddress.html

Condon, M. W. F., Clyde, J. A., Kyle, D. W., & Hovda, R. A. (1993). A constructivist basis for teaching and teacher education: A framework for program development and research on graduates. *Journal of Teacher Education, 44*, 273-278.

Cooney, T. J., Shealy, B. E., & Arvold, B. (1998). Conceptualizing belief structures of preservice secondary mathematics teachers. *Journal of Research in Mathematics Education, 29*(3), 306-333.

Crawford, R. M. (1998). Facilitating a reading anxiety treatment program for preservice teachers. *Reading Improvement, 35*(1), 11-14.

Darling-Hammond, L. (1998). Teachers and teaching: Testing policy hypothesis from a national commission report. *Educational Researcher, 27*(1), 5-15.

Duckworth, E. (1996). *The having of wonderful ideas.* New York: Teacher College Press.

Foegen, A., Espsin, C. A., & Allinder, R. M. (2001). Translating research into practice: Preservice teachers' beliefs about curriculum-based measurement. *The Journal of Special Education, 34*(4), 226-236.

Fenstermacher, G. (1994). The place of practical arguments in the education of teachers. In V. Richardson (Ed.), *Teacher change and the staff development process: A case in reading instruction* (pp. 23-42). New York: Teachers College Press.

Green, T. (1971). *The activities of teaching.* New York: McGraw-Hill.

Groulx, J. G. (2001). Changing preservice teacher perceptions of minority schools. *Urban Education, 36*(1), 60-92.

Harlin, R. P. (1999). Developing future professionals: Influences of literacy coursework and field experiences. *Reading Research and Instruction, 38*(4), 351-370.

Harper, N. W., & Daane, C. J. (1998). Causes and reduction of math anxiety in preservice elementary teachers. *Action in Teacher Education, 19*(4), 29-38.

Hart, P. M., & Rowley, J. B. (1996, Spring). Different, but alike: An exploration of preservice teacher decision making with regard to the selection of children's literature for classroom use. *Reading Research and Instruction, 35*, 209-222.

Hodge, S. R. (1998). Prospective physical education teachers' attitudes toward teaching students with disabilities. *The Physical Educator, 55*(2), 68-77.

Imel, S. (2000). Change: Connections to Adult Learning and Education ERIC Digest No. 221

Irvine, J. (2000, April). *Seeing with the cultural eye: Different perspectives of African American teachers and researchers.* Paper presented at the Annual Meeting of the American Educational Research Association, New Orleans, LA.

Irvine, J., & Fraser, J. (1998, May 13). *Warm demanders.* Available: http://www.edweek.org/ew/1998/35irvine.h17

Johnson, V. G., & Landers-Macrine, S. (1998). Student teachers explain changes in their thinking. *The Teacher Educator, 34*(1), 30-40.

Kennedy, M. (1999). Approximations to indicators of students' outcomes. *Educational Evaluation and Policy Analysis, 21*(4), 345-363.

Ladson-Billings, G. (1999). Preparing teachers for diverse student populations: A critical race theory perspective. In A. Iran-Nejad & D. Pearson (Eds.), *Review of research in education* (Vol. 24, pp. 211-248). Washington, DC: American Educational Research Association.

Ladson-Billings, G. (2000). Fighting for our lives: Preparing teachers to teach African American students. *Journal of Teacher Education 51*(3), 206-214.

Levin, B., & Matthews, C. E. (1997). Using hypermedia to educate preservice teachers about gender-equity issues in elementary school classrooms. *Journal of Research on Computing Education, 29*(Spring), 226-247.

Linek, W. M., Nelson, O. C., & Sampson, M. B. (1999). Developing beliefs about literacy instruction: A cross-case analysis of preservice teachers in traditional and field based settings. *Reading Research and Instruction, 38*(4), 371-386.

Mason, T. C. (1997). Prospective teachers' attitudes towards urban schools: Can they be changed? *Multicultural Education, 6*(4), 9-13.

Maxson, M. M., & Sindelar, R. (1998). Images revisited: Examining preservice teachers' ideas about teaching. *Teacher Education Quarterly, 25*(2), 5-26.

Merriam-Webster. (2001). *Merriam-Webster's Collegiate Dictionary, Tenth Edition.* Springfield, MA: Merriam-Webster.

Nespor, J. (1987). The role of beliefs in the practice of teaching. *Journal of Curriculum Studies, 19*(4), 317-328.

O'Loughlin, M. (1992). Engaging teachers in emancipatory knowledge construction. *Journal of Teacher Education, 43*(5), 336-346.

Pajares, M. (1992). Teachers beliefs and educational research: Cleaning up a messy construct. *Review of Educational Research, 62*(3), 307-332.

Peterson, K. M., Cross, L. F., & Johnson, E. J. (2000). Diversity education for preservice teachers: Strategies and attitude outcomes. *Action in Teacher Education, 22*(2), 33-38.

Pigge, F. L. & Marso, R. N. (1997). A seven-year longitudinal multi-factor assessment of teaching concerns development through preparation and early years of teaching. *Teaching and Teacher Education 13*(2), 225-235.

Prawat, R. (1992). Teachers' beliefs about teaching and learning: A constructivist perspective. *American Journal of Education, 100*(3), 354-395.

Quinn, R. J. (1997). Effects of mathematics methods courses on the mathematical attitudes and content knowledge of preservice teachers. *Journal of Educational Research. 91*(2), 108-113.

Raths, J. (2001). Teachers' beliefs and teaching Beliefs. *Early Childhood Research and Practice, 3*(1). Available: http://ecrp.uiuc.edu/v3n1/raths.html.

Richardson, V. (1994). The consideration of beliefs in staff development. In V. Richardson (Ed.), *Teacher change and the staff development process: A case in reading instruction* (pp. 90-108). New York: Teachers College Press.

Richardson, V. (1996). The role of attitudes and beliefs in learning to teach. In J. Sikula (Ed.), *Handbook of research on teacher education* (2nd ed., pp. 102-119). New York: Macmillan.

Robin, B., Tellez, K., & Miller, R. (1998). A comparison of text-based and graphical Internet tools in preservice teacher training. *Journal of Technology and Teacher Education, 6*(4), 259-272.

Ropp, M. M. (1999). Exploring individual characteristics associated with learning to use computers in preservice teacher preparation. *Journal of Research on Computing in Education, 31*(4), 402-424.

Schon, D. (1987). *Educating the reflective practitioner.* San Francisco: Jossey-Bass.

Sherry, A. C. (2000). Expanding the view of preservice teachers' computer literacy: Implications from written and verbal data and metaphors as freehand drawings. *Journal of Technology and Teacher Education, 8*(3), 187-218.

Tatto, M. T. (1996). Examining values and beliefs about teaching diverse students: Understanding the challenges for teacher education, *Educational Evaluation and Policy Analysis 18*(2), 155-180.

Tatto, M. T. (1997). Reconstructing teacher education for a global community. *International Journal of Educational Development, 17*(4), 405-415.

Tatto, M. T. (1998). The influence of teacher education on teachers' beliefs about purposes of education, roles and practice. *Journal of Teacher Education, 49*(1), 66-77.

Tatto, M. T. (1999). The socializing influence of normative cohesive teacher education on teachers' beliefs about instructional choice, *Teachers and Teaching, 5*(1), 111-134.

Tatto, M. T., & Papanastasiou, E. (2003). *The influence of program theory and strategies in teacher education: A case study.* Unpublished manuscript.

Teicher, J. M. (1997). Effect of multicultural music experience on preservice elementary teachers' attitudes. *Journal of Research in Music Education, 43*(3), 415-427.

Tisdell, E. J., Hanley, M. S., & Taylor, E. W. (2000). Different Perspectives on Teaching for Critical Consciousness. In A. L. Wilson & E. R. Hayes (Eds.), *Handbook of adult and continuing education.* San Francisco: Jossey-Bass.

Vacc, N. N., & Bright, G. W. (1999). Elementary preservice teachers' changing beliefs and instructional use of children's mathematical thinking. *Journal for Research on Mathematics Education, 30*(1), 89-110.

Yildirim, S. (2000). Effects of an educational computing course on preservice and inservice teachers: A discussion and analysis of attitudes and use. *Journal of Research on Computing in Education, 32*(4), 479-495.

Zeichner, K., & Gore, J. (1990). Teacher socialization. In W. Houston (Ed.), *Handbook of research on teacher education* (pp. 329-348). New York: MacMillan.

CHAPTER 7

THE IMPACT OF SCHOOLS ON TEACHER BELIEFS, INFLUENCE, AND STUDENT ACHIEVEMENT

The Role of Collective Efficacy Beliefs

Roger D. Goddard
University of Michigan

For more than a quarter century, researchers have developed a large body of literature on the meaning and effects of a particular belief held by teachers, namely teacher efficacy. This work makes significant contributions to our knowledge about the correlates of teacher efficacy. We know, for example, that teacher efficacy is a significant predictor of productive teaching practices. Indeed, teachers with strong perceptions of self-capability tend to employ classroom strategies that are more organized and better planned (Allinder, 1994), student centered (Czerniak & Schriver, 1994; Enochs, Scharmann, & Riggs, 1995), and humanistic (Woolfolk & Hoy, 1990) than do teachers with lower levels of efficacy. Teacher efficacy

Advances in Teacher Education 183–202

is also strongly related to trust (Da Costa & Riordan, 1996), openness (DeForest & Hughes, 1992), and job satisfaction (Lee, Dedrick, & Smith, 1991). These studies provide considerable explanation for the positive link between teacher efficacy and student achievement (e.g., Anderson, Greene, & Loewen, 1988; Armor et al., 1976; Ashton & Webb, 1986; Gibson & Dembo, 1984; Ross, 1992, 1994) because such approaches and attitudes are widely accepted as educationally productive.

In light of these promising findings about teacher efficacy, recent research has added an organizational dimension to inquiry about efficacy beliefs in schools. This line of inquiry emphasizes that teachers have not only self-referent efficacy perceptions but also beliefs about the conjoint capability of a school faculty. Such group-referent perceptions reflect an emergent organizational property known as *collective efficacy* (see, i.e., Bandura, 1997; Goddard, Hoy, & Woolfolk Hoy, 2000). Within an organization, perceived collective efficacy represents the beliefs of group members concerning "the performance capability of a social system as a whole" (Bandura, 1997, p. 469). The link between performance and efficacy is direct and powerful. Analogous to self-efficacy, collective efficacy is associated with the tasks, level of effort, persistence, shared thoughts, stress levels, and achievement of groups.

For schools, collective efficacy refers to *the perceptions of teachers in a school that the faculty as a whole can organize and execute the courses of action required to have a positive effect on students*. To fully understand the impact of collective efficacy, one must recognize that schools, and the beliefs that characterize their cultures, provide complex and influential normative environments for their students and faculty. According to Bandura (1997),

> analysis of the culture of organizations should be concerned not only with traditions of how things are done but also with shared beliefs about the organization's capabilities to innovate and perform effectively. Because of their diverse impact, an organization's beliefs about its efficacy to produce results are undoubtedly an important feature of its operative culture. (p. 476)

Thus, just as individual teacher efficacy partially explains the effect of teachers on student achievement, from an organizational perspective, collective efficacy helps to explain the differential effect that school cultures have on teachers and students. Hence, it is reasonable (and correct) to expect that some schools have a positive influence on teachers whereas the impact of other schools is much less so productive. For example, some teachers will find themselves in schools with low morale and a depressed sense of collective efficacy while other teachers will work in schools possessed by a high degree of mutuality, shared responsibility, and confidence in the conjoint capability of the faculty. A major purpose of this chapter is to explain why such differences are strongly related to teachers' perceptions of self-capability, influence over school decisions, and student achievement differences among schools.

Importantly, collective efficacy perceptions are not reducible to the sum of their parts as they gain meaning only through their combined power to encourage certain actions and constrain others. Perceptions of group efficacy serve to influence the behavior of individuals and collectives by providing expectations for action (Sampson, Morenoff, & Earls, 2000). Indeed, Sampson et al. argue that collective efficacy is important to group functioning because it explains how organized capacity for action is tapped to produce results. For example, dense and trusting relational networks reflect high levels of social capital in a group. According to Sampson et al., however, the potential for such social resources to influence outcomes is reached only when a group's collective efficacy is sufficiently robust to compel members to action in pursuit of desired organized attainments. Perceptions of collective efficacy directly affect the diligence and resolve with which groups choose to pursue their goals. Hence, collective efficacy is a potent way of characterizing the strong normative and behavioral influence of school culture. Knowledge about collective efficacy is, therefore, critical to understanding the influence of schools on teachers' professional work and, in turn, student achievement.

The purpose of this chapter is to describe the importance of collective efficacy to teachers' personal efficacy, teaching practice, and influence over school decisions, as well as important group outcomes such as student achievement, work group effectiveness, and neighborhood safety. In the course of doing so, the chapter examines the social cognitive underpinnings of efficacy theory. Specifically, I address the nature of efficacy beliefs, their formation and change, and the extension of social cognitive theory to thinking about group capabilities.

A SOCIAL COGNITIVE PERSPECTIVE ON THE FORMATION AND CHANGE OF EFFICACY BELIEFS

Notably, there are two distinct, but theoretically related, types of efficacy—individual and collective. Although conceptually distinct, individual and collective efficacy share a social cognitive theoretical orientation. The purpose of this section is to explain these shared underpinnings and to emphasize the extension of social cognitive theory to the group level.

Social cognitive theory is concerned with human agency, or the ways that people exercise some level of control over their own lives. Central to the exercise of control is one's sense of personal efficacy or "beliefs in one's capabilities to organize and execute a course of action required to produce a given attainment" (Bandura, 1997, p. 3). But social cognitive theory acknowledges that "personal agency operates within a broad network of sociostructural influences" (p. 6) and thus the theory "extends the analysis of mechanisms of human agency to the exercise of collective agency" (p. 7)—people's combined beliefs that they can work together to produce desired effects. When individuals and collectives choose to work in pursuit of certain attainments, their actions reflect the exercise of agency.

Human and Organizational Agency

The most fundamental assumption of social cognitive theory is that of agency. From the perspective of social cognitive theory, people are more likely to purposefully pursue goals that seem challenging, rewarding, and attainable. When applied to teaching, social cognitive theory predicts that the decisions teachers make about their classroom practices are directly influenced by their perceptions of teacher efficacy. The higher one's teacher efficacy, the more likely one is to tenaciously overcome obstacles and persist in the face of failure. Such resiliency, in turn, tends to foster innovative teaching and student learning.

The assumption of human agency is also critical to our understanding of group functioning. Extended to the school level, the parallel concept is organizational agency. Because agency refers to the intentional pursuit of a course of action, we may begin to understand school organizations as agentive when we consider that schools act purposefully in pursuit of their educational goals. For example, one school may work to close achievement gaps by race while another acts to increase the quality of teacher professional development. When such differences are purposeful, they reflect the exercise of organizational agency. Of course, organizational agency results from the agentive actions of individuals directed at the attainment of desired goals.

Sources of Efficacy-Shaping Information

Bandura (1986, 1997) postulates four sources of efficacy-shaping information: mastery experience, vicarious experience, social persuasion, and affective state. Just as these sources are critical for individuals, they are also fundamental to the development of collective efficacy perceptions.

Mastery Experience

Enactive experiences are important for organizations. Teachers as a group experience successes and failures. Past school successes build teachers' beliefs in the capability of the faculty, whereas failures undermine it. If success is frequent and too easy, however, failure is likely to produce discouragement. A resilient sense of collective efficacy requires experience in overcoming difficulties through persistent effort.

Recently, Goddard (2001) tested the hypothesis that mastery experience (operationalized as prior school reading achievement) is a significant positive predictor of differences among schools in collective efficacy perceptions. Not only was past school achievement a significant predictor of differences among schools in teachers' perceptions of collective efficacy, but also past achievement was a stronger predictor than aggregate measures of school race (i.e., proportion minority) and SES. This finding supports the extension of social cognitive theory to the group level by demonstrating that collective efficacy perceptions are strongly related to mastery experience. Also, while mastery experience explained the majority of the variation between schools in collective efficacy, more than a third of this variation was unexplained. In other words, in addition to mastery experience, there are other factors systematically associated with organizations that may explain variation among schools in collective efficacy. These factors most likely include the other sources efficacy-shaping information postulated by social cognitive theory and described immediately below.

Vicarious Experience

Just as teacher efficacy is enhanced by observing successful models with similar characteristics (Gorrell & Capron, 1988; Schunk 1981, 1983, 1987; Schunk & Zimmerman, 1997), so too is collective efficacy enhanced by observing successful individuals and organizations, especially those that attain similar goals in the face of familiar opportunities and constraints. Individuals and organizations may also learn from dissimilar counterparts that have attained highly valued outcomes. Replication of successful educational programs across a wide variety of settings by schools aspiring to achieve similar success is a familiar example. Indeed, in the current high stakes system of state-mandated testing and accountability, schools wanting improved educational outcomes may experience gains in collective efficacy by observing successful educational programs offered by teachers in higher achieving schools. These examples illustrate that social cognitive theory extends to the group level to explain that organizations do indeed learn vicariously about their capabilities (Huber, 1996).

Social Persuasion

Social persuasion is another means of strengthening a faculty's conviction that they have the capabilities to set and achieve goals. Talks, workshops, professional development opportunities, and feedback about achievement can inspire action. Although verbal persuasion alone is not likely to compel profound organizational change, when coupled with models of success and positive direct experience, it can influence the collective efficacy of a faculty. Persuasion can encourage group members to innovate and overcome difficult challenges.

Social persuasion is also important to explaining the influence of collective efficacy on organizational participants. A robust sense of group capability establishes a strong press for collective performance. Organizations high in collective efficacy are places where group members understand school goals and persist in their efforts to attain them. Teachers new to a given school quickly learn about this aspect of their school's culture in talks with other teachers and administrators. In schools possessed by a high degree of collective efficacy, new teachers learn that extra effort and educational success are the norm. These high expectations for action create a normative press that encourages all teachers to do what it takes to excel and discourages them from giving up when faced with difficult obstacles. Although the expectations of peer groups do not always win the day, organizational life is nevertheless filled with social exchanges that communicate expectations, sanctions, and rewards to members. Hence, expectations for action set by collective efficacy beliefs do not go unnoticed; rather, these expectations are fundamental aspects of an organization's culture and its influence on group member performance.

Affective States

Organizations have affective states that are impacted by collective successes and failures. Indeed, just as individuals react to stress, so do organizations. For example, immediate past performance on state-mandated tests, which is typically widely publicized, plays a key role in influencing the mood of schools. Efficacious organizations can tolerate pressure and crises and continue to function without debilitating consequences; indeed, such organizations learn to rise to the challenge when confronted with disruptive forces. Less efficacious organizations, on the other hand, are more likely to react dysfunctionally which, in turn, increases the likelihood of failure. Thus, affective states exert considerable influence over how organizations interpret and react to the myriad challenges they face.

The Pivotal Role of Cognition in the Interpretation of Efficacy-Shaping Information

Ultimately, the exercise of human agency depends upon how individuals and groups interpret their efficacy-shaping experiences. Indeed, Raudenbush, Rowan, and Cheong (1992) characterize efficacy as "a cognition that mediates between knowledge and action" (p. 150). Bandura (1997) emphasizes that whether efficacy beliefs are enhanced or diminished after a given level of enactive experience is not simply an artifact of the performance; efficacy beliefs are created when individuals weigh and interpret their performance relative to other information. According to Bandura, "changes in perceived efficacy result from cognitive processing of the diagnostic information that performances convey about capability rather than the performances per se" (p. 81). The same is true for all four sources of efficacy information—the role of social cognition is critical. That is, perceptions of efficacy for various individual and collective pursuits arise from cognitive and metacognitive processing of the sources of efficacy-shaping information described here.

Having discussed the social cognitive underpinnings of collective efficacy, the chapter turns now to a discussion of how collective efficacy is related to teacher efficacy and the influence that teachers have over instructionally relevant school decisions.

COLLECTIVE AND TEACHER EFFICACY: A MULTILEVEL PERSPECTIVE

Collective efficacy is distinct from, yet related to, teachers' perceptions of personal efficacy. And, while a great deal of research has connected both teacher and collective efficacy to student achievement, an important but overlooked question concerns the nested association between these two influential types of beliefs. The focus on teacher and collective efficacy is partly motivated by troubling evidence indicating that, depending on personal characteristics and experiences, teachers new to urban schools sometimes experience declines in teacher efficacy during their first year of teaching (Chester & Beaudin, 1996). Hence, schools do affect teacher efficacy. Moreover, Raudenbush, Rowan, and Cheong (1992) showed that teacher efficacy also varies within teachers, depending on the classes they teach. They found that intrateacher variation was most strongly related to differences in students' level of preparation and engagement, factors that seemed to explain why teachers had higher efficacy for honors and academic track courses. Raudenbush et al. also found a modest positive relationship between teacher efficacy and school-level variables representing teacher control and staff collaboration. Aside from their study, however, there has been little work to investigate the effects of school context on teachers' efficacy beliefs.

The focus of this section of the chapter is, therefore, to determine the extent to which teacher efficacy varies among schools and, the extent to which a school's collective efficacy explains these differences in teacher efficacy. To inform this inquiry, I offer a theoretical analysis of the relationship between teacher and collective efficacy. Next, I report the results of a multilevel analysis of the relationship between teacher and collective efficacy observed in the elementary schools of a large urban district.

A Theoretical Examination of the Link between Collective and Teacher Efficacy

Given that teachers usually work in the isolation of their classrooms, one must ask whether a school's collective efficacy really makes a difference to their self-efficacy beliefs. Indeed, many argue that the loose coupling between educational processes and outcomes makes the work of teaching difficult not only to do, but also to manage with typical bureaucratic controls. Yet, while the complexity of teaching and loose coupling that typifies schooling may make instruction a wieldy task, these factors do not negate the strong social influence of organizational culture. Bandura (1997) explains how even loosely coupled organizations influence their members as follows:

> People working independently within a group structure do not function as social isolates totally immune to the influence of those around them. Their sense of efficacy is likely to be lower amidst a group of chronic losers than amidst habitual winners. Moreover, the resources, impediments, and opportunities provided by a given system partly determine how efficacious individuals can be, even though their work may be only loosely coupled. (p. 469)

Bandura's argument suggests that teacher and collective efficacy should covary positively. The purpose of this discussion is to offer a theoretical analysis of this covariance. The discussion draws upon Coleman's social theory of normative control and Bandura's social cognitive theory to explain the positive link between teacher and collective efficacy. After this discussion, the results of a recent study (Goddard & Goddard, 2001), in which the empirical relation between teacher and collective efficacy was tested, are summarized.

Social Norms

Because collective efficacy sets expectations for action in schools, it is useful to consider the impact of social norms on individual behavior. According to Coleman (1985, 1987, 1990), norms permit group members to influence the actions of others when those actions have consequences for members of the group. When a teacher's actions are inconsistent with group expectations for action, the teacher's actions are likely to be sanctioned by the faculty. In fact, Coleman argues that the intensity of the social sanctions delivered to those who break norms will be commensurate with the effect of norm-breaking on the collective. Thus, if most teachers in a school believe the faculty can successfully teach students, the school's normative and behavioral environment will press teachers to put forth the effort required to attain valued goals. From a sociocognitive perspective, the power of this normative press lies in the social persuasion it exerts on teachers.

Mastery Experience

Another way to address the relationship between collective and teacher efficacy from a theoretical perspective is to consider how schools have collective mastery experiences. When a school has high average levels of student achievement, it is obvious that one or more teachers were directly successful with their students. In other words, group mastery experiences are the result of the enactive successes of individual teachers. Thus, mastery experience—one of the most powerful sources of efficacy-shaping information (Bandura, 1997; Goddard, 2001; Pajares, 1997)—has the potential to operate in concert at both the individual and collective levels. From this perspective, teacher and collective efficacy should covary positively in response to a given mastery experience.

School Context and Teacher Efficacy

In addition to the positive association between teacher efficacy and staff collaboration and control found by Raudenbush et al. (1992), several other school contextual variables (exclusive of collective efficacy) have also been found to predict variation in teacher efficacy. For example, Moore and Esselman (1992) showed that positive school climate, lack of impediments to effective instruction, and teacher empowerment were all positively and significantly related to teacher efficacy. Similarly, Hoy and Woolfolk (1993) showed that school contextual variables representing principal influence with superiors and the academic press of a school are strongly related to teachers' sense of personal efficacy. Together, these studies suggest that emergent school contextual factors are related to teachers' perceptions of self-efficacy for educating students successfully.

In sum, one must recognize that teachers are aware of and influenced by the social processes and collective beliefs that characterize a school. Indeed, an individual with modest teacher efficacy will likely persist more in the face of personal obstacles and setbacks in a school where teachers tend to believe in the group's conjoint capability to educate the students successfully. Conversely, the same individual might experience a decrease in teacher efficacy upon joining a faculty that dwells on past group failures and has little expectation for organizational improvement. In such a context, even a highly efficacious teacher may begin to view personal effort and persistence as inconsequential to student growth and development and hence experience a decline in teacher efficacy.

A TEST OF THE RELATION BETWEEN
COLLECTIVE AND TEACHER EFFICACY

The preceding discussion illustrates the theoretical possibility that collective efficacy systematically influences teacher efficacy by establishing expectations for action in schools. It is equally important, however, to recognize several key conceptual and empirical distinctions between teacher and collective efficacy. To illustrate, this section of the chapter reports a reanalysis of data employed by Goddard and Goddard (2001) in a study of teacher and collective efficacy. The data were drawn from 438 teachers in 47 elementary schools. The schools were located in the Midwest in one of the nation's 50 largest city school districts. The efficacy measures employed are described below.

Teacher Efficacy Measure

Teacher efficacy was measured using a five-item personal teacher efficacy scale based on Gibson and Dembo's (1984) teacher efficacy scale. Scores on the five-item teacher efficacy subscale have had adequate internal consistency and a one-factor structure in previous research (Hoy & Woolfolk, 1993; Woolfolk & Hoy, 1990). "If I really try hard, I can get through to even the most difficult or unmotivated students" is a sample item from the scale.

Collective Efficacy Measure

Collective efficacy was measured using the 21-item collective efficacy scale recently developed by Goddard, Hoy, and Woolfolk Hoy (2000). "Teachers in this school are able to get through to difficult students" is a sample item from the collective efficacy scale.

Both scales are scored on a six-point Likert-type scale from (1) strongly disagree to (6) strongly agree. Mean scores for the efficacy variables are

Table 7.1. Descriptive Statistics for Teacher and Collective Efficacy
(n = 438 teachers in 47 schools)

Variable	Mean	Standard Deviation	Minimum	Maximum
Teacher efficacy	4.67	.76	1.40	6.00
Collective efficacy	4.33	.48	3.45	5.30

Note: Author's calculations based on reanalysis of data reported by Goddard and Goddard (2001).

Table 7.2. Teacher and Collective Efficacy Scale Correlations
at the Teacher and School Level

Teacher Level	Teacher Efficacy	Collective Efficacy	r^2
Teacher efficacy ($n = 438$)	—	.42	.176
Collective efficacy ($n = 452$)		—	
School Level ($n = 45$)			
Teacher efficacy	—	.51	.260
Collective efficacy		—	

Note: author's calculations based on reanalysis of data reported by Goddard and Goddard (2001).

displayed in Table 7.1. Notably, teachers tend to have slightly higher perceptions of capability for themselves than for the faculty groups to which they belong. The mean scores do not reveal, however, any information about the extent to which teacher and collective efficacy covary. To assess the strength of the empirical relation between teacher and collective efficacy, I decided to correlate the two variables. Because the variables occur at two different organizational levels (individual and collective), the unit of analysis problem forces one to compromise either by creating aggregate (school level) teacher efficacy scores or, individual (teacher level) collective efficacy scores. While each approach suffers partly from bias resulting from the measure of one variable at an inappropriate level, the advantage is that the resulting correlations do provide a useful indication of the strength of the relationship between the two variables. The individual and school-level correlations are reported in Table 7.2. Notably, at both levels, the strength of the relationship between the two is moderate at best ($r_{ind.} = .42$, $r_{sch.} = .51$,). Indeed, collective efficacy explains between 18% ($r_{ind.}^2$) and 26% ($r_{sch.}^2$) of the variation in teacher efficacy. Thus, teacher efficacy and collective efficacy are related but distinct constructs.

Table 7.3.   Variance Decomposition of Teacher Efficacy and Collective Efficacy Scales: One-way ANOVA with Random Effects

	Teacher Efficacy	*Collective Efficacy*
Variance Among teachers within schools (σ^2)	.530	.278
Variance between schools (τ_{00})	.027	.195
Reliability (λ)	.325	.863
ICC^a	4.8%	41.2%
$ICC_{adj}{}^b$	13.6%	44.8%

Note: Author's calculations based on reanalysis of data reported by Goddard and Goddard (2001).
[a] Intraclass correlation coefficient , $\rho = \tau_{00}/(\sigma^2 + \tau_{00})$
[b] Adjusted intraclass correlation coefficient , $\rho_{adj} = \tau_{00}/(\lambda * \sigma^2 + \tau_{00})$

To understand more about variation in teachers' perceptions of self and group capability, two one-way ANOVAs with random effects were conducted using hierarchical linear modeling (HLM) software (Byrk & Raudenbush, 1992). Table 7.3 reports the results of this analysis. The intraclass correlation coefficient (ICC) represents the proportion of variance in teacher and collective efficacy that is systematically associated with school membership. The most important finding from this comparison involves the large differences in the ICC for teacher and collective efficacy. Notably, collective efficacy varies 45% between schools while only 14% of the variation in teacher efficacy is systematically associated with school membership.

Using the teacher and collective efficacy measures described above, Goddard and Goddard hypothesized that collective efficacy would be a significant positive predictor of differences among schools in teacher efficacy. In addition to collective efficacy, school SES, proportion minority and size were employed as covariate measures of school context. Their results are summarized in Table 7.4. Because all variables in the multilevel analyses were standardized (to a mean of zero and standard deviation of 1), results in Table 7.4 are interpreted in terms of standard deviation units. Models 1 through 5 separately test the strength of the relationship between several school contextual variables and teacher efficacy. Notably, SES, past achievement, and collective efficacy are significant predictors of differences among schools in teacher efficacy while school size and minority composition are not. Among the three statistically significant predictors, collective efficacy is clearly the strongest predictor of variation among schools in teacher efficacy. Indeed, before accounting for the effects of SES and past math achievement, a one standard deviation increase in collective efficacy is associated with a .191 standard deviation

Table 7.4.   Prediction of Variation in Teacher Efficacy among School Means with Selected School Characteristics (*n*= 438 teachers in 47 schools)

| | Model | | | | | |
	1	2	3	4	5	Combined
Intercept	.005	.008	.011	.009	.020	.023
Proportion minority	−.082					—
Proportion low SES		−.104*				.042
Number of students			−.045			—
Prior math achievement				.108*		−.035
Collective efficacy					.191**	.247**

** $p < .01$
* $p < .05$

increase in teacher efficacy (see Model 4). Moreover, after adjusting for differences related to school SES and past achievement, the increase in teacher efficacy associated with a one standard deviation increase in collective efficacy is nearly .25 standard deviations.

To understand the strength of this multilevel relationship between teacher and collective efficacy, it is essential to review the variance decomposition statistics reported by Goddard and Goddard. Table 7.5 shows that while school SES and past achievement alone explained less than

Table 7.5.   Proportion of Variation in Teacher Efficacy among Schools Explained and Remaining for Models Reported in Table 7.4 (*n* = 438 teachers in 47 schools)

| | Model | | | | | Combined Model |
	1	*2*	*3*	*4*	*5*	
Proportion of variation explained[a, b]	—	.247	—	.231	.735	.823
Between-school variation remaining[a]	—	.0358[c]	—	.0366[d]	.0126[e]	.0082[f]

[a] Proportion of variation in teacher efficacy explained and remaining reported only for models with statistically significant predictors.
[b] Proportion calculated as the reduction in variation among schools in teacher efficacy found in the unconditional multilevel analysis (.04758, Chi-square = 67.33, $df = 46$, $p < .05$).
[c] $\chi^2 = 62.30, df = 45, p < .05$
[d] $\chi^2 = 62.44, df = 45, p < .05$
[e] $\chi^2 = 50.48, df = 45, p = .266$
[f] $\chi^2 = 49.13, df = 43, p = .241$

25% of the variance among schools in teacher efficacy, *the effect of collective efficacy on teacher efficacy was about three times stronger.* Indeed, the addition of school SES and past math to a model already containing collective efficacy increases the explanatory power of the model very little, from .735 to .823. Hence, when compared with the impact of several powerful and commonly employed school contextual controls (SES, proportion minority, school size, and past achievement), collective efficacy is the aspect of school context most strongly related to teachers' sense of personal efficacy. These findings support the theoretical explanations sketched earlier to explain that collective efficacy has a strong influence on the normative environment of schools and hence makes a difference to teachers' beliefs about personal capability.

In sum, the findings reported above indicate that collective efficacy is a potent way of characterizing school culture. Indeed, collective efficacy is far more strongly related to teachers' perceptions of self-capability than many more common measures of school context. Schools with low levels of collective efficacy have debilitating effects on teachers' perceptions of self-capability. Of course, the opposite is also true; when teachers find themselves in schools with a high level of collective efficacy, individual teachers tends to have higher levels of personal efficacy. Higher levels of efficacy reflect more productive school cultures, which tend to have positive effects on the self-perceptions that teachers hold.

These findings underscore the need to attend to the development of collective efficacy in schools. As postulated by social cognitive theory, social influence shapes self-efficacy. Where teachers tend to think highly of the collective capability of the faculty, they sense an expectation for successful teaching and hence are increasingly likely to work to be successful themselves. Conversely, where collective efficacy is low, it is less likely that teachers will be pressed by their colleagues to persist in the face of failure or, that they will change their teaching when students do not learn. Hence, efforts that develop collective efficacy may be rewarded with the development of positive beliefs about self-capability in teachers, productive teaching, and ultimately, student learning. It is also likely that the relationship between teacher and collective efficacy is reciprocal with a change in one likely to lead to a change in the same direction of the other.

The next section of this chapter turns attention to the relationship between collective efficacy and the level of influence teachers have over instructionally relevant school decisions. The focus is on organizational agency and the opportunities teachers have to exercise discretion over their collective future.

ORGANIZING SCHOOLS TO FOSTER COLLECTIVE AGENCY

We know that schools high in collective efficacy frequently have relatively high levels of student achievement. To make such knowledge useful, however, it is important to understand how schools can be organized to foster collective efficacy. The purpose of this section is to consider what happens to collective efficacy when teachers are provided with opportunities to exercise organizational agency. The wording is important. This section does not report an investigation of shared decision-making per se or management styles that devolve *all* decision making to teachers; indeed, such recommendations abound in the face of limited evidence about which particular strategies work best in various situations. Rather, this section offers a theoretical and empirical analysis of the relationship between collective efficacy and an organizational design that provides teachers with opportunities to influence decisions that are highly relevant to their professional work.

The work of teaching is complex and demanding. Teachers do not wish to have their professional time deployed to investigate *every* problem their schools encounter. Most teachers are, however, interested in decisions that affect their professional work. Such decisions typically include, for example, those involving the selection and evaluation of curricular materials and activities, student academic placement, and school discipline policy. When teachers have the opportunity to influence *instructionally relevant* school decisions, collective conditions encourage teachers to exercise organizational agency. Indeed, Rosenholtz (1989) argued more than a decade ago "principals who facilitate networks among teachers to exchange ideas about the best way to reach school goals, who accomplish school goals, who themselves help teachers to accomplish goals, orient them to the school as a collective endeavor" (p. 15). The more teachers have the opportunity to influence instructionally relevant school decisions, the more likely a school is to be characterized by a robust sense of conjoint capability and a "can-do" attitude. In turn, social cognitive theory predicts that a robust sense of collective efficacy encourages the attainment of organizational goals by fostering productive educational practices that enhance student learning. According to Bandura (1997) "collective community action provides the vehicle for effecting desired changes" (pp. 500-501).

To learn more about this intriguing possibility, Goddard (2002) hypothesized that collective efficacy is a significant positive predictor of differences among schools in the level of influence teachers have over instructionally relevant school decisions. The results of this study are summarized here. Scale items employed to tap teacher influence over instructionally relevant decisions reflect teachers' reported level of control over

curriculum, instructional materials and activities, professional development, communication with parents, student placement, and disciplinary
policy. Data were obtained from 428 teachers in 45 schools in a large
urban school district in the Midwestern United States. The multilevel
structural equations employed to test the hypothesis were as follows:

Level 1: $Y_{(Influence)ij} = B_{0j} + r_{ij}$
Level 2: $B_{0j} = \gamma_{00} + \gamma_{01}W_{(Mean\ SES)j} + \gamma_{02}W_{(Prop.\ Minority)j} + \gamma_{03}W_{(Sch.\ Size)j}$
$+ \gamma_{04}W_{(Math)j} + \gamma_{05}W_{(Prop.\ Female)j} + \gamma_{06}W_{(Collective\ Efficacy)j} + \mu_{0j}$

This approach assessed whether collective efficacy was predictive of
variation between schools in teacher influence after controlling for school
contextual factors (school size, minority proportion, and SES). The results
of the analysis are reported in Table 7.6. After adjusting for school context, collective efficacy was, indeed, a significant positive predictor of variation among schools in the extent to which teachers had influence over
important school decisions. Specifically, the findings show that a one standard deviation increase in collective efficacy was associated with a .41
standard deviation increase in the extent to which teachers report exert-
ing influence over instructionally relevant school decisions.

**Table 7.6.   Full HLM: Prediction of Variation Among Schools in
Teacher Influence with Selected School Characteristics
(n = 428 teachers in 45 schools)**

Intercept (school average)	.016
	(.074)
Collective efficacy	.409**
	(.130)
School size	.050
	(.062)
Proportion low SES	.204
	(.132)
Minority concentration	−.001
	(.084)
Proportion female	−.024
	(.069)
Mathematics achievement	.101
	(.084)
Proportion of variance explained	.24
Between-school variation remaining	.208[a]

Note: Standard errors in parentheses.
[a] χ^2 = 134.65, df = 44, $p < .001$
** $p < .01$

From the perspective of social cognitive theory, the results highlight the importance of enablement to the exercise of collective agency. The results are also consistent with the view of Rosenholtz (1989) who argued for the importance of principals organizing schools to "grant teachers a part in constructing school reality" (p. 15). In contrast, when group influence is stifled, people are more likely to see the events around them as outside their control. This is the case, for example, in many traditional schools where principals retain power over nearly all decisions. The results here, however, suggest the need for practices that enable group members to exert influence and exercise organizational agency. Bandura (1997) refers to such efforts as group enablement. He observes, "collective enablement programs take many different forms, but the shared assumption is that they work in part by enhancing people's sense of efficacy to bring about change in their lives" (p. 503). Schools that formally turn over instructionally relevant school decisions to teachers tend to have higher levels of collective efficacy. Collective efficacy, in turn, fosters commitment to school goals, and ultimately, the attainment of student growth and development goals.

Having discussed the important connections between collective efficacy and teacher efficacy and influence, the chapter moves now to a consideration of the types of group outcomes that collective efficacy appears to foster.

A CALL FOR ATTENTION TO THE INFLUENCE OF COLLECTIVE EFFICACY ON TEACHER PRACTICE AND STUDENT ACHIEVEMENT

Perhaps the most compelling reason for the recent development of interest in social cognitive theory is the well-documented link between collective efficacy and group goal attainment. Within education, a series of studies have documented a strong link between collective efficacy and student achievement (Bandura, 1993; Goddard, 2001; Goddard, Hoy, & Woolfolk Hoy, 2000). Bandura demonstrated that the effect of collective efficacy on student achievement was stronger than the direct link between SES and student achievement. Similarly, Goddard and his colleagues have shown that, even after controlling for students' prior achievement, race/ ethnicity, and gender, collective efficacy has a stronger effect on student achievement than student race or SES. In other words, disadvantaged children tend to be better off in schools where the culture is characterized by a robust sense of group capability. Teachers' beliefs about the collective capability of their faculty vary greatly among schools and are strongly linked to teacher efficacy and influence, and hence, student achievement.

The power of collective efficacy to influence organizational life and outcomes lies in the expectations for action that are socially transmitted by efficacy perceptions. Collective efficacy is an important aspect of a group's culture, not just for schools, but also for any type of organized group. For example, Sampson, Raudenbush, and Earls (1997) showed that the more robust the sense of collective efficacy in city neighborhoods, the less likely was the occurrence of neighborhood violence. This is because neighborhoods in which residents reported a strong sense of collective efficacy were ones in which citizens felt an expectation for action that predisposed them to intervene to decrease violent activity. Such social sanctions serve as deterrents to those who might otherwise violate group expectations with violent activity. In addition, Little and Madigan (1997) have shown that collective efficacy is a strong positive predictor of work group effectiveness. They observe that collective efficacy has "a mediating, or facilitating effect on team performance" (p. 518). As educators look for approaches to school improvement that can help all students achieve to high levels, it is timely and important to examine how schools can be empowered to exert control over their circumstances.

The recent study of collective efficacy indicates that school culture influences members strongly by setting expectations for action governed by thinking about group capability. Collective efficacy clearly shapes teachers' self-referent thought and the control work groups exert over their circumstances. Still, we need more knowledge about how collective efficacy can be developed in schools. Almost certainly, efforts to build collective efficacy will be rewarded with gains in teacher efficacy, teacher influence, and, in turn, student growth and development. The research reported here, however, represents only a modest beginning. More knowledge is needed about how collective efficacy mediates the relation between organized activity and goal attainment. Moreover, the time is ripe for longitudinal studies of collective efficacy that investigate how perceptions of group capability change over time and how these perceptions foster the sustained effort and resiliency needed to attain desired learning outcomes for students.

REFERENCES

Allinder, R. M. (1994). The relationship between efficacy and the instructional practices of special education teachers and consultants. *Teacher Education and Special Education, 17,* 86-95.

Anderson, R., Greene, M., & Loewen, P. (1988). Relationships among teachers' and students' thinking skills, sense of efficacy, and student achievement. *Alberta Journal of Educational Research, 34*(2), 148-165.

Armor, D., Conroy-Oseguera, P., Cox, M., King, N., McDonnell, L., Pascal, A., Pauly, E., & Zellman, G. (1976). *Analysis of the school preferred reading program in selected Los Angeles minority schools* (Report No. R-2007-LAUSD; ERIC Document Reproduction No. 130 243). Santa Monica, CA: Rand Corporation.

Ashton, P. T., & Webb, R. B. (1986). *Making a difference: Teachers' sense of efficacy and student achievement.* New York: Longman.

Bandura, A. (1986). *Social foundations of thought and action: A social cognitive theory.* Englewood Cliffs, NJ: Prentice-Hall.

Bandura, A. (1993). Perceived self-efficacy in cognitive development and functioning. *Educational Psychologist, 28*(2), 117-148.

Bandura, A. (1997). *Self-efficacy: The exercise of control.* New York: W. H. Freeman.

Chester, M. D., & Beaudin, B. Q. (1996). Efficacy beliefs of newly hired teachers in urban schools. *American Educational Research Journal, 33*(1), 233-257.

Coleman, J. S. (1985). Schools and the communities they serve. *Phi Delta Kappan, 66*, 527-532.

Coleman, J. S. (1987). Norms as social capital. In G. Radnitzky & P. Bernholz (Eds.), *Economic imperialism: The economic approach applied outside the field of economics.* New York: Paragon House Publishers.

Coleman, J.S. (1990). *Foundations of social theory.* Cambridge, MA: Harvard University Press.

Czerniak, C. M., & Schriver, M. L. (1994). An examination of preservice science teachers' beliefs and behaviors as related to self-efficacy. *Journal of Science Teacher Education, 5*(3), 77-86.

Da Costa, J. L., & Riordan, G. (1996, April). *Teacher efficacy and the capacity to trust.* Paper presented at the annual meeting of the American Educational Research Association, New York.

DeForest, P. A., & Hughes, J. N. (1992). Effect of teacher involvement and teacher self-efficacy on ratings of consultant effectiveness and intervention acceptability. *Journal of Educational and Psychological Consultation, 3*, 301-316.

Enochs L. G., Scharmann, L. C., & Riggs, I. M. (1995). The relationship of pupil control to preservice elementary science teacher self-efficacy and outcome expectancy. *Science Education, 79*(1), 63-75.

Gibson, S., & Dembo, M. (1984). Teacher efficacy: A construct validation. *Journal of Educational Psychology, 76*(4), 569-582.

Goddard, R. D. (2001). Collective efficacy: A neglected construct in the study of schools and student achievement. *Journal of Educational Psychology, 93*(3), 467-476.

Goddard, R. D. (2002). Collective efficacy and school organization: A multilevel analysis of teacher influence in schools. *Theory and Research in Educational Administration, 1*, 169-184.

Goddard, R. D., & Goddard, Y. L. (2001). A multilevel analysis of teacher and collective efficacy. *Teaching and Teacher Education, 17*, 807-818.

Goddard, R. D., Hoy, W. K., & Woolfolk Hoy, A. E. (2000). Collective teacher efficacy: Its meaning, measure, and effect on student achievement. *American Education Research Journal, 37*(2), 479-507.

Gorrell, J. & Capron, E. W. (1988). Effects of instrumental type and feedback on prospective teachers' self-efficacy beliefs. *The Journal of Experimental Education, 56(3)*, 120-123.

Hoy, W. K., & Woolfolk, A. (1993). Teachers' sense of efficacy and the organizational health of schools. *The Elementary School Journal, 93*(4), 355-372.

Huber, G. P. (1996). Organizational learning: The contributing processes and literatures. In M. D. Cohen & L. S. Sproull (Eds.), *Organizational learning* (pp. 124-162). Thousand Oaks, CA: Sage.

Lee, V. E., Dedrick, R., & Smith, J. (1991). The effect of the social organization of schools on teachers' efficacy and satisfaction. *Sociology of Education, 64*, 190-208.

Little, B. L., & Madigan, R. M. (1997). The relationship between collective efficacy and performance in manufacturing work teams. *Small Group Research, 28*(4), 517-534.

Moore, W., & Esselman, M. (1992). *Teacher efficacy, power, school climate and achievement: A desegregating district's experience.* Paper presented at the annual meeting of the American Educational Research Association, San Francisco.

Pajares, F. (1997). Current directions in self-efficacy research. In M. L. Maehr & P. R. Pintrich (Eds.), *Advances in motivation and achievement* (pp. 1-49). Greenwich, CT: JAI Press.

Raudenbush, S. W., Rowan, B., & Cheong, Y. F. (1992). Contextual effects on the self-perceived efficacy of high school teachers. *Sociology of Education, 65*, 150-167.

Rosenholtz, S. J. (1989). *Teachers' workplace: The social organization of schools.* New York: Longman.

Ross, J. A. (1992). Teacher efficacy and the effect of coaching on student achievement. *Canadian Journal of Education, 17*(1), 51-65.

Ross, J. A. (1994, June). *Beliefs that make a difference: The origins and impacts of teacher efficacy.* Paper presented at the annual meeting of the Canadian Association for Curriculum Studies.

Sampson R. J., Morenoff, J. D., & Earls, F. (1999). Beyond social capital: Spatial dynamics of collective efficacy for children. *American Sociology Review, 64*, 633-660.

Sampson, R. J., Raudenbush, S. W., & Earls, F. (1997). Neighborhoods and violent crime: A multilevel study of collective efficacy. *Science, 277*, 918-924.

Schunk, D. H. (1981). Modeling and attributional effects on children's achievement: A self-efficacy analysis. *Journal of Educational Psychology, 73*, 93-105.

Schunk, D. H. (1983). Developing children's self-efficacy and skills: The roles of social comparative information and goal setting. *Educational Psychology, 8*, 76-86.

Schunk, D. H. (1987). Peer models and children's behavioral change. *Review of Educational Research, 57*, 149-174.

Schunk, D. H., & Zimmerman, B. J. (1997). Social origins of self-regulatory competence. *Educational Psychologist, 32*(4), 195-208.

Woolfolk, A., & Hoy, W. K. (1990). Prospective teachers' sense of efficacy and beliefs about control. *Journal of Educational Psychology, 82*, 81-91.